# Association Discussed: Or, The Socialism Of The Tribune Examined

Horace Greeley, Henry Jarvis Raymond

**Nabu Public Domain Reprints:**

You are holding a reproduction of an original work published before 1923 that is in the public domain in the United States of America, and possibly other countries. You may freely copy and distribute this work as no entity (individual or corporate) has a copyright on the body of the work. This book may contain prior copyright references, and library stamps (as most of these works were scanned from library copies). These have been scanned and retained as part of the historical artifact.

This book may have occasional imperfections such as missing or blurred pages, poor pictures, errant marks, etc. that were either part of the original artifact, or were introduced by the scanning process. We believe this work is culturally important, and despite the imperfections, have elected to bring it back into print as part of our continuing commitment to the preservation of printed works worldwide. We appreciate your understanding of the imperfections in the preservation process, and hope you enjoy this valuable book.

# ASSOCIATION DISCUSSED;

OR,

## THE SOCIALISM OF THE TRIBUNE EXAMINED.

BEING

A CONTROVERSY BETWEEN THE NEW YORK TRIBUNE AND
THE COURIER AND ENQUIRER.

BY

H. GREELEY AND H. J. RAYMOND.

HARPER & BROTHERS, PUBLISHERS,
82 CLIFF STREET, NEW YORK.
1847.

# PREFACE.

The papers embraced in the following pages are republished from the daily journals for which they were written, at the request of a number of persons who feel a lively interest in the principles and projects therein discussed.

The manner in which the controversy arose may be understood from the following statement:—

The Tribune of August 19th, 1846, contained a letter signed by Mr. A. Brisbane, addressed to the Editor of the Courier and Enquirer, and proposing sundry inquiries, to which specific answers were requested, concerning certain features of the scheme of Social Reform of which he was the acknowledged advocate.

The Courier and Enquirer on the 25th of August answered these inquiries at length. On the 26th The Tribune contained an editorial rejoinder, to which the Courier replied on the 28th. The Tribune, on the 1st of September, again responded editorially, and this was followed on the 5th by a rejoinder from the Courier. The sequel may best be understood from the following paragraphs, which are inserted in the order and manner of their first appearance:—

*From the Courier and Enquirer, Sept. 7th, 1846.*

We have received from Mr. Albert Brisbane a long reply to our first article in answer to his queries on *Association*, published in The Tribune. We do not acknowledge the slightest obligation on our part to publish the arguments of those with whom we disagree: and as a general thing, we would not consent, upon any terms, that our columns should be used to spread before the public sentiments which we deem unsound and mischievous. But in this case The Tribune has so often complained that we never allow their side of the question to be heard, that we will give place to this letter from Mr. Brisbane, as soon as our limits will allow, provided The Tribune will give place in its columns to our reply. This, we think, must, on the score of fairness, satisfy even the most fastidious.

*From the Daily Tribune, Sept. 8th, 1846.*

The *Courier and Enquirer* states that it has received an article on *Association* from Mr. A. Brisbane, which it will publish provided The Tribune will give place to its reply. Waiving all question as to the fairness of this requisition—that we shall publish the answer to an article written by a third party having no connection with (save as an occasional correspondent), nor control over The Tribune—we are unable at present to give the stipulation required, on account of the preöccupation of our columns. * * * But though we can not now open our columns to a set discussion by others of Social questions, (which may or may not refer mainly to points deemed relevant by us,) we readily close with the *spirit* of the Courier's proposition, and trust the following form will be equally acceptable to it with its own, viz: As soon as the State Election is fairly over—say Nov. 10th—we will publish an article, filling a column of The Tribune, very nearly, in favor of Association as we understand it; and upon the Courier's copying this and replying, we will give place to its reply, and respond; and so on, until each party shall have published twelve articles on its own side and twelve on the other, which shall fulfil the terms of this agreement. All the twelve articles of each party shall be published without abridgment or variation in the Daily, Semi-weekly and Weekly editions of both papers. Afterward, each party will of course be at liberty to comment at pleasure in his own columns. In order that neither paper shall be crowded with this discussion, one article per week only, shall be given on either side, unless the Courier shall prefer greater dispatch. Is not this a fair proposition? What says the Courier? It has of course the advantage of the defensive position and of the last word.

*From the Courier and Enquirer, Sept. 9th, 1846.*

We are surprised, we confess, at The Tribune's refusal to comply with our offer,

1st. Because Mr. Brisbane, in the columns of The Tribune, commenced this discussion; and The Tribune simply volunteered to defend him from our reply. Why should not the *principal*, then, instead of the volunteer friend, be permitted to answer for himself?

2d. Because The Tribune has readily found room for replies to *all* the articles we have written upon this subject except the last, and was not preoccupied until after our offer to publish arguments *in favor* of Association, on condition that it should publish our reply.

We will comply, however, most cheerfully with the terms of The Tribune, in discussing this question, provided it will discuss Association *as it is*,—that is, as it is defined and explained in the writings of Fourier, Brisbane, Godwin, the Roxbury community, The Tribune and other advocates and apostles of the cause. If it will take up *the whole subject*, we will readily discuss it on almost any terms:—but it would be manifestly unfair for The Tribune to select some one isolated *branch* of the system, and insist that we shall discuss *only that*. When we know exactly what the Tribune understands Association to be, for the purposes of this discussion, we shall have no difficulty in agreeing upon the terms. Until then, however, it would be difficult to say whether we should even *differ* in regard to the subject. The Tribune may so narrow the platform as to leave nothing to be discussed. Until we know, therefore, the ground it proposes to take, and how thorough it is willing to make the inquiry, we can only say that we "close readily with the *spirit* of its proposition,"—and will cheerfully discuss *Association* on the terms proposed.

*From The Tribune, Sept. 10th, 1846.*

The Courier will find what we understand by Association plainly stated in our extended reply of the 1st inst. to one of its earlier articles. If it finds nothing to differ about in that statement, so much the better: we have recently been forced by violent attacks and unjust imputations to devote space to Social discussions which we could very ill spare, and would gladly have appropriated otherwise. If the Courier does not dissent from our idea of Association, as set before it on the 1st inst., we have no occasion for controversy. We certainly can not find room for a discussion in which it is implied that we are to be held responsible for whatever the Courier may find in the voluminous writings of a dozen persons, several of them disagreeing on certain points with each other, and one at least (Fourier) in his later expressly condemning a part of his earlier speculations. The Courier would doubtless object to our holding it responsible for all that has been advanced on Social topics by the Express, Observer and others who have written in favor of the existing order of things. To bring the discussion within the space we can afford it, the rule we have proposed of letting each party speak for himself, and be responsible only for what he propounds, appears to us indispensable.

*From the Courier and Enquirer, Nov. 10th, 1846.*

Fourierism.—The Tribune some weeks since proposed a discussion, with this paper, of the principles and plans of the Associationists, to be commenced immediately after the State election; and agreed if we would publish its articles in exposition and defense of those principles and plans, to give place in its columns to our replies. We acceded at the time to this proposal; and now stand ready to redeem our promise, whenever The Tribune may think proper to commence the discussion.

We believe the discussion of this subject may be so conducted as to serve the cause of truth and the best interests of society: and also that in point of importance, it stands second to none of the topics which now agitate the public mind. We are temporarily and partially relieved, moreover, from the immediate pressure of political matter, and shall gladly avail ourselves of the opportunity to canvass subjects of social and universal interest.

*From The Tribune, Nov. 12th, 1846.*

The reasoning Editor of the Courier understands this whole matter too well to have made the above proposition in good faith. He quite well knows, for we have expressly informed him, that for any such general foray as he meditates on every thing and every body who seems to consider a Social Reform desirable, he must find his excuse elsewhere than in The Tribune. He is quite at liberty to make himself the Bossuet of the Social Reformation if he can, but he need not expect our aid in attaining that distinction.

[Here follows a summary restatement of the positions taken by The Tribune in the foregoing paragraphs.]

*From the Courier and Enquirer, Nov. 14th, 1846.*

It will be seen [from the article of Sept. 9th] that our only difficulty in the matter arose from fear that the Tribune would take up only a *branch* of the general subject, and so frame the statement of Association as to leave nothing to be discussed. If this apprehension should be removed, we agreed explicitly to "*discuss Association on the terms proposed.*" On the 10th, the Tribune satisfied our scruples by saying that it would take the ground laid down in a former article (Sept. 1) to which we had already replied, thus showing that we did find in it matter for discussion. We acquiesced in this arrangement.

"Of the personal and insulting tone of the above paragraph we have nothing to say, except that it is unworthy any man who pretends to common fairness and courtesy. But we submit to the judgment of our readers, whether it is not a shuffling evasion of a proposition and a promise deliberately and carefully made by The Tribune itself. The unreasoning editor of that paper knows that we 'made' no proposition, but only called upon him to fulfill his own. His assertion that we '*meditate*' a general foray on every thing and every body who seems to consider a Social Reform desirable, is as unfounded as it is impertinent. And the grace of his permission, that we may make of ourselves a Bossuet if we can, is fairly matched by the ungracious modesty with which he declines to aid us in the attempt. We agreed to discuss Association upon The Tribune's own terms, because we believed it to be an important subject, involving principles of vital interest to society, and calling for the investigation of those who assume, through the public press, to instruct and guide the public mind. The Tribune, moreover, had repeatedly complained that we only presented one side of the subject, and challenged us to its full and fair discussion, upon terms and in a manner definitely pointed out in the extract we have quoted above. We accepted the challenge; and, if our acceptance then failed to meet The Tribune's scruples, we now repeat it, and agree to discuss the subject upon the terms laid down by The Tribune itself. If that paper has any faith in the soundness of its views, it will not hesitate to submit them to free discussion. If its proposition for such a discussion was originally made in good faith, it can not now be withdrawn or evaded without a breach of that faith. And if its deliberate promise to enter upon it was made with any intention of fulfilling it, we submit that it can not now be repudiated without a flagrant violation of common honesty."

*From The Tribune, Nov. 16.*

The Courier and Enquirer surely can not expect us to multiply words about so plain a matter as that of our proposed controversy. Our original offer was to discuss "Association *as we understand it*," and we referred to our article of Sept. 1st last to simply show what that is, and that there is abundant room for discussion between us. But we insist on our right to lay down our own propositions, and to be held to maintain those propositions, and none other. We seek not to hold the Courier responsible for anybody's ideas or statements but its own, and we will be concluded by or required to defend none other than our own. If the Courier accedes to this unreservedly, we will directly open the discussion; if not, not. This is our fourth and last time of making the offer, each time as definitely as how.

The Courier is too well acquainted with our views and convictions to apprehend that we shall not broadly present and maintain Association. It only fears that we shall not afford it a pretext for dragging in whatever beside it deems calculated to increase the general prejudice against or gratify the current hatred of the advocates of a Social Reform. To discuss "the principles and plans of the Associationists," which it seeks to substitute for the question we have uniformly proposed, would be like agreeing to discuss "the characters and objects of the public lecturers on Animal Magnetism." These last might be ever so indifferent, without affecting the verity and importance of the phenomena termed Animal Magnetism. But we know what is the true topic, and shall discuss that or nothing.

*From the Courier and Enquirer, Nov. 17th.*

We believe The Tribune has "*made this offer*" three times before; and if it had exhibited a tenth part of the readiness to *fulfil* its engagements which it has shown in making them, the discussion would long ere this have been under way. Meantime, we call The Tribune's attention again to the following, from our paper of Saturday, which we desire to be understood as now repeating:—

"We agreed to discuss the subject of Association UPON THE TRIBUNE'S OWN TERMS, because we believed it to be an important subject, involving principles of vital interest to Society, and calling for the investigation of those who assume, through the public press, to instruct and guide the public mind. The Tribune, moreover, had repeatedly complained that we only presented one side of the subject, and challenged us to its full and fair discussion, upon terms and in a manner definitely pointed out in the extract we have quoted above. *We accepted the challenge;* and if our acceptance then failed to meet The Tribune's scruples, *we now repeat it,* and OFFER TO DISCUSS THE SUBJECT UPON THE TERMS LAID DOWN BY THE TRIBUNE ITSELF."

If the Tribune can quibble out of this, it probably will; if not, not. It can take whatever course it thinks best.

*From The Tribune, Nov. 18th.*

The Courier and Enquirer offers to assent unreservedly to the terms on which we originally professed, and have all along been willing, to discuss with it the subject of Association. Very good. Relying on the good faith of the Courier's assurance, we shall commence the discussion at our first available hour—certainly before the week closes. We only ask that the conditions be carefully remembered.

In the progress of the discussion, (which extended to a much greater length than was originally contemplated by either party), the scope of the terms agreed upon and the extent to which they had been observed, became mingled with the other topics of controversy. For the means of forming a judgment upon this point, therefore, we refer to the papers in which it is discussed.

The examination of the subject on either side has been less methodical and complete than was desired; but for this defect a sufficient apology is found in the discursive and desultory method which the form of controversy renders unavoidable.

The papers are reprinted, without alteration or revision, from the daily journals for which, in the ordinary course and with the necessary haste of editorial duty, they were originally written. They pretend, therefore, to no literary merit, and do not venture voluntarily within the lines of literary criticism.

Social theories and plans of general reform are daily acquiring new interest, and gaining a stronger hold on the attention of the public. The parties to this discussion hope that it may not be wholly without influence, in stimulating and guiding to beneficent results the active benevolence of the present age, as well as in keeping its projects within the limits of sound sense, of strict morality, and the imperative exactions of Christian principle.

H. J. RAYMOND.<br>H. GREELEY.

# ASSOCIATION DISCUSSED.

From the Tribune, Nov. 20th, 1846.

## LETTER I.

*To the Editor of the Courier and Enquirer:*

I OPEN the proposed discussion by the statement of a few rudimental propositions, intended to show that Justice to the Poor and Wretched demands of the more fortunate classes a radical Social Reform. Let it be termed a summary setting forth

### Of Rights and Obligations.

"In the beginning GOD created the heaven and the earth."

The earth, the air, the waters, the sunshine, with their natural products, were divinely intended and appointed for the use and sustenance of Man (Gen. i. 26, 28)—not for a part only, but for the whole Human Family.

Civilized Society, as it exists in our day, has divested the larger portion of mankind of the unimpeded, unpurchased enjoyment of those natural rights. That larger portion may be perishing with cold, yet have no legally recognized right to a stick of decaying fuel in the most unfrequented morass, or may be famishing, yet have no legal right to pluck and eat the bitterest acorn in the depths of the remotest wilderness. The defeasance or confiscation of Man's natural right to use any portion of the Earth's surface not actually in use by another, is an important fact, to be kept in view in every consideration of the duty of the affluent and comfortable to the poor and unfortunate.

It is not essential in this place to determine that the divestment of the larger number of any recognized right to the Soil and its Products, save by the purchased permission of others, was or was not politic and necessary. All who reflect must certainly admit that many of the grants of land by hundreds of square miles to this or that favorite of the power which assumed to make them were made thoughtlessly or recklessly, and would not have been so large or so unaccompanied with stipulations in behalf of the future occupants and cultivators, if a reasonable foresight and a decent regard for the general good had been cherished and evinced by the granting power. Suffice it here, however, that the granting of the Soil—of the State of New York, for example—by the supreme authority representing the whole to a minor portion of the whole is a "fixed fact." By a law of Nature, every person born in the State of New York had (unless forfeited by crime) a perfect right to *be* here, and to his equal share of the Soil, the woods, the waters, and all the natural products thereof. By the law of Society all but the possessors of title-deeds exist here only by the purchased permission of the land-owning class, and were intruders and trespassers on the soil of their nativity without that permission. By law, the landless have no inherent right to stand on a single square foot of the State of New York except in the highways.

The only solid ground on which this surrender of the original property of the whole to a minor portion can be justified is that of PUBLIC GOOD—the good, not of a part, but of a whole. The people of a past generation, through their rulers, claimed and exercised the right of divesting, not themselves merely, but the majority of all future generations, of their original and inherent right to possess and cultivate any unimproved portion of the soil of our State for their own sustenance and benefit. To render this assumption of power valid to the fearful extent to which it was exercised, it is essential that it be demonstrated that the good of the whole was promoted by such exercise.

Is this rationally demonstrable now? Can the widow, whose children pine and shiver in some bleak, miserable garret, on the fifteen or twenty cents, which is all she can earn by unremitted toil, be made to realize that she and her babes are benefited by or in consequence of the granting to a part an exclusive right to use the earth and enjoy its fruits? Can the poor man who day after day paces the streets of a city in search of any employment at any price, (as thousands are now doing here), be made to realize it on his part? Are there not thousands on thousands—natives of our State who never willfully violated her laws—who are to-day far worse off than they would have been if Nature's rule of allowing no man to appropriate to himself any more of the earth than he can cultivate and improve had been recognized and respected by Society? These questions admit of but one answer. And one inevitable consequence of the prevailing system is that, as Population increases and Arts are perfected, the income of the wealthy owner of land increases while the recompense of the hired or leasehold cultivator is steadily diminishing. The labor of Great Britain is twice as effective now as it was a century ago, but the laborer is worse paid, fed, and lodged than he then was, while the incomes of the landlord class have been enormously increased. The same fundamental causes exist here, and tend to the same results. They have been modified, thus far, by the existence, within or near our State, of large tracts of unimproved land, which the owners were anxious to improve or dispose of on almost any terms. These are growing scarcer and more remote; they form no part of the system we are considering, but something which exists in opposition to it, which modifies it, but is absolutely sure to be ultimately absorbed and conquered by it. The notorious fact that they do serve to mitigate the exactions to which the landless mass, even in our long and densely-settled towns and cities, are subject, serves to show that the condition of the great mass must inevitably be far worse than at present when the natural consummation of land-selling is reached, and all the soil of the Union has become the property of a minor part of the People of the Union.

The past can not be recalled. What has been rightfully (however mistakenly) done by the authorized agents of the state or nation, can only be retracted upon urgent public necessity, and upon due satisfaction to all whose private rights are thereby invaded. But those who have been divested of an important, a vital natural right, are also entitled to compensation. THE RIGHT TO LABOR, secured to them in the creation of the earth, taken away in the granting of the Soil to a minor portion of them, must be restored. Labor, essential to all, is the inexorable condition of the honest, independent subsistence of the Poor. It must be fully guaranteed to all, so that each may know that he can never starve nor be forced to beg while able and willing to work. Our public provision for Pauperism is but a halting and wretched substitute for this. Society exercises no paternal guardianship over the poor man until he has surrendered to despair. He may spend a whole year and his little all in vainly seeking employment, and all this time Society does nothing, cares nothing for him; but when his last dollar is exhausted, and his capacities very probably prostrated by the intoxicating draughts to which he is driven to escape the horrors of reflection, *then* he becomes a subject of public charity, and is often maintained in idleness for the rest of his days at a cost of thousands, when a few dollars' worth of foresight and timely aid might have preserved him from this fate, and in a position of independent usefulness for his whole after-life.

But the Right to Labor—that is, to constant Employment with a just and full Recompense—can not be guaranteed to all without a radical change in our Social Economy. I, for one, am very willing, nay, most anxious, to do my full share toward securing to every man, woman, and child, full employment and a just recompense for all time to come. I feel sure this can be accomplished. But I can not, as the world goes, give employment at any time to all who ask it of me, nor the hundredth part of them. "Work, work! give us something to do!—any thing that will secure us honest bread," is at this moment the prayer of not less than Thirty Thousand human beings within sound of our City-hall bell. They would gladly be producers of wealth, yet remain from week to week mere consumers of bread which somebody has to earn. Here is an enormous waste and loss. We must devise a remedy. It is the duty, and not less the palpable interest, of the wealthy, the thrifty, the tax-paying, to do so. The remedy, I propose to show, is found in ASSOCIATION. H. G.

From the Courier and Enquirer, Nov. 23, 1846.
## REPLY TO LETTER I.

THE N. Y. Tribune has entered upon a formal and elaborate vindication of the new Social System, which, for the last five years, it has earnestly urged upon the attention of its readers, under the name of *Association*; and upon the first page of our paper this morning, will be found its first article, which is simply prefatory to its promised statement of what that System is. We intend to make the System, and the principles out of which it grows, the theme of a somewhat close and critical examination, in order to determine for ourselves, and, if possible, to furnish to others the means of determining for themselves, whether Truth and the Public Good require that we should aid in securing their general adoption; or whether injury, of the most serious character, is inflicted upon Society by the constant and skillful appeals made to the public in their behalf. We do not know that the larger portion of the reading community will, in the outset at least, follow this discussion with any special or definite interest. But we are confident it will soon become apparent, that it is not a mere controversy concerning words, nor a useless debate of harmless abstractions, but a discussion of principles which lie at the very foundation of all Society; which enter into all the opinions of men upon Politics, Morals, and Religion; which color, however insensibly, the speculations of the closet, the teachings of the Pulpit, the Press, and the Bar, and the opinions of those who guide and control the affairs of civil and social life; and which involve, to an indefinite and unknown extent, the security, the harmony, and the aggregate well-being of the whole fabric of civilized Society. We hope to be followed in an inquiry, which we deem so important, at least with patience, if not with interest. The Tribune's first article not only prefaces its promised statement of what Association is, but sets forth the elementary Principles out of which Association grows. It lays the foundation of the new Social System which, the Tribune contends, should be made a substitute for that which is now in existence. It is necessary, therefore, at the outset, to see what those principles are; and for this purpose we ask a close perusal of the Tribune's article. In that article these points are distinctly set forth:—

1. The entire surface of the Earth, with all its products, was created for the use of the whole human race; its ownership is, therefore, vested "by a law of Nature," in the race; and every man who is born upon the Earth, has a perfect right to his share of it.

2. While this would be the alledged *rightful* disposition of the land, the *actual* property of it is vested in a portion of the race; and the residue, that is, those who own no land, have been wrongfully divested and despoiled of what is theirs. This has been done by Civilized Society; which has, therefore, been guilty of a foul wrong, in thus robbing the larger portion of the human family of the land to which, by a law of Nature, they are entitled.

3. As a natural consequence of this, it is held to be the duty of Society to restore to these landless men that which is rightfully theirs; or, if this can not be done, Society is bound to compensate them for that of which they have been robbed. In other

words, those who own Land are, in duty, and by natural law, bound to give to those who possess none, payment for that of which, by a law of Nature, they are the rightful owners.

4. "Association" proposes to carry this into effect, that is, to confer upon the landless, if not the land, something equivalent in value to the land, of which they have been despoiled. How this is to be accomplished the Tribune has yet to explain.

These, we believe, are all the points made by the Tribune, or at least they embrace the substance of its first article. All its deductions rest upon its primary position : that, by a law of Nature, every man born upon the Earth has a *right* to a portion of that Earth. This position is set forth very distinctly, thus :—

"By a law of Nature, every person born in the State of New York had a *perfect right* to *his equal share* of the soil, the woods, the waters, and all the natural products thereof."

This can only mean that the land of New York is, by a law of Nature, and rightfully, owned in equal shares by all the persons born within the State; and that those who actually own none of it are wronged and robbed of what is justly theirs. Now, this position, we insist, is equivalent to a *denial of the Right of Property in Land*. It denies the right of any one man to hold a certain piece of Land for himself, and as his own, and to exclude from it all other persons in the world. This is a necessary and inevitable inference. For, if all the men born within certain limits, at any time own all the land within those limits, and if one thousand more men are afterward born within the same limits, then, according to the Tribune's theory, the land within those limits will be then owned, in equal shares, by one thousand more men than held it before. Of course, then, these equal shares must become smaller than they were before; or, in other words, each man of the original holders of the land must part with a portion of that which he then accounted his. But the right of property involves necessarily the right of retention, of supreme and permanent dominion : and if this right of retention be taken away, the right of property no longer exists. Now the Tribune's theory does actually destroy this right of retention; and it, therefore, as we alledged at the start, *denies* that Land can be rightfully *owned* by anybody.

The same conclusion may be reached by a reverse process of reasoning. Suppose that the Tribune concedes that a man may be the actual and exclusive owner of a certain portion, say one acre, of the soil of New York. Another man may, of course, acquire an equally rightful title to the adjoining acre; and this process may rightfully go on until every acre of the soil of New York may become the rightful property of somebody. Now suppose other men to be born within the limits of the same State : they could not rightfully own any portion of the soil, because others have already acquired a rightful and exclusive ownership in the whole of it. But the Tribune declares explicitly that they would be *wrongfully* deprived of it—that each one of them has a "perfect right" to his "equal share." The Tribune, therefore, must deny the principle with which we started, that one man can *rightfully be the exclusive owner* of any part of the earth's surface. This is the fundamental principle from which the Tribune starts in its advocacy of Association—namely, that THERE CAN BE NO RIGHTFUL PROPERTY IN LAND.

Now if a man may not rightfully own Land, how can he rightfully own any thing which the land produces ? Is there any ground for a distinction between property in Land, and property in the products of Land ? Why may a tree be owned, when the land upon which it grows can not ? Why may the wheat which grows out of the soil be owned by some man, when the soil from which it grows can not ? What inherent quality makes the one *ownable* when the other is not ? The Tribune may reply, the Labor bestowed in producing it makes one the subject of property. But Labor only changes the *form* of a thing :—it does not create it. And if the original be not ownable, how can its product become so ? If no one man can own land, to the exclusion of all others, how can any man own its products ? There is no principle which will sanction the distinction. If land is not ownable, nothing is. If the right of property in Land be denied, the right of property in every thing else, is denied also. If, as the Tribune maintains, "every person in New York, has a perfect right to his equal share of the soil" of New York, then, most certainly, he has an equally perfect right to his equal share of whatever that soil, directly or indirectly, may produce.

The original proposition, therefore, from which the Tribune starts, in its advocacy of Association, is a denial of the Right of Property in Land ; and inclusively a denial of the right of Property in any thing whatever. Now we must not be understood to say that the Tribune does this actually and consciously ; it will, probably, promptly disavow any such opinion. But we do assert, and we think we have proved, that the ground-principle of its whole System, the elementary proposition with which it starts, the very principle which shapes its whole theory of Rights and Obligations, does, of necessity, involve these results. If that principle is true, these results must follow ; and the Tribune can not disavow the results, without disavowing the principle also.

Now it can scarcely be necessary, at least at present, to establish the right of absolute Property, either in Land or in any thing else. God gave to man, not simply the *use*, but the *dominion*, the property, the ownership of the Earth. His declared object in doing so, was to secure its cultivation. At first, when there were but few men upon the Earth, they did not find it needful to cultivate it much, and so they did not care to own it ;—and thus it remained uncultivated and unowned. But when men increased in number, it became essential to till the Earth ;—no man could till land of which he had not the property, either original and complete, or derived and limited : and thus, out of the very necessity of the case, grew the right of property in land, and so the right of property in the products thereof. That right was essential—was necessary to secure the cultivation of the Earth, and so the fulfillment of God's design. From it grew Agriculture, Commerce, and Industry in all its forms. Passion and avarice threatened to disturb or destroy it, and hence grew up Law for its protection. Out of the institution of Property, therefore, which grew from the law of Nature and of God, arose the fabric of Civilized Society. This, which is the order of Nature, reverses, it will be seen, the order of the Tribune. That paper insists that Society creates property, when in truth it is its creature. Property is the root of the tree of which Society is the trunk; and Society, in turn, as it is the product, becomes guardian of the right of individual property. Property has always originated every thing like order, civilization, and refinement in the world. It has always been the mainspring of energy, enterprise, and all the refinements of life. Evils are of course developed in connection with it; but they are accidental and comparatively trifling. Without it, they would be increased a thousand fold, and would exist alone and without relief. Without it civilization would be unknown—the face of the Earth would be a desert, and mankind transformed into savage beasts. There is no such "law of Nature" as that in which the Tribune finds its sanction for the doctrines it promulgates. There is no "law of Nature" which gives to every man a "perfect right" to his "equal share" of the Earth's surface. No man born now can stand in the same relations to the earth which Adam held: the "law of Nature" has forbidden it. That law brings men into the world under a certain system of circumstances, which have rightfully and in due course of nature grown up around him: *that* is the world into which he is born, and no "law of Nature" impels or requires him to overthrow that system, in order to secure his fancied rights.

Now let it not be said that these are idle speculations—mere truisms which no one disputes, and which it is a waste of time to promulgate and discuss. Let it not be said that the Tribune entertains no such extravagant theories as those set forth, and urges no such application of them to the practical affairs of life. We are anxious to redeem this discussion from any such reproach; and we insist upon the *fact*, that these principles are applied to the concerns of daily life, that they have already, to a very great extent, shaped and guided the public sentiment, and that they are slowly but surely creating a new *habitude* of thought and of action, in every department of civil and of social life, as one of direct pertinence, and of immense importance, in the bearings and arguments of this discussion. Let those who deem these matters of no importance, look back to the state of the public mind ten years ago, when precisely these same fundamental principles were proclaimed in this city by Fanny Wright. We intend no disrespect, and none is implied, to any one, by this allusion to the fact, that these same principles at *that* day, when preached by that woman, found no adherents except in a small company gathered from the most radical and ignorant portion of the Loco Foco party. She then denounced the rich as spoilers of the poor: landowners as robbers of those who owned no land; the laws of Society as essentially unjust; and the things that are, as the exact antipodes of the things that should be. She, too, demanded the reconstruction of Society; and enforced her claims by earnest appeals to the poverty and the wretchedness which may at any time be found upon the earth. She and her doctrines were, then universally despised, and she was scarcely honored with the "pitying contempt of smiles." Do those persons who thus regarded her fundamental doctrines then, realize that they are now daily proclaimed and urged upon the public ear, by one of the ablest, most adroit, and most influential leaders of the Whig party! And are they thoughtless enough to suppose, that this can go on, from year to year, without producing an effect!

The Tribune has commenced its discussion of *Association* by an elaborate exposition of its theory of Property in Land. It regards this theory as essential to the Social System which it advocates; and we have examined its fundamental principles precisely as they have been stated by itself. We have not sought nor desired to hold it responsible for any thing out of its own columns. But for what it does state, for the influence which these statements have exerted, and for the actual effect which they have produced, the Tribune must certainly expect, and can not refuse, to be held accountable in this discussion. We urge, then, as a part of our case against "Association as the Tribune understands and teaches it," that the Tribune's advocacy of the fundamental principles upon which it rests has produced a vast and most injurious effect upon society, in almost every department of action and of thought. We contend that these principles should be disproved and rejected by the great body of right-thinking men, because their constant, skillful and zealous proclamation by the Tribune has done, and is doing, infinite evil to the best interests of Society and the State. As proof of the effect they have already produced, we refer to the change they have effected, first, in the Tribune itself, and then, in the public mind. With the Tribune these principles are not lightly entertained, nor are they simply the play of a speculative and ingenious mind. They lie at the basis of its whole System of Politics and Morality. They color all its views of Life, all its notices of the most common events, all its sketches of character and of fact. They mould its political theories and dictate its political measures. Instead of advocating, as once it did, a distribution of the proceeds arising from the sales of the Public Lands, among the States, which are its rightful owners, it now demands that all landless men shall receive from that source the "*equal shares*" to which, "by a law of Nature," they are said to have a "*perfect right*." The Tribune has long contended that national and individual good require a *diversity* of national pursuits,— that Manufactures must be built up, and men induced to embark in that branch of industry, for employment and an independent support. But now it insists upon the "perfect right" of every man to *land* whereon to produce what he needs for his subsistence. We cite, therefore, the case of the Tribune itself, as directly in point, and as showing that these principles, which concern the foundation of property and the rights thereof, are injurious and wrong, because they are undermining and gradually destroying sound and important doctrines of which the Tribune itself has hitherto been the advocate. And if it proceeds, as it certainly will, to carry these principles to their full extent, it must convert the political party with which it acts, into a new party, made up from all existing parties, and taking its stand upon the fundamental propositions, which have formed the theme of these remarks.

In further proof of the dangerous tendency of these views of the Tribune, we refer to the effect which they have had upon the public mind. Is it not evident to every one, who has watched the current of public thought, that they have changed the tone of public sentiment, upon many most important points? Look at the facts already cited. What shocked the public when Fanny Wright proclaimed it, in the Tribune enlists their championship, or at least their toleration. Principles which, when urged by Locofocos, were denounced as radical and destructive, when put forth by a leading Whig press, become simply milestones of "*Progress*" and "*Reform*." In 1840, O. A. Brownson, then an active Locofoco, published an elaborate proclamation of his belief that no man could rightfully bequeath property, which he owned, to his posterity; and claimed that it should be thrown into a common stock. The public sentiment was aroused;—leading Whig presses published the review in full, and held it up as a beacon whereby to warn the citizens of the Union from the rocks of *Radicalism* upon which the Locofocos would wreck the ship of State. Now the doctrine that *no man can rightfully own land at all*, finds an advocate in one of the leading Whig presses of the City of New York! And many sober-minded, sound-headed, thoroughly conservative Whigs, are excessively annoyed that any one should deem the fact of the least importance!

These are the considerations which we oppose to the fundamental principles of Association, as they are set forth in the Tribune's article of Nov. 20th, to which that paper will consider this our reply.

---

From the Tribune, Nov. 26th, 1846.

## LETTER II.

*To the Editor of the Courier and Enquirer:*

I DO not see how any man could, with my opening article before him, have misstated its positions as you have done. That, in a state of Nature, all men *had* an equal right to the Soil, and that each had a right to appropriate to his own use any portion of it requisite for the supply of his own wants and not already thus appropriated by another, is a truth of the most palpable character. That Civilized Society has substituted a different law for that of Nature on this subject, is equally manifest. But what then? Does it follow that the change must *necessarily* have originated in injustice? That, surely, is not my position. Civilized Society, according to my understanding of it, divests the individual of many important natural rights, and may justly do so upon proof that the *general* good is thereby promoted, and that the individual receives a fair compensation for that of which he is deprived. I hold, therefore, that there may be a legitimate and just appropriation of lands and succession thereto; and, though I cannot doubt that large grants of land to any individual were originally wrong, and that no more such should be made, I have never advocated the revocation of any which have been lawfully and honestly procured. I do not hold that a newly-discovered or long-forgotten truth invalidates the acts of the legitimate authority which were done in good faith in opposition to the dictates of that truth. I do not hold that all lands can be equally divided between this or any future generation, nor that they ought to be. What I propounded and still maintain is simply this:— *Civilized Society, having divested a large portion of mankind of any right to the Soil, their natural resource for employment and sustenance, is bound to guarantee them an* OPPORTUNITY TO LABOR, *and to secure to them the just Recompense of such Labor.* That is my fundamental proposition. Refrain from beating the air and admit or dispute it.

Of course, you will perceive that I am just as strenuous an advocate of "a diversity of National pursuits" as ever, and of Distributing among the States, for enduring uses, the Proceeds of the Public Lands, so long as those lands shall continue to be sold. What I mainly desire with regard to the Public Lands is a *Limitation* of the area thereof which any man may hereafter acquire and hold, whether directly or at second-hand. That Limitation established, it will be a matter of secondary consequence that they continue to be sold at a moderate price, or be apportioned at free cost to those who need them.

Your allusion to Fanny Wright, utterly unwarranted by any evidence adduced by you, or by any facts within my knowledge, does not surprise me. I was well aware from the outset, that your course would be to appeal unscrupulously to prejudices, bugbears, and nicknames, to parry the dictates of Reason, Justice and Humanity. I do not believe Fanny Wright ever propounded or held views identical with mine respecting the Public Lands and the Right to Labor, but I shall not desert or deny a truth because she or any one else has proclaimed it.

I should prefer next to take up and demonstrate the *necessity* of a radical and thorough Reform of Society, if it be deemed desirable, to preserve the Laboring Class anywhere from the degradation and misery which has already befallen a large proportion of the landless multitude in Europe, and preëminently in Great Britain and Ireland. To my mind it is absolutely demonstrable—nay, demonstrated—that such degradation and misery are the results of causes and influences inherent in our present Social framework, and not to be eradicated until that framework shall be essentially changed. At this moment the farming laborers of England produce twice as much grain to the hand as the same labor produced three centuries ago, yet receive far less bread for their year's wages than they then did, and are actually in worse condition than were their ancestors of the Sixteenth Century. So is it in France, in Germany, in Italy. The incomes of the Wealthy and the destitution of the Poor are steadily increasing, side by side, throughout the civilized world. I see no remedy for this under our present system of Society. I am sure it may be remedied, without despoiling or injuring any one, on the basis of Association. Of that basis let me now give an outline sketch:—

By Association, then, I understand, under this term I advocate, a Social Order which shall substitute for the present Township, Commune, Parish, School District, or whatever the smallest Social Organization above the Family may be termed, a Phalanx or Social Structure expressly calculated to secure to all its members (who shall at the outset be two or three hundred, but ultimately be increased to near two thousand) the following blessings:—

1. A *Home*, commodious, comfortable, and permanent, so long as each has means to pay the fair annual rent thereof, or is willing to labor to defray such rent—and from which he can never be ousted because of sickness, infirmity, or other misfortunes.

2. An *Education*, complete and thorough, Moral, Physical, and Intellectual, commencing in infancy and continued without interruption to perfect maturity, and longer if desirable.

3. A *Subsistence*, in infancy and childhood, at the cost of their respective parents; in after-life from the fruits of their own Industry or from the income of their several investments, if such there be; but in case of orphanage, sickness, infirmity, or decrepitude without property, then at the charge of the Phalanx, as now of the Township, City, or County.

4. *Opportunity to Labor* secured to each individual, man, woman, and child, at all times, whatever his or her capacity, skill, or efficiency.

5. Just and fair *Recompense* to each for the labor actually performed by him or her, with assured opportunity for constant *Improvement* in Arts, Processes, and industrial ability.

6. Agreeable *Social Relations*, including facilities for frequent and familiar intercourse with those eminent for wisdom, virtue, learning, piety, or philanthropy.

7. Simple and ever-increasing Libraries, Cabinets, Philosophical Apparatus, &c. &c. with stated evening Lectures on Chemistry, Botany, Agriculture, Geology, and all branches of desirable Knowledge.

Such is a rude outline of the facilities to be afforded, with some of the more palpable ends to be attained, by the Association of a number of families in the ownership and occupancy of a single Domain of Five or Six Thousand Acres, the occupants inhabiting a single edifice or Phalanstery located on its most eligible site, and cultivated by the labor of all or nearly all the male members of suitable age, while a portion of them, larger or smaller according to the season and the weather, with most of the women and children, will be employed in the various Manufactures prosecuted by the Phalanx. Some of the external advantages and physical economies to be secured by the ultimate perfection of this Social Order are as follows:—

1. Economy of Land. Under the guidance of scientific and thorough agriculturists, an Association, with its immense gardens, orchards, vineyards, &c. would produce four times as much as is usually obtained from a like area, and would require not more than two acres (ultimately much less) to each occupant, instead of the ten or twenty acres' average of our present farms, to each person subsisted thereon.

2. Economy of Fences and of Fuel. The Domain cultivated jointly by five hundred families would not require so much fencing as would be necessary on one-tenth of the same area cut up into twenty little farms in the occupancy of so many diverse families; and the Unitary Edifice of an Association would be thoroughly and equally warmed with one tenth of the fuel now required to warm imperfectly the isolated dwellings of four or five hundred families.

3. Economy of Household Labor, Cooking, Washing, &c. The saving herein must be immense, even if one half the families should chose to take their meals privately in their several apartments, as they would be at perfect liberty to do.

4. Economy and perfection in Implements of Culture and Industry generally. The farmer of limited means can not now afford to supply himself with the best implements of his calling. He can barely afford to purchase the variety of Plows actually required to perform all kinds of Plowing with the greatest economy and in the best manner, and add thereto Cultivators, Harrows, Scythes, &c. &c., but to furnish himself with Planting, Sowing, Reaping and Mowing Machines, Stump Extractors, Fanning Mills, &c. &c., is utterly beyond his ability. Yet every day is adding to the number and perfection of these labor-saving inventions, without which the farmer of the next age will find himself thrown completely in the rear, and unable to compete in products and prices with his wealthy neighbor. I would gladly enlarge on this point, which is more or less applicable to every department of human effort and industry. The time is at hand when the Laboring Man must own the best Machinery, or be owned by the owners of it.

5. Economy in the cost of Education. Five to eight hundred children, living under the one roof, having there the choicest Maps, Globes, Orreries, Chemical Apparatus, &c., with Free Lectures at least weekly on the various Useful Arts and Sciences, alternating with their teachers from the gardens and work-rooms to the schools of various grades, would learn immensely faster than any now do, while the cost of instruction would be vastly less than now. Under proper regulations as to the distribution of time, all life would become Education, and a youth of twenty would often have acquired a far more thorough and solid intellectual culture than is now usually perfected in our highest seminaries.

6. Economy in Commercial Exchanges. The Phalanx, purchasing for all its members at wholesale for ready pay and selling in the same manner, would effect an exchange of the products it could spare for the commodities it should need at a twentieth part of the present cost, and thus save to Productive Labor at least one-fifth of its earnings now necessarily paid in mercantile profits and in the cost of transmitting its surplus products to their consumers.

7. Economy in the cost of Medical Attendance, Legal Proceedings, (rendered in good part needless,) &c. &c.

—But I am transcending my limits, and must stop. Bear in mind that I regard the Reform which Association proposes, and of which I have here sketched but the dry skeleton without the animating soul, as one to be effected cautiously, gradually, and with due regard to all existing interests. I do not anticipate its consummation in one year, nor in ten. But that the end it proposes is one to which Society should gravitate—nay, to which it *does* gravitate—that it should be studied, labored for, lived for, prayed for, until attained, is the ardent conviction of         H. G.

---

From the Tribune of the same date as above.

"*From the Courier and Enquirer of Nov. 20th.*

"It will be seen * * * that the Tribune *promises* to commence the discussion. We congratulate ourselves on having brought it, by dint of constant and close efforts, to this point, and await the fulfillment of *this* promise with some degree of hope that it will not, because it can not be avoided. We trust and believe that some degree of advantage to the public will accrue from the discussion, to which, it will be remembered, we were originally challenged by the Tribune upon *certain specific and well defined terms,* which we join with that paper in hoping will be 'carefully remembered.' We therefore copy them, and ask the Tribune to do the same, in order that they may be distinctly understood by the readers of both papers:—

*'From the Tribune of Sept. 8.*

'As soon as the State Election is fairly over—say November 10th—we will publish an article, filling a column of the Tribune, very nearly, in favor of Association as we understand it; and upon the Courier's copying this and replying, we will give place to its reply, and respond; and so on, until each party shall have published twelve articles on its own side, and twelve on the other, which shall fulfill the terms of this agreement. All the twelve articles of each party shall be published, without abridgment or variation in the Daily, Semi-weekly, and Weekly editions of both papers. Afterward, each party will of course be at liberty to comment at pleasure in his own columns. In order that neither paper shall be crowded with this discussion, one article per week only shall be given on either side, unless the Courier shall prefer greater dispatch.'"

☞ Our commencement of the Discussion opened on the very same morning with the above. The Courier's readiness to discuss with us on "*certain* SPECIFIC *and well defined terms,*" is evinced by opening on its part in an article of nearly *three times* the length expressly agreed upon! all which we are expected to publish, and *do* publish herewith. How much farther this imposition is to be carried, for the sake not so much of discussing or controverting what the Tribune proposes, as of telling the public what an exceedingly mischievous and dangerous paper the Tribune is, and how similar its views are to those of Fanny Wright, &c., &c., remains to be seen. We now give fair notice, however, that we intend to keep substantially within the limits agreed upon, and shall hold ourselves bound hereafter to publish of the Courier's articles so much only as comes within the rule. That paper will do as it sees fit about publishing, when we request it, an extra quantity equal to the overplus which it has so unjustly saddled upon us to-day.

From the Courier and Enquirer, Nov. 30, 1846.
## REPLY TO LETTER II.

IN its first article upon Association, the Tribune attempted to place the matter of Social Reform upon the ground of abstract right. It set forth the fundamental proposition out of which its theory grows, and drew therefrom the inferences which its object required. We copied that proposition in the Tribune's own language; and proved that it could not be true, because it led, inevitably and by logical necessity, to the absolute denial of the Right of individual Property in Land or in any thing else. The Tribune in reply charges us with having "*misstated* its positions." The charge is so absurd that it becomes simply ludicrous. We copied the very language of the Tribune itself. We gave to it precisely the meaning which common sense required. We drew from it simply the deductions which were unavoidable. None of these things does the Tribune dispute. How then can it charge us with having "misstated its positions?"

The Tribune makes a *new* statement of its position, which is briefly this:—

1. In a state of Nature all men had an equal right to the soil.
2. Civilized Society has deprived a large portion of them of that soil, to which they had this right.
3. Society is therefore *bound,* by natural justice, to recompense them for that land; and the Tribune proposes that the guaranty of an "opportunity to labor" shall be that recompense.

Here, as before, it is clearly manifest, that the only rightful claim of the kind specified, which the landless portion of mankind can have upon society, must be based upon some *wrong* inflicted upon them. Unless society has deprived them of land to which they had a perfect right, it owes them no recompense. If it owes them the recompense claimed by the Tribune, it can only be upon the ground that they were unjustly deprived of land to which they had a natural and a perfect right. If that deprivation was not unjust, no recompense is due. The Tribune insists that a recompense is due: and it, therefore, unavoidably implies now, what it openly asserted before, that the holders of land have despoiled those who own none, of the "equal share" to which, "by a law of nature," they had a "perfect right." If Society does owe to the landless man the guaranty demanded, as a recompense for having devested him of land, it can only be upon the ground that the land was rightfully his own. If it was rightfully his own, by a law of nature, it must have been wrongfully seized and held by another. And so we return to the precise point from which the Tribune set out, and from which it now endeavors to escape, namely, that the actual appropriation of land by individuals—in other words, the existing ownership of Land—is contrary to the Law of Nature, and a *wrong* inflicted upon those who own no land. This, as we have already shown, is equivalent to a denial of the Right of Property in Land, or in any thing else.

We said in our first article that the Tribune would undoubtedly disavow any such opinion; and so it attempts to do. But how can it do so in the face of its fundamental principle? While it persists in urging that the landless have a *claim* upon the owners of land for a recompense—while it insists that Society is *bound* to guarantee to them an equivalent for the land of which they have been deprived, how can it possibly disown the fundamental principle upon which this claim is founded? The two must stand or fall together. Either the landless man has been wrongfully deprived of land to which he had a perfect right, or Society owes him no recompense. The Tribune can not maintain the latter, and yet reject the former. If "Society is *bound* to guarantee the landless an opportunity to labor," it can only be upon the ground that it has done them wrong—that it has deprived them of land to which they had a right, and for which, as yet, it has paid them no return.

The Tribune, then, does still virtually, as it did in terms before, assert, that "every person born within the State of New York had a perfect right to his equal share of the soil thereof;" that Society has wrongfully deprived him of that right, and that it owes him therefor a recompense. Nor can that paper evade the full responsibility of such a declaration, as it seeks to do by adroitly changing the terms of its proposition, and substituting for it the truism, that "in a state of nature all men had an equal right to the soil." That proposition is not true, in any sense available for the Tribune's purposes. Men are not now born into any such "state of nature" as that in which it could be true. They are not born into any state which gives them an "equal right to the soil." They were born, not into a state of nature, but into a civil state—a state molded into form by the institution of Property; a state which has grown out of that institution, as the tree grows from its root. They were born into it with many rights which are perfect; but among them is not a right to an "equal share of the soil." They are not *deprived* of that right by Society, because they never possessed it. Society owes them no recompense, for it has done them no wrong. Thus falls to the ground the *new* fundamental proposition of the Tribune, which is simply a repetition of its old one, that Society is *bound*, by natural justice and right, to guarantee to the landless an opportunity to labor, as a recompense for the land of which it has deprived them.

Now the Tribune must not represent us as saying that such a guaranty is not *desirable*, or as opposing its attainment by any just and feasible means. We do no such thing. We only, thus far, have denied the validity of the Tribune's claim, upon the ground of *abstract and absolute Right*. We deny that any such change in Society is demanded by Justice; and that there is any thing in the essential relation between the owners of land and those who own none, which would impose upon the former the obligations claimed. We do so, because the claim is based upon principles false in themselves, and destructive to Society. It can not be maintained without involving, as we have shown, the absolute denial of the Right of Property; and in maintaining it, as the Tribune does, it does in effect maintain, in spite of its qualified disclaimer, that the monopoly of land by individuals is in violation of the law of nature, and a *wrong* which must be redressed "Association" proposes to redress that wrong; to secure to the persons who have been deprived of land, as an equivalent for their loss, an "opportunity to labor, with a certainty of securing a just reward therefor."

The Tribune proceeds to set forth the blessings to be secured by Association; and among them are these: a House, an Education, a Subsistence, opportunity to Labor, just pay therefor, agreeable Social relations, and constant progress in knowledge. We need scarcely assure the Editor of that paper that we shall most heartily coöperate with him in urging any reform, or any system of measures, which will secure these blessings to all mankind. They are objects which all must deem desirable; and it is the constant and unceasing aim of all good men, in Society as it now exists, to place these blessings within the reach of all. The Tribune claims that it can be accomplished only by the Association of a large number of families, in the ownership and cultivation of a large domain, living together in one house, and laboring together upon this single farm. This is its *claim:* but it remains to be substantiated. As yet the Tribune has given no proof of its efficacy, nor has it even informed us of the terms or method of Association. In whom is the property to be vested? How is labor to be remunerated? What share is capital to have in the concern? By what device are men to be induced to labor? How are moral offenses to be excluded, or punished? These, and a great variety of other queries, must be answered before we can have any precise and definite notion of the nature and form of the Association proposed. Any discussion of the system as such, therefore, must of course be postponed until the Tribune sets forth clearly and in detail the organization, essential character, and proposed advantages of, such an Association.

The Tribune professes to have been "aware, from the outset, that our course would be to appeal unscrupulously to *prejudices, bugbears,* and *nicknames* to parry the dictates of Reason, Justice, and Humanity." Language like this is quite uncalled for. It is utterly unwarranted by any thing we have said. We need hardly say that we regard the Tribune's doctrines, against which we are contending, as any thing but the "dictates of Reason, Justice, and Humanity." In claiming them as such, the Tribune very coolly *assumes* every point in controversy, and reproaches us very coarsely for not yielding to its pretensions. In attempted vindication of its assertion, that we appeal to "prejudices, bugbears, and nicknames," it only specifies our mention of the name of Fanny Wright, well knowing at the same time, that we expressly disavowed disrespect to any one, and only referred to it as designating a point of time, in the progress of radical sentiments. The *fact* of such progress, which was the important point of our remark, the Tribune does not question, or even notice. We regard it as undeniable, and as highly important in connection with this discussion. It proves the necessity of directing public attention to these opinions, and to the means by which they are constantly and insidiously urged upon the public notice. It proves that, while the public mind is agitated and absorbed by exciting matters of temporary interest—by discussions concerning the measures and men of political parties, principles are slowly and quietly gaining ground, which will in the end modify and transform, if they do not destroy, all existing parties. We cited, as an instance in point, the fact that the Tribune itself, long the advocate of the Distribution of the proceeds of the Public Lands among the several States, has now ventured openly to advocate their being *given away* to persons who own no land. No more forcible or striking proof could have been adduced of the power and tendency of these radical sentiments than was here afforded. And the Tribune, far from denying the essential fact charged upon it, simply reiterates its adherence to the Whig principle of Distribution, *so long as these lands continue to be sold;*—adroitly suppressing the fact that it opposes their being sold any longer, and urges, instead, their free apportionment! It proposes, moreover, to *limit* the amount of Land which any one man may own. Without inquiring now into the inherent justice of such a limitation, we have only to remark, that if it be just and politic, it seems equally just and politic to limit the amount of property *of any kind* which a man may acquire. Indeed, the right to impose restrictions in the one case implies a similar right in the other : and the necessity of so doing is certainly quite as strong. If the government has a right to forbid one man from holding as much land as he can buy and pay for, it must also have the right to forbid his holding the *products* of land beyond a certain limit. The exercise of such a power in either case, we apprehend, would be a stretch of authority on the part of government, which would as far outstrip the extremest despotism of an absolute monarchy, as it would transcend the rights of republican rulers.

We think we have clearly shown the baselessness of the Tribune's claims on the ground of abstract right, and have repelled its coarse aspersions of our fairness and courtesy. We think it not at all unlikely that we shall insist, in the course of this discussion, that the Tribune is an "exceedingly mischievous and dangerous paper;" but it will be only by way of inference from the principles which it promulgates; and for those principles, as well as for all just inferences from them, the Tribune, and not we, must be held responsible.

Several other points of the Tribune's letter we shall pass unnoticed—partly because they are not important, and partly because we do not wish needlessly to extend this article. We wish it, however, understood that we have never agreed to make our articles of any specific length; nor has any thing been said concerning their length on either side, except with regard to the opening article, on the Tribune's side—which that paper said should "fill a column of the Tribune, very nearly." Nothing whatever has been said of the length of the subsequent articles on either side;—but the specific agreement was, that "all the twelve articles of each party should be published *without abridgment or variation* in the Daily, Semi-weekly and Weekly editions of both papers." We shall see that *our* part of this agreement is fulfilled to the letter.

---

From the Tribune, Dec. 1st.
LETTER III.

*To the Editor of the Courier and Enquirer:*

WHEN our revolutionary Congress passed its world-renowned Declaration of Independence, in the assumption, as "self-evident" truths, that "All men are created equal," and "endowed by their Creator with certain inalienable rights —that among these are life, liberty, and the pursuit of happiness," they asserted either a pregnant truth or a most pernicious falsehood. If the latter, their separation from Great Britain was an act of God-defying treason, as the Tories of that day conscientiously believed it, and we are still the rightful though rebellious subjects of Queen Victoria. If their fundamental basis were a truth, not a "fanfaronade of nonsense," as it has been pronounced, but a vital verity, then it is a truth which directly sustains my elemental proposition already considered. For, if all men be really endowed by their Creator with an inalienable right to life (that is, inalienable until forfeited by their own misconduct), then are they also endowed by their Creator with a right to the means of sustaining and preserving life. If a man should refuse to masticate his food, and thence die, such death involves or proceeds from no infringement of his natural rights; just so, if he starve because he refuses to perform the labor necessary to bend the elements to the production of food; but if a man, able and willing to labor, is permitted to famish for want of Employment, the original right of all to the Soil having been taken away by Civilized Society, and the right to use the Earth for purposes of culture and production vested in a part only, how can it be said that the "inalienable right" of that man to "life" was not practically subverted? I can not realize that there is need of further argument on this point. I reiterate, then, the points argued in my two previous articles :—1. Originally, in a state of Nature, all men had an equal right to the Earth and its natural products, and any man had a right to occupy and improve any portion of the Soil not already so occupied by another. 2. This right was taken away by Civilized Society, or its agent, Government, in granting to individuals or allowing them to acquire an exclusive right to portions of the Soil beyond their respective wants for cultivation. 3. Society, having thus divested a large portion of mankind of any right to the Soil, their natural resource for Employment and Sustenance, is bound to guarantee to each of them an OPPORTUNITY TO LABOR, and to secure them the just RECOMPENSE of their Labor. These are the positions I have thus far labored to establish, with what pertinence and success our readers will judge. On these positions I base my assumption that the Wealthy and Powerful in our present Social Order are morally bound to seek out and establish a better Social Condition for the less fortunate millions around and beneath them, whose *chance* to obtain an honest livelihood now depends on the casualty of some one or more of the possessors of Property wishing to hire them—a condition in which the right to Labor and to the equitable products of such Labor shall be practically secured and enjoyed by all. Here I stand, and mean to stand. Our readers will judge whether you have or have not misstated my positions, in order to evade them, and whether the statement that "the *existing* ownership of Land is contrary to the Law of Nature" (which even Blackstone asserts as an incontrovertible truth) is indeed "equivalent to a denial of the Right of Property in Land, or in any thing else." You are very welcome to argue, if you choose, that the compensation I plead for to those whom Society has divested of all Right to the Soil is inadequate or inappropriate, and that the Lands themselves ought to be restored and held in common, or equally divided. I have no objection to as much of this as you please as *your* proposition, but I am satisfied with my own. I deduce the universal Right to Labor from premises which appear to me really incontrovertible by a believer in the Whig principles of the American Revolution, or in any Republican principles whatsoever. If these principles lead farther than is necessary for my purpose, so be it; but that can not invalidate their truth. The assertion, however, that an averment of the original Right of all men to Land, and their consequent subsisting Right to Labor, "is equivalent to a denial of the Right of Property in Land, or indeed in any thing else," proves nothing but a deplorable want of reflection on the subject. The natural right to Individual Property has its origin in Labor. He who cuts a tree in the forests, and fashions it into a canoe or a cradle, has an exclusive right to the article he has thus made, provided he has left timber to others wherefrom to make themselves canoes or cradles. Were he to make a canoe of the only tree within the territory of his tribe, I should question his Right to deny the use of it to his brethren, though I should insist on his right to be compensated by them, in case they used it, for his labor in making the canoe. Need I say more to indicate the broad line of demarcation between the true and universal Right of Property, and such falsely-assumed Rights as would deny to the mass of men, not merely Property, but the elements out of which Property is to be fashioned!

Your denial of the right of all men to be guaranteed an Opportunity to Labor in case they are divested of their original right to the Soil, seems to me based on exactly the considerations and couched in almost the language wherein the advocates of despotism have in all ages resisted the right of Mankind to Liberty, or a voice in the government which rules them. I have an indistinct recollection that your very argument about men being born, "not into a state of Nature, but* * * a state molded into form by the institution of Property," &c., is found in Burke's answer to Paine's "Rights of Man"—that I have read it in one or more essays in support of Monarchy and Aristocracy, I have a distinct recollection. I do not deem it better or worse on that account; but, as you incessantly harp on the affinities and tendency of my arguments, you will hardly object to be reminded of the natural relationship of yours.

Enough for the present that you deny, as distinctly and broadly as I assert, the *Right* of all men to Labor, and the consequent Duty devolved on the State or the legal owners of the Soil to guarantee it to them. You admit, however, that such guaranty is desirable, if it can be attained by just and feasible means. Very good: I will endeavor soon to set forth distinctly what these means are. But this will be difficult if you insist on your right to make your articles twice or thrice the length I indicated long before commencing, and which I thought you clearly enough understood to be a measure, not for one article or one party, but for each and all. I proposed a column as the space which I could conveniently devote to this subject, without trenching upon room needed for other purposes Thus far, you have filled more than twice the space exacted by the articles to which you were replying. If you think this is fair play, go on. I mean in my next to go on with the development of Association, whatever may be the cavils interposed. I will now, however, reply to your practical questions:

1. The Property of an Association will be vested in those who contributed the Capital to establish it, represented by Shares of Stock, just as the property of a Bank, Factory, or Railroad now is.

2. Labor will be remunerated by a fixed and definite *proportion* of the *Products* of such Labor, or of their Proceeds, if sold by or to the Association.
3. Capital ditto. Skill or Talent ditto.
4. Men are to be induced to labor by a knowledge that their reward will be a certain and major proportion of the Product, which of course will be less or more according to the energy, skill, and diligence wherewith they labor. Now the Slave has no inducement to labor but the fear of the lash, and the Hireling has a thousand temptations to eye-service or unfaithfulness. Even the worker for himself is often discouraged or rendered sluggish by the loneliness, monotony, or seeming inefficacy of his solitary toil. But a group of ten or twelve chosen companions, laboring for themselves under a chief chosen by and from themselves, and knowing that two-thirds to three-fourths of all they produce will be divided among them, after making just compensation for the use of the fertilized Land, most improved Machinery, &c., will need few "devices" to tempt them to labor. The facts that excellence in useful Labor will be the sure and only road from Indigence to Competence, and that it will be the fountain of civic honors and Social distinction, can not be without their influence. And the circumstances that all the children will be educated to see honors thus bestowed and distinctions accorded to those who have evinced genius, skill, or devotion in the peaceful walks of Industry rather than in the fields of Carnage or the arenas of forensic strife, can not fail to exercise a profound and lasting influence.

5. Moral offenses may be punished by legal penalties, as at present, if necessary. If the circumstance of living constantly in the eye of hundreds, whose reprobation would be moral exile and blasting ignominy, the agreeable, healthful excitement of a constant, animated, ever-varying Industry, and the guaranty of a thorough Moral, Physical, and Intellectual Education to each and all, shall combine to render offenses comparatively infrequent, I trust that will not be objected to by the Courier, any more than by H. G.

From the *Courier and Enquirer*, Dec. 8, 1846.

### REPLY TO LETTER III.

In its last article upon Association the Tribune comes fairly back to the proposition with which it started, and from which it sought to recede—namely, that all the men at any time born upon any territory have, by a law of Nature, a "perfect right" to "equal shares" of its soil. It attempts now, moreover, to make an argument in its support. The Declaration of Independence proclaims the "inalienable right of every man to life." This includes, the Tribune asserts, a right to the *means* of living, and therefore to *land*, as that from which such means are to be derived. Our objection to this argument is, that it proves too much. Land is not the first necessity of a famishing man. His primary want is the want of food, of the *products* of land. If, then, such a man have an inalienable and unconditional right to the means of living, as the Tribune asserts, he has a right to his "equal share" of the *food* in the world, of which Society has deprived him. His right is not merely a "right to *labor*," but a right to *food*. The Tribune's proposition, therefore, when carried out, proves the right of every man, not simply to land, but to its products—not to labor, but to food, and so also to clothing and to shelter. It proves, therefore, too much; it establishes what is not true, and therefore it can not be true itself.

Or take the other branch of the proposition.

The same Declaration of Independence proclaims the "inalienable right" of every man to the "pursuit of happiness." This, upon the Tribune's theory, includes a right to the means of becoming happy. What these means are, must of course depend upon each individual's notion of happiness. The Tribune's reasoning, therefore, would establish the "inalienable right" of every man to his share of whatever he deems essential to his "pursuit of happiness." The conclusion certainly is inadmissible: therefore the premises can not be true. The right of man to life and the pursuit of happiness does not include a right to the *means* of living and becoming happy, except so far as these may be acquired by him without interference with the rights of others. This conclusion is clear, because the opposite proposition leads inevitably to results which are palpably false.

But the Tribune does not recognize the validity of this mode of reasoning. "If these principles," says the editor of that paper, "lead farther than is necessary for my purpose, so be it: *but that can not invalidate their truth.*" In our judgment, that depends upon what they lead to. The Tribune may have heard of the *reductio ad absurdum.* It is a method of reasoning which found favor with Euclid, and which has preserved its credit tolerably well to the present day. According to that, if any proposition can be shown logically, no matter by how long a process, to prove an absurdity or a falsehood, the proposition itself can not be true. The Tribune thinks differently. In its view, it is a matter of indifference, whither the principle leads when carried out. That paper accepts it just "so far as is necessary for its purpose:" to all beyond that point, it shuts its eyes. If a proposition is laid down, which logically warrants the conclusion that black is white, or that a part is more than the whole, or that wrong is right, "*so be it,*" says the Tribune: "that can not invalidate the truth" of the principle "so far as it is necessary for my purpose." We can not assent to this novel theory of reasoning.

We have proved, in our first article, by an argument the conclusiveness of which the Tribune has not yet impeached, that its fundamental proposition, asserting the "perfect right" of every man born in the State of New York to his "equal share" of its soil, of necessity involves a denial of the right of any man to be the exclusive *owner* of any land. That point we regard as established, because the argument proving it has not been impeached: nor is its validity at all disturbed by the Tribune's "indistinct recollection" that the same argument was used by "Burke in his answer to Paine's 'Rights of Man.'" Unfortunately for us, as well as for the Tribune's memory, Burke, to the best of our knowledge, never wrote such an answer, and we can not therefore fall back upon his great authority. The Tribune complains that we "harp upon the affinities and tendencies" of its principles. This is very true; but in all our harping, we have struck no note half so full of import as this simple, tacit identification by the Tribune itself, of the "affinities" of its principles with those of Thomas Paine. We can not agree with that paper, that "we do not deem them better or *worse* on that account."

Having thus examined the fundamental principle out of which the scheme of Association grows, we can now advance to an inquiry into its PRACTICAL ORGANIZATION. The Tribune proposes that large tracts of land shall be occupied by large numbers of persons, inhabiting one house, laboring, living, and transacting all their business in common. These social structures, called Phalanxes, are to take the place of townships everywhere; and all the land of New York is to be occupied by the inhabitants of New York, in that form. The first question is, *who shall own it?* The second is, *who shall own its products?* Both are thus answered by the Tribune:

"1. The PROPERTY of an Association shall be vested in those who shall contribute the CAPITAL to establish it, represented by shares of stock.

"2. Labor, Capital, and Skill, will be remunerated by a fixed and definite *proportion* of their *products*, or of their proceeds, if sold."

These are the two fundamental principles which are to govern this new practical organization of society, and upon which it is to be conducted. They deserve examination. It will be seen that the men who have CAPITAL are to be the OWNERS of the land. A man with money enough may buy an entire domain, say five thousand acres—and even two or ten of them, for aught that yet appears. Laborers, the men without money, the men who have nothing but their strength or their skill, settle upon it to cultivate it, under the specific agreement that for their Labor they are to receive a fixed and definite *proportion* of its Products. What this proportion is to be we are not yet told, except that the Tribune says it will be a "*major* part." Suppose it to be *three-fourths*. How stands the contract then? Simply thus: *One rich man, or one rich Company, owns Five Thousand Acres of Land, which he leases forever to two thousand poor men, at the yearly rent of one-fourth of its products.* The relation subsisting between the *owners* of this land, and the *laborers* upon it, is simply that of Landlord and Tenants. The lease is perpetual—the rent is payable in kind. Precisely the same relation exists in regard to the house in which they dwell, the tools with which they work, the very domestic utensils and every thing else which they use. The Landlord, whether he be a man or a joint-stock Company, is the OWNER of the whole Property of the Association. The Laborer uses that property, and pays therefor a proportion of that which he produces. This is the system of land-tenure which the Tribune seeks to substitute for that now existing—this is the new form which that paper would give to Society; and it is a form which, in all its essential features, is identical with that by which all the large estates in the *Anti-Rent* districts have always been held. The property in those estates, just as in an Association, is vested in the men of capital. The laborers upon them, just as upon a Domain, receive a fixed *proportion* of the products of their labor—at least *nineteen-twentieths* of what they produce—whereas in Association the Tribune simply says they would receive a "major part." Upon these large estates, moreover, the tenants own their cattle, tools, &c., &c., whereas in Association *all* the property is vested in those who furnish the capital. The only differences, therefore, in the two cases are clearly in favor of the former. *The essential features of both forms and both relations are the same.* Association, as set forth by the Tribune, virtually proposes to " perpetuate and extend the relation of Landlord and Tenant over the whole arable surface of the Earth ;" a proposal to which, as the Tribune informed us on the 30th ult., the Hebrew Prophets were decidedly averse. Now we insist that the tenants of the Anti-Rent district should fulfill their contracts, and pay the rent they justly owe. But we are decidedly opposed to extending and perpetuating the system of land tenures which prevails there, over the rest of the State. The Tribune, on the contrary, virtually encourages the evasion of those contracts, but urges the universal adoption of that system. This seems to be the difference between us.

This is one of our many objections to the scheme of " Association as the Tribune understands it." We think there can be no room to doubt that its essential feature is that which we have indicated, and that its direct and inevitable tendency would be to render the relation of LANDLORD and TENANT universal and perpetual. This feature seems to be the framework of the whole—the skeleton which has hitherto been concealed from view by the plausible pretensions and philanthropic purposes which the Tribune has heaped upon it. Our aim is simply to *dissect* the scheme—to open it to public view—to scatter the fogs that envelop it, and let daylight shine through it— that its exact form and nature may be seen. One feature of it, we think, stands plainly in view; others will probably appear in due course of this discussion, in the progress of which we may, in spite of the Tribune's protest, feel bound to indicate the " affinities and tendencies" of its principles. If these should be, as the Tribune intimates they may, rather with Thomas Paine than Edmund Burke, for that, we submit, *we* can not be held responsible.

The Tribune professes to be, and thus far shows itself ready to answer all pertinent questions. We are yet ignorant of very many points connected with the practical working of Association. How, for instance, are the Laborers upon a domain to acquire a property in it? What provision is to be made for the natural increase of their numbers? Can the Capitalists who own it, be compelled in any way to sell? How is " constant industry" to be converted from *hard work* into an " agreeable excitement!" What is meant by " civic honors," and how are the people to be taught that excellence in useful labor is the only avenue to distinction? These and other points still require elucidation ;—we hope that paper will give them its attention ; and in that hope, for the present, we rest.

The Tribune says that thus far we have " *filled more than* TWICE *the space*" which its own articles occupy. Unfortunately for this assertion, *space* is susceptible of measurement; and the very article in which the assertion is made occupies *six square inches more* space in the Tribune itself, than our article to which it was written in reply. If the readers of the Tribune can command a carpenter's rule, they can measure for themselves.

---

From the Tribune, Dec. 8th, 1846.

### LETTER IV.

*To the Editor of the Courier and Enquirer:*

SINCE progress is essential to a discussion of the matter in controversy within the limits proposed, I will leave the subject of Man's Natural Rights where it now stands. I think I can well afford to do so. If there be *one* reader of both sides who believes your unsupported assertion that I affirm the " perfect right" of all men at any time born upon any territory to " equal shares of the Soil," in full view of what I *have* asserted and labored to demonstrate, I will waste no more words on *that* reader. Or, if there be one who can not discriminate between the assertion of an original right inhering in all men to a portion of the God-created elements, with their spontaneous productions, and the assertion of a similar right to the products of other men's labor or care, I despair of making an impression on that one. I write only for such as are capable of perceiving a palpable distinction, and candid enough to admit it when perceived. If there be any disposed to insist that Man *can not* have a natural right to such portion of the God-created elements as may be necessary to his subsistence (of which Society may rightfully divest him only by guaranteeing him a just equivalent) because, according to *their* logic, you can not admit this without proving a natural right to something *more*, they are welcome to spin such web of logical subtleties as long and as strong as they please. I only protest against having *my* limbs fettered by it.

That Paine and Burke were eminent champions of opposite theories of Government and Human Rights half a century ago, I will prove if you desire it, but I suppose I need not. That Burke's essays on this subject were truly *answers* to Paine's " Rights of Man," I think I shall have no difficulty in showing, even though he never named the work or the author. And that the substance of your argument in this connection may be found in Burke's writings, I will endeavor to show if you request it. That my fundamental positions are identical in substance with those of " The Rights of Man"—that the " affinities" of my Political principles are with those of Thomas Paine as against those of Edmund Burke, is most true. That yours are the opposite is also clear enough. And now, if you can induce any to repudiate the principles of the Declaration of Independence because Thomas Jefferson was an unbeliever, you will of course have no difficulty in disposing of " The Rights of Man" in the same way. The essential identity of the two cases needs no illustration. The American People have hitherto been able to discriminate between the Political truth inculcated by Paine and Jefferson, and the Theological error into which a misalliance (especially throughout Europe) of ritual Christianity with Aristocracy and Tyranny impelled them.

have confidence that they will continue to make that discrimination.

And now to the practical working of Association.

Your *decided* objection to "extending and perpetuating the [Manorial] system of Land Tenures," is a cheering symptom. I shall bear it in mind upon the great question of shielding forever our yet unsold Public Lands from the possibility of being so perverted. But when you proceed to argue that *Land* will absorb *one-fourth* of the products of an Association, because *Capital* may do so, you betray a sad want of acquaintance with the matter. The *Capital* of a mature Association would probably be Half a Million Dollars, of which the first cost of the Land would be, if U. S. land, say $8,000 or *one-sixtieth*. Thus, instead of Land (far better than the Manors, and in the same condition they were when they were leased to the Tenants) receiving *one-fourth* of the products, or *one-twentieth*, its proportion would be *one-two-hundred-and-fortieth*, until the not distant day when the Government shall change its system of disposing of those Lands, and allow the Landless to take and occupy an adequate portion thereof, without charge, except for the actual disbursements in acquiring, surveying, and allotting it. When that consummation shall have been reached, your solicitude in behalf of the "two thousand poor men" whom Association threatens to fleece of "one-fourth of their products" will no longer be in requisition.

Let me say, once for all, that Association proposes to divest no man of any property which the Law says is his. It does not interfere directly with Landholding, "Anti-Rent," "National Reform," &c. Its grand aim is to effect a Reconciliation of the interests of Capital and Labor, by restoring the natural Rights of the latter without trenching on the acquired Rights or Interests of the former. It will take no foot of land (until the Public Lands be made free) but by purchase of the legal owners at their own volition. Let me see if I can not show how this will be done, even to the casual reader. I will summarily contrast the Industrial Economy of an ordinary Township with that of an Association:—

A Township, we will say in Michigan, is settled, stragglingly, by some fifty to one hundred emigrants from New England or this State, most of them farmers by vocation. The first comers obtain good locations, and at the minimum price. But, on the other hand, they are doomed to live for years without Schools, without Churches; to travel many miles to Mills or Mechanics, with wretched apologies for Roads, and in daily want of many of the most essential comforts of life. The children necessarily grow up rude and unintellectual; hunting and fishing get the upper hand of work with them; Mails and Newspapers come along tardily and reach but few; the overshadowing woods, the decaying timber, the undrained marshes and rarely disturbed vegetable mold continue for many years to generate miasmas and multiply diseases, which, in the absence or scarcity of proper Medical talent, are tampered with by every Quack abomination; immense suffering is endured from the want of proper medicine, comforts, and nursing; many die whom proper care would have saved; while the aggregate loss of time by sickness (often at such seasons as to cause a loss of the fruits of the year's toil) is appalling. Such is a fair general picture of pioneering in the West—or, indeed, almost anywhere.

Years pass; the forest slowly melts away; the little notches first cut in it gradually connect with each other; a fruitful soil emerges from beneath the once eclipsing shade. Mills, School-houses, Churches, are erected; Stores are opened, Mechanics come in, with Doctors, Lawyers, &c., in abundance. Now the hitherto unoccupied lands are worth ten times, and, in the spot marked out by water-power or central position for the village, one hundred to five hundred times the original value. But what has created this additional value? The labor, amid privations and sufferings, of the pioneers. They have tamed the forest, constructed bridges, opened roads—made the country traversable, habitable, with comfort and facilities of intellectual improvement. But do they who did the work reap the advantages of it? By no means. The enhanced price of the unoccupied lands goes into other pockets than theirs; they have added much to the general wealth, but little or nothing to their own. Many of them are driven by their necessities, others by their indolent and improvident habits (how acquired we have seen) to sell their improvements for a song, and push off into the woods again. The grandchildren of the first settlers of Onondaga and Ontario, the children of the pioneers of Genesee and Chautauque, may to-day be found, generally destitute, in the log-huts of Illinois and Iowa. So will it be again and again.

Now let us see Association attempt to settle a new township. In the first place, the land is all bought at the first price with whatever else is necessary to an effective and comfortable outset, and this forms the original capital, which the pioneers, if destitute of property, must pay interest or rent upon, as we know no way to obtain the use and benefit of others' property but by paying for it. At once the axes of a hundred pioneers are put in requisition—not in a hundred isolated spots, but at that one best calculated for a beginning; and the forest is driven back half a mile each way from the site of the edifice that is to be. If a location partly prairie is chosen, that circumstance may be turned to far greater advantage in Association than in isolation. The prairie and woodland of the West would seem to have been blended in their giant proportions with a direct view to Associated Industry. If any swamp or other generator of miasma is at hand, one day's united labor will drain it; a week will suffice to make one good road out into daylight; a physician will be one of the pioneers; a School may be established and regular religious observances instituted before the first month has passed away. A saw-mill, grist-mill, smiths' shops, &c., &c., will be put in operation forthwith, saving an enormous waste of time in running to and from one and another of them by isolated backwoodsmen. Whatever articles are needed will be purchased in some large mart by wholesale at prime cost, instead of being bought at double price of the small dealers in a new region, and another price lost in time and team or shoe-leather in procuring them. A twentieth part of the labor required to fence miserably the petty clearings of the isolated settlers (which must be fenced again and again as each clearing is extended) will fence thoroughly the one Domain of the Association, and there will be a mill at hand to aid in getting out the materials. So with digging wells, purchasing implements, procuring books, newspapers, &c., &c. Are not the economies of Association palpable and immense! Do not three-fourths of our People stand in need of the additional comforts and intellectual advantages which Association proffers? Why, then—if it be affirmed that the mass of men are too selfish, depraved, short-sighted, to realize these blessings—will not regenerate, self-sacrificing Christians take hold, and set us an example of a reform so vast, universal, and enduring in its consequences?

But to the particular point of capitalists being the owners of the land, and taking one-fourth of all the products therefor. We have seen that the first cost of the land is but a bagatelle compared with the actual capital of a mature Association; and such would still be the fact although the land were bought at a price (on account of improvements already made upon it) as high as $20 per acre. Probably $50,000 capital in all would supply the indispensable wild land, implements, provisions, materials, &c., &c., for a beginning on new land at Government price, out of which beginning, in the course of ten or fifteen years, a mature Association could, by steady, well-directed Labor, be developed, having now a population of One Thousand or Two Thousand Acres under thorough culture in gardens, orchards, nurseries, grain, vegetables, &c, with an equal amount in Grass, and as much more remaining in the primitive forest. The entire property, including a permanent Edifice affording ample accommodations for all, Groceries, Barns, Mills, Workshops, Machinery, &c., would now be worth some Half a Million Dollars. One-fourth of the "product to Capital" (should experience indicate that as the just proportion) would be a heavy burden, say you! But to *what* Capital! Not merely to the $50,000 Capital borrowed or invested for the commencement (allowing the resident associates to have nothing of their own), but to the *whole* capital now invested, including the nine-tenths created by the persevering, well-directed Labor of the associates as well as that originally procured from others. The "one-fourth to Capital" would thus be nine-tenths divided among the workers themselves and their parents and seniors, now too old for severe labor, instead of being allotted entirely to the original capitalists. Very soon, the residents would be able to buy up the stock of the non-residents, who would thus be enabled and encouraged to invest in another Association just starting—and so on. There would be no compulsion, no obligation to sell, nor any need of it. Changes by death, vicissitudes, and a natural inclination of capitalists to aid those who need aid, rather than hang as a burden on those who do not, would render it easy for an Association to buy in its stock held by non-residents whenever able and desirous to do so.

As to the "agreeable excitement" of "constant industry," it is *now* realized by thousands who have congenial occupations amid associates of their choice. Many a man who can not do a day's work in a field alone, *enjoys* a hard day's work at a house-raising or log-rolling. Many a one now drags through the day in a filthy, ill ventilated, half-warmed, repulsive workshop, who would work heartily in an agreeable locality and in the vocation of his choice. But I can not here enter upon the philosophy of Attractive Labor—this article is already too long.

I am compelled to exceed the length originally stipulated, by your habitually and inveterately doing so; I can not otherwise obviate your cavils and answer your questions, and make any progress in the controversy. Yet are you not ashamed, on reflection, of so paltry a quibble as is contained in your assertion, that my last in the *leaded minion* of Tribune Editorials fills more *space* than your preceding in the *solid nonpareil* (which is twice as much matter to the square inch), in which its length constrained me to place it? The following is the actual measurement (excluding the *leads*, which each party properly gives to his own, and not to his opponent's articles) of the three articles hitherto published on each side respectively:

Our 1st art. ...4128 ems.     Courier's do.....9315 ; diff. 5187
Our 2d do.... 5661 "          Courier's do.....6585 ; diff. 924
Our 3d do ...4704 "           Courier's do.....5715 ; diff. 1011

Excess of Courier's articles over ours,....... ..7,122
Or, 297 minion lines—equal to ONE AND ONE THIRD columns of the Tribune, solid.

Now be so good as not to exceed this in *actual* length, and I will try to get back to the column on each side originally proposed, and keep there. H. G.

From the Courier and Enquirer, Dec. 14th, 1846.

## REPLY TO LETTER IV.

THE Tribune's reply to our last article upon this subject, will be found in our columns this morning. We pass by, for the present, its doctrine of Natural Rights, and ask attention to that portion of the article which relates to the PRACTICAL WORKING of Association.

It is universally agreed that the existing Social System is not perfect—that it fails to remedy certain evils which prevent that universal diffusion of happiness which all deem desirable. These evils, in our judgment, grow out of the defects or vices of individual character, and are only to be remedied by individual and personal reform. The Tribune ascribes them to the organization of Society; and contends that they are only to be remedied, by an entire change and reorganization of the forms and methods of Social Life. It habitually exaggerates these evils, in order to render more vivid the conviction that some social reform is needed; and then it insists that the only remedy which will prove efficient is to be found in ASSOCIATION. We contend, on the contrary, that Association will only increase and perpetuate the *worst features* of the existing Social System. And first we notice the new relations which Association will establish between the Proprietors and the Cultivators of the Soil.

In our last article we proved that the direct and inevitable tendency of Association would be, to render the relations of LANDLORD and TENANT *universal and perpetual*. We proved this from the premises of the Tribune itself—1. That the property of an Association would be vested in those who should furnish the capital; and, 2d. That Labor would receive as its reward, a share of its products. These principles would govern all Associations; and when Association should become universal, these principles would become universal likewise, and the relation of landlord and tenant would be everywhere and forever prevalent. In reply to this position, the Tribune says nothing whatever, but aims merely to show, that *the land* would not draw so large a rent as was implied by an illustration which we used. It affects to regard our objection to the system as founded upon the allegation, that "land would absorb *one fourth* of the products of an Association." Now this formed no part of our argument. We insisted simply that the relation established between the two classes of society would be that of Landlord and Tenant; and the Tribune has not denied that it would be so; nor can it make any such denial, unless it first repudiates the principles it has already laid down. The men who furnish the capital, buy the land, build the edifice, provide the table, purchase the tools, the furniture, the machinery, the cattle, and indeed *every thing* which the Association may need; and of all these things they are the OWNERS. The laborers, with their families, live in that house, eat at that table, and work with those tools upon that farm; and when the harvests are gathered in, they take to themselves a part thereof in payment of their labor, and deliver the rest as *rent* to the owners of the property. Now it matters not *how much* rent they pay nor how little. The fact remains, that they are merely *Tenants* upon the estates of certain Landlords. Do they not, then, occupy precisely the position, in all essential respects, of the tenants in the Anti-Rent district; and since the leases in both cases are perpetual, and the rent payable in kind, is not their relation to the owners of the estate essentially the same?

This question the Tribune has not attempted to answer; though it does attempt to evade its force by drawing an illusory distinction between the capital of a mature Association, and the original cost of starting one. Thus, in a paragraph of which we condense the language though we vary neither the words nor the meaning, it says:—

"Probably $50,000 would supply the indispensable land, implements, &c., for a beginning: out of which beginning in ten or fifteen years a mature association could be developed, having an entire property worth some $500,000."

And the Tribune goes on to say, that the share of the products due to *Capital* would now be mainly paid to the *workers* themselves; thus plainly implying that the workers would have acquired, and made their own, a large part of the *property*. The Tribune here evades, or attempts to evade, a very important point, one to which we directed its special attention in our last article, by the question, "How are the Laborers upon a domain to acquire a property *in it?*" It does not answer the question, but contents itself with implying that they *would* acquire it in some way. Let us examine this very important point a little more closely:—

Suppose fifty men furnish $50,000 for an Association upon which 150 others, who have no money, are to labor and to live. With that sum they buy the land, build the house, furnish the tools, and in short procure every thing needed at the outset. They are the absolute *owners* of the entire *Property* of the Association. The 150 laborers work upon it and live upon it;— and their labor, in the course of ten or fifteen years, greatly enhances the value of the land, so that the whole shall then be worth say $500,000. Do they thereby become in any sense, or to any extent, the *owners* of it, or of the houses, mills, &c., that may have been built upon it? Certainly not. They have drawn their reward in the *share* of the products due to their labor. If that has been more than enough to support them, they may have laid it up; and all they may thus have saved is their property. But they have no more title to the domain, or to the houses built upon it, than before. Its rise in value has benefited those who invested their money in it, but no others. The original owners are the perpetual owners of all the property, unless they choose to sell, and unless at the same time others are able, and choose, to buy. For the Tribune says expressly, that "there will be no compulsion, no obligation to sell." Now if the concern should not prove successful, the Laborers would not be able to buy. If, on the contrary, it should succeed, and its value should rise from $50,000 to $500,000 in ten or fifteen years, the owners would not sell, except at a correspondingly high price. How, then, we again ask, are Laborers to acquire any share in the *property* of an Association, upon any better terms than they can acquire property on under the present System? The Tribune says, to be sure, that "changes by death, vicissitudes, and a *natural inclination of capitalists to aid those who need aid* (!)" would render it easy for laborers to buy their stock. But we see no force in this. If a stockholder should die, his children of course would inherit his right, and would be no more likely to sell it, if profitable, than he himself: and as to the *natural inclination* of capitalists, we advise the Tribune to consult some of them, before building such magnificent castles upon their disinterested benevolence.

Now let it be borne in mind that these Associations, upon the Tribune's theory, are to be universally substitutes for the existing Social System. All the land in this State, and in the U. S., is to be held in this form and under these relations. Is it not perfectly clear that one class of persons, those, namely, who *have money*, will become the OWNERS of all the real estate;—and that the other class, those, namely, who have *no money*, will become their TENANTS, cultivating their land, occupying their houses, &c., and paying rent in kind for their use, but having in them no property whatever? And is it not also perfectly clear, that just in proportion as the system should be found to prove successful, would the Laboring Class find increased difficulty in rising to the class of Proprietors? And would this not be simply an aggravation of the worst features of the Social System which now exists?

The Tribune draws a very pleasant picture of the ease, economy, and success with which a new settlement could be established in Michigan by an Association. Now if Association were urged simply as a new and improved method of settling a new country, clearing its forests, draining its swamps, making its roads, &c., we might perhaps have less to say against it. We concede to a certain extent its economy, and the zest which, under some circumstances, labor derives from excitement. But both these features have their limits and necessary conditions, of which the common sense of mankind takes special and correct account, and of which Association takes no account whatever. Thus, in farming districts, nothing is more common than for farmers to *club together* and buy threshing machines, mowing machines, &c., owning and using them in common;—or to make husking-bees, log-rollings, chopping-matches, &c., for their mutual aid. But common sense tells them where to stop. These associated efforts make labor attractive only while they are *novel*. Once make them the ordinary routine of daily toil, and they would soon grow far more distasteful than the solitary labors of the independent workman now are. Beside, to these communities of property and of effort the nature of man has affixed a limit; at a certain point they must stop. They can not be carried into the details of daily life; all experience proves this, and to contradict it we have nothing but the Tribune's assertion. When they are carried beyond that point, jealousies arise, and contentions follow. Where all labor in common, sharing the results equally, the nimble would look upon the slow as infringing upon his rights; the skillful would grumble at the awkward; the lazy would constantly seek to shift the burden to his neighbor's shoulders, and yet claim his share of their joint productions; ten occasions of bickering would spring up where one now exists; and in spite of all philosophy, work would soon become just as hard, monotonous, and repulsive as it is now. The Tribune's highly-colored and attractive picture is simply a fancy sketch—evincing a hopeful, but an amazingly credulous mind, and calculated only to mislead. It is just as baseless, though not so beautiful, as More's "Utopia," or the "Happy Valley of Rasselas." We wish it were otherwise, but facts are stubborn things; they will not yield to theory, nor the fanciful speculations of ideal dreamers.

In further exposition of the Practical Working of this system, we hope the Tribune will tell us what provision is to be made in an Association for the natural increase of its population—upon what terms new members are to be received—what provision is to be made for Education, and under whose direction that matter is to be placed—what relation it will bear to the State—by what definite arrangement of details the principle of Association will be carried into the various departments of domestic life—and generally, what will be the routine of Associative Existence. Thus far, the Tribune, although it proposed to take the lead, has done little but reply to, or evade, our arguments, or, as it contemptuously styles them, our "*cavils*." We hope it will now go on to set forth more precisely the distinctive features of Life in an Association, as in that way it will best secure the "*progress* essential to a discussion of the matter in controversy within the limits proposed." We shall hereafter advert to the Tribune's theory of Natural Rights, and to its still more novel theory of Logic. The Tribune persists in saying that Burke's Essays on Government and human Rights were truly *answers* to Paine's Rights of Man, although it abandons its first assertion, that Burke formally *answered* Paine. Perhaps the Tribune will better understand the true state of the case when it learns that Burke's Essays were written *first*; and that Paine's "Rights of Man" was written, professedly in answer *to them:* of this answer of Paine, Burke took no notice whatever. Paine, as is well known, was a drunken infidel, who denied the being of a God, scoffed at the idea of human responsibility, and poured the foul filth of his blasphemy upon every thing that belonged to religion. The Tribune ventures so far as to intimate that, upon these points, Paine *did* indeed fall into a "*theological error*" (!) but it makes haste to excuse him therefor, by the plea that he was "*impelled*" thereto by the "misalliance of Christianity with Aristocracy and Tyranny." This is certainly a convenient plea for the infidelity of this age, as well as for that of Paine; we should be sorry to believe that the Tribune deems it valid. Some of Paine's political sentiments were, doubtless, just; but his fundamental principles concerning human rights and human duties, the nature of law and the grounds of justice, were the natural offspring of his infidelity. No man ever yet had a creed of fundamental Politics entirely distinct from his religious belief.

We have made this article longer than we wished to do; but we could not make it shorter. With regard to length, however, the Tribune has again changed its ground. It originally complained of the *space* our articles occupied in its columns, which meant the *room*, the proportion of the paper, which they filled, if it meant any thing. We replied that the Tribune's article making the complaint occupied *more* space in its own columns than did ours. The Tribune concedes this, but calls it a "paltry quibble," and makes the *new* complaint that our articles, being in "solid nonpareil" have "*twice as much matter to the square inch*" as its own, which are in "leaded minion." It is hard to be charged with *quibbling* for simply taking what the Tribune *says* as an index of what it *means*. If it had said *matter* instead of *space*, in the first place, we should have known at once that *ems*, and not inches, were meant; and would thus have saved ourselves the trouble of measuring the one, and the Tribune that of counting the other. We advise the Tribune, however, if it wishes to save space, to put its own articles, as it does ours, in *solid nonpareil;* meantime we will be as brief as possible, though the Tribune's course makes it necessary for us to say again, that when that paper speaks of "*the column on each side originally proposed*," it speaks of something that never existed.

From the Tribune, Dec. 16.

## LETTER V.

*To the Editor of the Courier and Enquirer:*

I CAN answer and set at rest nearly the first half of your article by the simple statement of a fact In Association, those who furnish the original Capital or nest-egg are the owners simply of so much *stock* in the concern—not of all the land and property, as you suppose. We will suppose this $50,000 At the expiration of the first year an appraisment is made, and it appears that $25,000 has been added to the value of the property by building, fencing, planting, enriching, &c., &c. For this amount new stock is issued, which is apportioned to Labor, Capital, and Skill, as impartial justice shall dictate The member (resident or not) who holds $5,000 of the stock will have one tenth of the new stock awarded to Capital; and if he has been a resident and worker beside, he will have a farther dividend on his Labor and Skill, provided the subsistence of his family shall not have balanced or exceeded the value of such Labor. The man who has none will have new stock apportioned to him for the excess in value of his Labor over the cost of his Subsistence. Thus at the end of ten years, supposing no cash dividends have been paid, but the whole net product absorbed in increasing the property of the Association, the owners of the original $50,000 Capital will now be owners probably of $100,000 Capital, while the other $400,000 increase of Capital Stock based on the erection of Buildings, planting of Orchards and Nurseries, improvement of Lands, &c., will have been apportioned to the Laborers, who will now be owners of four-fifths of the entire property, the just and natural product of their Labor after giving Capital its honest due. How radically this differs from the way things go on at present, I think I need not indicate. Are you answered on this point?

Let me now briefly answer your following questions:

The "natural increase of population" in an Association will be provided for by successive additions to the Edifice, the workshops, &c., by the establishment of new branches of Industry with the extension and perfection of old, by the extension of the Gardens, Orchards, &c, &c., and the gradual improvement of the land, until the highest attainable point in fertility and productiveness shall have been reached, and the number of members shall be as many as it can comfortably and advantageously subsist. If a commencement be made with one hundred persons, adding not more than fifty per year by acceptance of new members, until the tenth year, and thence only by natural increase, it will be many years before the whole number will reach fifteen hundred to two thousand. Then, if the limit of the domain's productive capacity shall have been reached, a portion of the members—naturally the younger and more enterprising but less affluent—will conclude to take a new location and start for themselves They will be assisted with Capital from the parent hive—in fact, they will naturally continue members of it until their orchards, gardens, buildings, &c., on their new homestead will have made it a comfortable residence. If none shall choose to emigrate this year or next, some new branch of manufacturing industry will be started—say a cotton, woolen, or silk factory—which will employ more labor without requiring an extension of territory, and ultimately the comparative inconvenience and disadvantage of so large a population will induce a portion to prefer a new location. I think no one who is familiar with the economy of a beehive need borrow trouble on this head.

New members (from without) will be received upon application, probation, and assent of a constitutionally prescribed number or proportion of the resident associates. (This is a question which pertains almost exclusively to the outset of Association. Ultimately, I presume most would prefer to remain amid the friends and the scenes of their childhood rather than to "seek their fortune" elsewhere; unless a marriage, religious sympathy or some peculiar industrial or educational faculty rendered a change of residence manifestly desirable.)

As to Education, it would be the special charge of Counselors elected by all the adult members, who would take care that the very best talent was from time to time employed in that vital department. My own opinion is that true Teachers are created such, not manufactured; and I surely need not urge that the facilities for distinguishing those whom God designed for Teachers of this or that acquirement would be vastly greater in Association than they now are. I have already said that the thorough Education of every child, Physical, Moral, and Intellectual, is one of the most important ends to be attained through Association.

The relation of each Association to the State will ultimately be that of the present Township, or rather, a combination of the School District with the Township. Intermediately, it will be regarded and treated much the same as a manufacturing company.

As to the "definite arrangement of details," *that* would require columns to state it fully. I think it will answer here to say that a body of voluntary associates, banded together by mutual faith in and assent to these fundamental PRINCIPLES — that every human being has a right to a thorough and true Education— to ample and unfailing Opportunity to Labor— to the just and equal Recompense of such Labor—to Social enjoyment, Mental culture, and ample Subsistence—in short, to "Life, Liberty, and the pursuit of Happiness"—will have little trouble in settling details, save in the first crude experiments. If the original "details" should not render exact justice, Experience would soon dictate and insure their amendment. That knavish, indolent, selfish, quarrelsome persons may engage in such an enterprise at the outset is true; but I have been satisfied by slight experience that they can not stay there. They will either be transformed by the genius of the place or be impelled to flee its presence. The theologic averment of the discomfort of the wicked in the place where there should be none such is fully paralleled by the uneasiness of a conceited, covetous person in Association, and the impossibility of his long remaining there.

As to poor Tom Paine, since I have never

heard that he was an Associationist nor even a Land Reformer, I am unable to account for the bitterness of vituperation with which you assail him. That to him, more than to any other man, this country is indebted for the impulse to its Independence from Great Britain—that its separation from the Mother Country was more ably and cogently advocated and justified by him than by any other writer—that his voice cheered the discomfited defenders of our Liberties, as they tracked with blood the frozen soil of New Jersey on their retreat before the overwhelming numbers of the enemy in the winter of 1776, and reanimated the People to make the efforts and sacrifices necessary to secure our Freedom—I confess, seem to me to entitle him to some measure of kindly regard at the hands of every American citizen—I trust these are not among the incitements to the vindictive hatred which with you pursue and blacken his memory. I have read very little of his writings about Religion, but I am very sure your assertion that he "denied the being of a God" is untrue. That the atrocious perversion of Christianity by too many of its Doctors of Divinity to sustain the "Divine Right of Kings" and other people-crushing abominations was a chief cause of his rejecting it, I can not doubt. Shall not those Doctors be entreated to take heed lest they drive men "of this age as well as that of Paine" into like deplorable errors!

Your talk about "matter" and "space" I pass in silence.

You say that "to these communities of Property and Effort the nature of Man has affixed a limit; at a certain point they must stop" I oppose to this assertion my own, that these "communities of Property and Effort" naturally become more and more numerous and intimate as men become more enlightened, humane, and just. Originally, and now among savages and barbarians, he who travels must make his own roads as well as defend his own person and valuables; Civilization provides Roads and Police. Originally, and till within the few last generations, he who wished to educate his children hired his own teachers; now we have Common Schools, the result of a "community of Effort," the school-houses common property. At last we have in our State superadded thereto Common School Libraries —a step our own fathers would have stared at. These are but a few items of progress toward a *general association* of "Property and Effort," toward which, as I have already asserted, Society steadily gravitates whenever it makes any true and beneficent advances. If any body had predicted, a century ago, that the Patroon of Rensselaerwyck, fiddler Jack, the Governor, and a kitchen-maid, would in 1846 travel from Albany to New-York in the same conveyance, paying the same fare, and eating at the same table, he would have been deemed stark mad; yet now we see it done, and nobody is badly hurt or shocked by it. Every day our high-bred ladies ride down Broadway in the same omnibus with servant-girls and shop-boys, and do not find themselves contaminated in the least. Whale-ships are constantly fitted out on a plan of "community of Effort," dividing the proceeds of a long voyage in a manner approximating that of Association. To say nothing of the Moravians, Shakers, Rappites, Zoarites, &c, who have been for twenty to two hundred years practicing their various systems of pretty thorough "community of Property and of Effort," and have not yet discovered that they "must stop," we know that the Benevolence of our day is irresistibly, unconsciously impelled into the channel of Association. Philanthropy erects or implores the erection of a "Sailors' Home," a "Home for Aged Respectable Females," a "Home for the Reformation of Female Outcasts," &c, — not a separate dwelling for each half-dozen objects of its benevolent concern, but a large edifice to accommodate its hundreds—the whole—on account of its great economy and manifold advantages. Birkenhead, a new city, is just springing up across the river from Liverpool, and its dwellings mark a very decided approach toward those of Association. So in Boston, where benevolent capitalists have for some time had in contemplation, and I believe have ere this commenced, the erection of spacious edifices for the Poor, to have kitchens, cooking-ranges, &c, common to all the inmates, with all the rooms heated by a common furnace, &c., &c. And, not to protract this article by multiplying examples, the following paragraph has been running the rounds of our cotemporaries, and has received a very decided endorsement from the Express—so that Christianity and Morality may look it in the face without trembling. Read and think!

"A NEW IDEA.—A new idea has just been started in London. A plan has been suggested, and indeed commenced, of building immense palaces, similar to the Athenæum and other great club-houses, to be called 'Club-Houses for the Married.' In these edifices suits of rooms are arranged, consisting of one, two, or three sitting-rooms, as the case may be, with kitchen, offices, &c., to be let at all prices, £50 a-year upward. A family may be accommodated in each suite, and may either keep house by themselves or take their meals at a public boarding-table. The advantages proposed are, living in palaces instead of old, dingy and dusty houses (paying small rents, comparatively speaking), and the enjoyment of thorough ventilation, and, therefore, one source of health. Several of these very desirable establishments are already projected in the immediate suburbs of London, surrounded by gardens, lawns, shrubberies, &c. This is an age of improvement."

In the truth of that last remark rests the hope of
H. G.

---

From the Courier and Enquirer, Dec. 24.
### REPLY TO LETTER V.

OUR readers, we trust, will appreciate the difficulty of conducting an argument with an opponent who recognizes none of the common rules of reasoning, and who repudiates his positions as fast as they become unpleasant. In our last two articles of this discussion, starting from the explicit declarations of the Tribune of Dec. 1st, that '*the Property of an Association will be vested in those who shall contribute the Capital to establish it,*" and that Labor would be rewarded by a share of its products, we proved from these premises that the direct tendency of Association would be, to render the relation of LANDLORD and TENANT perpetual and universal. In reply, the Tribune says that "in Association, those who furnish the original capital *are not the owners* of all the land and property, *as you suppose.*" This is the exact *negative* of the Tribune's former statement; and, as that has been fully examined, and as, moreover, we have no room to waste in reconciling the Tribune's contradictions, or in demolishing all the novel positions it may choose to take, we shall pass to the PRACTICAL WORKING of Association, with reference to its individual members; and our aim will be to show that a Phalanx would contain within itself the elements of discord, without any adequate counteracting or harmonizing force; and that these would inevitably effect its destruction. In doing this, we shall be obliged to trace, somewhat in detail, the course of daily life in one of these establishments.

The theory of Association requires that its principle should be carried into, and should shape and govern all the details of social life. That principle, of community of effort, is to enter into all the employments, and all the enjoyments, the necessities and pleasures of daily life. It is to be carried into their eating, working and living—into the education of their children, the direction of their labor, the distribution of profits, and in short into all their relations. To begin with, the *cooking* for all of them is to be done by a select number, called a *group*, and all are to eat at one table. Now the first task will be to select the cooks. By whom will it be done? And suppose some who desire to be cooks are excluded from that group: —will they not naturally have a prejudice against the cooking of their successful rivals? And suppose, through their influence or otherwise, a portion of the inmates dislike the dishes set before them: must they be forced to submit, or may they set up an opposition party and seek the overthrow of the obnoxious cooks? If the latter, we have an internecine quarrel at once. If the former, we have a tyranny of the extremest and most odious character. This may seem a frivolous cause of trouble; but will it not be real? And precisely the same difficulties will be encountered in every branch of domestic life in Association.

Look again at the arrangements for Labor. A *group* is to be employed in gardening: another in plowing: a third in wood-cutting, &c. These, of course, are all to be distinct. Each man has his proper place, in his proper group, for the fulfillment of his proper mission. Now, who shall assort and arrange them? And suppose a number are dissatisfied with the place assigned to them, by whom is the matter to be finally decided; and how are the disaffected to be compelled to acquiesce? What will prevent them from grumbling—from exciting dislike in others, from persuading them to grumble, and so fermenting discord and hatching rebellion? Beside, there will be many kinds of labor less pleasant, and more repulsive than others. For instance, boot-blacking, ditch-digging, scavenger work, &c., are all obnoxious and disgusting labors; yet they must be performed. None, probably, will volunteer in their behalf, for none will regard that as their special and proper sphere. But a *group* must be detailed for their performance; by whom shall this be done? And suppose the persons designated avow their preference for gardening, rather than cleaning sinks, and in the end refuse to do that duty: where is the remedy, and by whom, and in what way, can it be enforced? Are any to be *compelled* to do it? And suppose some do offer, for high pay, to discharge these "filthy functions" of society: will not others look upon them as a little below their level; as consenting to do for pay what nothing would induce *them* to do? And will they not gradually, though compelled to meet with them in social intercourse constantly, come to look down upon them, to discountenance their familiarity, and so to repudiate their acquaintance, and in the end regard and treat them as servile and degraded? Will not this be the natural tendency of things? And does Association provide any adequate counteracting influence?

And now, to advance a step farther in this inquisition: it is an essential feature of Association that each man's labor is to be appraised and set to his credit. Now, when all work together, by whom and how is this to be done? And when it is done, how are the awards to be enforced? Here may be a dozen men in one group—all apparently healthy and industrious, —but among them must, of course, be a great disparity in the amount of work which they can accomplish. This disparity, while all work at a common task, is not perceived, yet it is perfectly clear that it exists. Now shall it be estimated or not? And will it not be accounted hard that one man should receive less than another, no more industrious but a little more efficient? And if all are rewarded alike, will not he who actually earns the most think it hard that others should share equally, and so deprive him of his just reward? And will he not feel inclined to relax his exertions, since he makes nothing from their excess? Now when it is considered that all the business of life—all the countless diversities of daily labor, are to be brought under this arrangement, is it not clear that the system will become infinitely complicated, and that the causes of discord and collision will be numberless?

And now let us follow this inquiry still farther. The Tribune tells us that the "Education of every child" will be "one of the most important ends of Association;"—and that it will be the "special charge of Councilors elected by all the adult members." The plan for educating children, proposed by Association, is certainly worthy of examination, and should be thoroughly understood, before a judgment of the system is formed. We regret that the Tribune is so studiously vague upon this point, as well as others:—but it says enough to indicate the general character of the system proposed. The principle of Association is to govern Education. "Every child" is to be under the "special charge" of Councilors, chosen by the "adult members." To begin with, suppose the adult members are not unanimous: are the minority to submit implicitly to the choice of the majority? If so, they must of course surrender their children to the "special charge" of the Councilors: and thus they may be educated, not only in disregard of the wishes of their parents, but in direct hostility to principles which they deem essential. If not so, may the minority establish another school,—select another council,—have other teachers, and so set up an opposition school? And may they seek to convert others to their way of thinking and acting? And can any number of persons act thus? And will not the Association thus be split up into factions upon this subject? Nothing of all this, certainly, could be allowed, as it would speedily reëstablish the existing Social System upon the ruins of the Phalanx. The Educational Council must have charge of the matter, and must be supreme in it. The children are all to be given into their hands, for all the purposes of Education. They are to decide who shall be their teachers, and what they shall be taught: and their dominion will embrace, as the Tribune says, " the thorough Education, Physical, *Moral*, and Intellectual of every child." Now suppose the " adult members" choose a Council of Infidels, and give them this charge of the whole matter. The case is supposable and must be met. There may be some parents who would have scruples against committing the *moral* training of their children to such a Council. What are they to do? Are they to set up an opposition School? Or must they teach their children themselves? In either case, they abandon the principle of Association, and revert to the present Social State. It is clear that they must submit to the Council, until they can overthrow it; and then the opposite party must go through the same process of despotism, struggle for relief, and final victory. And here would be the seeds of a thorough and a fatal revolt against the whole fabric of Association.

And now to carry this scrutiny into the sphere of religion: How will religious worship be arranged in Association? Will some one mode of worship be established by the "adult members," to which all must conform? Clearly such a step would involve the very extremity of State tyranny over conscience, and would produce an explosion at once. Must, then, all be at perfect liberty to conduct their worship upon such principles, and is such a manner, as they see fit? Then, of course, a place of worship must be provided for each sect that may grow up. Will this be done by the Association itself? Will the Presbyterian build, or aid in building, a Catholic chapel? Will the Methodist assist in providing a place for Mormon worship? And suppose each sect does this for itself, clearly then, the principle of Association is abandoned, and they go back to the present Social State, and that, too, under immense disadvantages. For it must be remembered, they are all within a limited space;—they inhabit one house;—their places of worship must be close together, probably under the same roof. Suppose, then, the Methodists choose to conduct their religious services with loud shoutings, &c, as they do now?—will not the Unitarians, or the Universalists, who worship in the next room, be disturbed, and feel annoyed, and so in the end become angry with their neighbors? And beside all this, will not conscientious parents become distrustful of the effect which modes of worship, directly at war with *their* principles, will have upon their children? And will they not soon see that when all are so closely crowded together, they can not escape that influence?

Now we are aware that these objections may seem petty, and that the Tribune will probably characterize them as "*quibbles*," and "*cavils*." But they touch the very root of the whole system, which claims to be a system of *Social life*, and not a mere speculation. Difficulties precisely of this sort would spring up at every step, and in every department. There would be a countless variety of tastes, of principles, of sentiments, of prejudices, and of whims, to be gratified or harmonized. And even in the least important matters, they would produce a marked effect. Suppose a child were sick, and the Association physician should be a homœopathist;—would the parent, who was an allopathist, or a hydropathist, or a chrono-thermalist, or a magnetist, be compelled to employ him? or would the Association provide all these various doctors for all such various wants? And precisely the same difficulty must be encountered in every branch of social life. Nothing would be exempt from it. These prejudices, predilections, and convictions would *exist*, and would have an influence; and that influence would tend constantly to destroy the Association. They can be obviated only in two ways:—they must be overruled, *put down* by the strong hand: or they must be consulted and gratified—and that would simply be a return to the existing social state,—a conversion of Association into the isolated system,—the dissolution of the Phalanx into a Township.

The Tribune concedes, as perforce it must, that "knavish, indolent, selfish, and quarrelsome persons" may enter into an Association;—but it insists that they "could not stay there." Why not? Suppose they were to become the *majority*; and what is to prevent it? The Tribune claims, to be sure, in less direct but equally explicit terms, that a *wicked person could stay in Heaven, as easily as a covetous or conceited person could stay in an Association*. We see not the slightest ground for such an extravagant and absurd assertion.

The Tribune insists that the tendencies of the age are toward association; that there is no limit to the application of the principle;—and that it may be carried into all the relations of daily life. We have given our reasons for thinking differently. The Tribune refers to the "benevolent provisions of the day" as evidence of its position—thus:—

" Philanthropy erects a 'Sailors' Home,' a ' Home for aged Females,' &c.,—not a *separate dwelling* for each half-dozen objects of its benevolent concern, but a *large edifice* to accommodate its hundreds."

This is a strange argument. Public charity takes that shape, simply because it can not *afford* any better. Will not the Tribune admit that every poor sailor would be better off, if Philanthropy could give him a house and farm of *his own*, than in this large edifice with a thousand others? And are they not all put together in one edifice, and placed upon the footing of an Association, simply because nothing better can be afforded? The same *kind* of provision is made for convicts. Auburn has an "Edifice," in which the economies, labor-groups and general principles of Association are carried out thoroughly and rigorously; but would the Tribune urge *that* as a reason for reorganizing all Society upon the same plan?

Equally fallacious are all its citations. Community of effort makes roads, establishes a Police, digs canals, &c., simply because individual effort can not do it; but that fact does not imply that victuals should be cooked, tables set, children taught, and the whole human race "taken in and done for" upon the same plan. So, too, communities organized for some one predominant purpose, such as the maintenance of a special religion, like the Shakers, Moravians, &c., may hold together, so long as that motive is strong enough to overbear all the ordinary impulses and laws of action—but no longer. And as to the scheme of "club-houses for the married," so exultingly cited by the Tribune, we have only to say, that those who *can not* live elsewhere, and who *can* live there, would probably do so—and would find it advantageous. Others, we opine, will remain in *statu quo*.

At the opening of this discussion, we took up the Tribune's theory of Natural Rights, and proved it to be unfounded. The Tribune replied by saying, that our argument was akin to that of Burke against Paine. We rejoined that if so, we thought all the better of it on that account. The Tribune responded by saying that its own political affinities were with the principles of Paine, and that Paine's politics were entirely distinct from the "*theological error*" into which he had been driven. We replied that no man *could* have a theory of fundamental politics entirely distinct from his religious belief;—that Paine was a *drunken infidel*:—and that his notions of Natural Rights, with which the Tribune claimed affinity, grew out of this infidelity. This certainly was a proper way of meeting the Tribune's claim. How is it treated by the editor of that paper?

"I am surprised," he says, "at the bitterness of vituperation with which you *assail poor* Tom Paine!...... To him, *more than to any other man,* this country is indebted for the impulse to its Independence from Great Britain .... His voice cheered the discomfited defenders of our Liberties," &c. "*I trust these are not among the incitements to the vindictive hatred with which you pursue and blacken his memory.*"

Low as is our estimate of Paine's moral character, we believe he would have scorned to resort to so unmanly a method of answering an opponent. Yet we find affixed to it the initials of the Tribune's Editor.

---

From the Tribune, Dec. 28.

### LETTER VI.
*To the Editor of the Courier and Enquirer:*

I must confess that it seems to me unprofitable to answer objections—if they may be dignified with that appellation—which are founded only in the grossest ignorance and misconception of what I have presented, as well as of all that Associationists have been urging for several years past. For instance, when I stated that "the Property of an Association will be vested in those who shall contribute the *Capital* to establish it," how *could* I have anticipated that you would limit the term "Capital" to the moneys invested in the mere beginning of the enterprise—in the purchase (if it must be purchased) of the wild land on which an Association is to be founded, and of the few rude materials with which it is commenced? What is Capital but the unconsumed product of past Labor possessed of an enduring, or at least remaining value? Suppose a Western pioneer has bought an eighty-acre tract for $100, and made improvements on it worth $200, are not these latter as truly Capital now as the $100 he paid, or the land he obtained for it? And if $50,000 be paid for the land, building materials, implements, provisions, &c, with which an Association is commenced, and if three hundred men work thereon a year, fairly earning $200 each, and consuming but one hundred dollars' worth of provisions, clothing, &c., who can fail to see that the $30,000 additional value which their labor has created is just as much Capital at the end of the year as the original $50,000 was at the beginning, and as such entitled to be represented by stock, receive future dividends, &c, &c.? If you, therefore, need any reconcilement of my statements you have quoted, or have understood me to teach that those who furnished the "original" nest-egg, must own all the eggs and all the chickens evermore, I must believe that not another reader of this controversy is involved in your difficulty.

Your mistaken assumptions that "all are to eat at *one table,*" or that there can be but one set of cooks, &c, &c., evince a sad unacquaintance with a system which you have for years been denouncing as abominable, and imploring everybody to understand and execrate as you did. So with regard to Labor, to Education, Religion, &c. Had you but read attentively any of the writings of the Associationists, you would have seen how your obstacles are surmounted. Nay, you might easily have learned that the Zoar and Rapp Communities have existed from twenty to forty years respectively, daily encountering and overcoming all the difficulties in regard to Food, Cooking, Labor, Education, &c, you deem so insuperable. And even our little beginnings of Association, destitute though they be of capital, machinery, experience, and that immense facility afforded by Custom and Habit to any undertaking, have withstood all the influences you imagine so certain to work their dissolution, through the three to five years of their existence respectively; and I feel very sure, from my partial acquaintance with their affairs, that not one of them will break up, as none has ever yet broken up, because of differences regarding Religion, Education, Cookery; or because no one can be found to perform indispensable duties. Is not this experience, brief though it be, worth something? After the first steamship had crossed the ocean, all the learned and logical demonstrations of the utter impracticability of ocean steaming were unanimously voted null; and I respectfully suggest that your quandaries are fast passing into the same category.

"It *does* move, nevertheless," said Galileo, when Bigotry had just compelled him to renounce and denounce the doctrine of the heliocentric motion of the Earth; and thus Association will demonstrate its own practicability in spite of all your cavils. I know there is, and must be, difficulty in the transition; that those who have been trained to consider the game of grab and gouge the great business of life, must have a new spirit breathed into them before they can comprehend and act upon the vital principles of Social Unity. Association is but the body, of which the Golden Rule is the soul. I know men to whom it is an impracticable idea; but I know others to whom it is no longer so. I feel sure that this latter class is rapidly increasing, and will one day predominate. I know well that an Association of knaves and dastards—of indolent or covetous persons—could not endure without a moral transformation of its members; but I know also that its organism strongly tends to correct the faults inimical to its existence, and that one complete and successful Phalanx would do more to dignify and ennoble Labor, to diminish idle Scheming and increase useful Working, to mitigate the evils of Rapacity, Extravagance, Intemperance, and Pauperism, than has been accomplished by all the Philanthropic effort of the last century. In this faith I proceed.

That you have been wrong throughout, concerning Burke and Paine, I think I need not take more space to show. That Paine's "*notions*" of Natural Rights were those which gave the impulse to our Revolution, and that by them only can that Revolution be justified, is most notorious. When you connect his "theory of fundamental politics" with Infidelity, you virtually libel the cause of American Independence. And "*drunken Infidel*," as you term Paine, I never heard that he turned traitor to the Liberal principles and associates of his earlier years, or died the pensioner and tool of Royalty and Aristocracy. As you do not deny that your view of the origin and fundamental basis of Society and Government is substantially Burke's, and as you are surely mistaken both in your allegation that Burke did not write to refute Paine, and your reason for it (that Burke's great work on this subject was written first)—for though Paine's "Rights of Man" was published after Burke's Essays, all its fundamental ideas had been put forth in his earlier writings in defense of the American cause prior to and during the Revolution—I believe I need say no more on this head.

And now to resume my general argument:

We have already seen that Association is the vital element of Society—that it enters into and measures Human Progress from the rudest condition of the Savage to the most refined Civilization, so that we might accurately say of a particular People, not that they were more or less Civilized, but that they were more or less Associated. A Civilized People grind their grain at common mills, instead of pounding it in family mortars, travel on common Roads and Steamboats, instead of by separate trails and in individual canoes, educate their children in Common Schools, have common Asylums, Colleges, Railroads, Canals, Banks, &c. The question which separates us is not so much one of kind as of degree, and may be fairly stated thus: Is it practicable and desirable to multiply the common interests and common efforts of civilized society as much more as they have already been multiplied in the progress from Barbarism to Civilization? You insist that the point already reached in Civilized Society is the extreme limit; I say, "Not so; for men in several instances have gone *farther* on the same path, to their manifest advantage and security from threatening evils." Is not mine the more intrinsically reasonable presumption?

The physical problem of our Age, it seems to me, is the due and thorough ORGANIZATION OF INDUSTRY. Of *dis*-Association, incoherence, antagonism, Society now presents many striking examples. One of them may be seen about the steamboat wharves of our City, where hundreds of hackmen are encountered on the arrival of a boat, seeking the employment which not more than a dozen can usually obtain; the result being, that while the passengers pay exorbitant prices, the hackmen as a class are poorly recompensed and subsisted. This is a fair specimen of the workings of isolated effort and selfish competition. So with regard to the employment of rude Labor in our Cities. The coming on of Winter contracts business, stops building, diminishes manufacturing, and throws out of work several thousands of poor laborers, who through the warmer months have earned their $4 to $7 per week, and would gladly earn still, but can find nothing to do. Their families suffer; the grocers, coal-dealers, &c., are losers in custom and profits; the Alms-House is crowded, and private charity taxed to the point of exhaustion; thousands annually die of fevers and other diseases born of Destitution; thousands more are driven by despair to intoxication—and all this vast and ever-increasing tide of human anguish and wo might be arrested or at least greatly diminished, if Society could but discover and adopt means of securing constant employment and tolerable recompense to its less fortunate members. Can this be a task beyond the capacity of the Nineteenth Century? I am sure that if the results of a Presidential Election had depended on the solution of this great problem, it would have been triumphantly solved before this time. When every sound horse or ox finds employment and has a positive market value beyond the cost of its keeping, it can not be that Man alone must be left to die because his freely proffered muscular and intellectual powers will not command the bread which would keep him from famishing.

Our age has already witnessed great strides toward an Organization of Industry, and the work is still rapidly progressing. Manufactories, Railroads, Mining Companies, &c., &c., are among the proofs and the fruits of this general tendency, as Banks, Life Insurances, Mutual Insurances, Odd Fellowship, &c., are evidences on another side of the universal tendency of Civilized Society toward Association. In all, the principle of mutuality and reciprocity is the animating one; and those most vehement against systematic and many-sided Association, are individually sure that on this side or on that, a farther approach to it is feasible and would prove beneficial. Perhaps the Manufacturing Capitalists of our day are, as a class, as hostile as any other to complete Association, and yet they have done more than any other class to demonstrate the vast economies and efficiency of Organized Industry. One hundred persons employed in a factory now fabricate as much cloth as many hundreds could do by isolated effort; and the march of improvement in this department of Industry is exceedingly rapid, as I doubt not it will be in Agriculture when duly organized and conducted on a scale of like magnificence. The evils we now experience in Manufacturing Industry result from its one-sided and partial Organization. Having been organized by Capital alone, and with a primary view to the advantage and profit of Capital, the coveted results, Economy and Efficiency in Production, have been attained; but with no corresponding benefit, often a positive injury, to the laborer, who frequently finds his recompense diminished as his product is increased. Rare skill or talent, industrial or financial, may be able, because of its rarity, to command a liberal salary; but mere Labor is unable even to stipulate the hours of its own daily application, but must work as it is ordered in a schedule or code of by-laws which it had no voice in framing. In turn, it has but a slender and remote interest in the goodness of its own product, the faithfulness of its own work; if the day is worn out or the piece woven, so as to pass muster and command the stipulated price, all is effected that the workman usually cares for. If his fabrics or wares rise in the market, his employer may make a fortune, but nothing comes thence to him; if the goods fall, the employer may be ruined, while he can lose nothing unless it be his employment. Hence indifference, eye-service, indolence on the one hand, with avarice, tyranny, and meager recompense on the other. Let me endeavor, in contrast with this, to give some idea of Manufacturing in Association:

The fundamental basis of Association, we have seen, is a *proportional* distribution of products to Labor, Capital and Talent, according to the just claims of each. Every Association will prosecute several branches of Manufacture, in order to give the widest possible range of employment, and secure, as nearly as may be, to each member opportunity to live by whatever useful Labor may be most agreeable to him. Every member will be attached to one or more groups organized for the prosecution of certain species of Manufacture. In mild, pleasant weather, the great majority will be employed in the fields and gardens, Agricultural employment being then most agreeable and pressing. Few beside women and children will be left within doors, unless there be an extraordinary demand for some species of Manufacture, tempting some to persist therein by the assurance of a larger recompense. But a stormy day will at any time transfer hundreds from the fields to the factories and shops, where in Winter the great majority will find employment. Now mark the difference between Manufacturing in Association and out of it:

1. In Association, the workers will choose their own superintendents, foremen or overseers, and regulate their own hours of daily toil. They have now no voice in regard to either.
2. In Association, the workers receiving a settled *proportion* of the price realized for their product, will have a direct interest in making the fabric as perfect as possible, so as to secure for it a preference in the market, and a high price. Should an advance be realized, on this account or any other, a large proportion of it will accrue directly to the workers, whereas it now falls entirely to the share of Capital.
3. The frequent and ready alternations from Manufacturing to Agricultural labor would tend greatly to preserve the health and prolong the life of each worker, who now suffers from undue exposure to the elements in farming, and undue confinement and restraint from air and exercise in manufacturing.
4. There would be no loss of time by reason of the weather, but all seasons would be productive.
5. Each individual would be trained to expertness and efficiency in two or more different vocations, so as at the most to be twice as hard to starve as at present.

I might extend this enumeration, but enough. I think all must see that Association, while guaranteeing Liberty in Labor and Justice in the award of Profits, would not merely insure immense economies in Consumption but an immensely-increased efficiency in Production also. It is far within the truth to estimate the production of an Association of 1500 persons at *double* the aggregate they would produce in our present isolated, competitive relations, while the aggregate consumption requisite to the enjoyment of plenty and comfort would be at least fifty per cent. less. Now let us concede that *exact* justice in distribution would not be attainable—that some members might receive ten per cent. less than their absolute earnings—would they be likely to revolt at this, while they still had abundance of every thing, including Education, Libraries, Social advantages, &c., with an unfailing home for their children, and at least double the annual saving that they could realize out of Association? If they would, they must be of the sort you instance who would delight in so conducting their religious worship as to annoy worshipers of a different creed, and who would be likely to insist on having all the children educated after their own pattern. I apprehend you will find very few of *this* sort who can ever be induced to believe Association practicable. H. G.

From the Courier and Enquirer, Jan. 6, 1847.

## REPLY TO LETTER VI.

We have now said nearly all that we deem necessary concerning what may be called the Political Economy of Association, and are therefore prepared to advance to a discussion of its MORALITIES, a term which may comprise all its provisions for Education, Social intercourse, &c., &c. We have already shown that the Tribune's position, that "the *property* of an Association is to be vested in those who furnish the Capital to establish it," and that Labor would be rewarded by a share of its products, would, inevitably perpetuate the relation of Landlord and Tenant. The Tribune now asserts that in "Capital" it meant to include the product of Labor; the evasion is too palpable to require special notice. How the Labor bestowed *upon* a domain can be called part of the "Capital contributed to *establish* it" is beyond our comprehension. And if, moreover, men may acquire property, ownership in land, by simply working upon it, and thus rendering it more valuable, the original owner is certainly divested of his right without his consent. The position involves, as may easily be shown, that *denial of the right of property in Land*, which has already been deduced from the Tribune's fundamental position. Of this point, therefore, we shall say no more at present, but proceed to another branch of the general subject.

In our last article we endeavored to show that the inherent vices and weaknesses of human nature would render impossible such a community of interest and of life as the Tribune advocates. The essential *selfishness* of man would be at war with the essential principle of Association, and would inevitably destroy it. While men continue vicious or imperfect, while they are governed or influenced by prejudice, passion, or self-seeking in any of its forms, they can not combine and carry forward such a community as that proposed. The Tribune, while professing to reply to this objection, actually concedes its full force and validity. Says the Editor of that paper:

"I know that" vicious persons "*must have a new spirit breathed into them before* they can comprehend and act upon the vital principles of Social Unity. I know well that an Association of indolent or covetous persons *could not endure without a moral transformation of its members.*"

Now it seems to us that this concession is fatal to the whole theory of Association. It certainly implies that Individual Reform must *precede* Social Reform—that the latter must have its root in the former—that Association can not advance beyond the personal reformation of the individuals who compose it. This point the Tribune concedes; and the same thing has been conceded by some of those who have hitherto been most zealous in support of Association. Thus, Charles Lane, of whose labors in this cause the Tribune has often spoken in the highest terms, publishes in that paper, of Dec. 23d., a letter which contains this striking admission :—

"As in the experiments in the United States, it has been discovered that *a justly-prepared and well-qualified will in every individual comprised in an association, is necessary to its success,* as well as good, enlightened, and pure habits. Manners which are quite passable in individuals become intolerable in association; for offenses may be borne during a few minutes where we have little or no interest, which, perpetually recurring where our all is affected, wax into grievous injuries. Thus the conclusion at which most men have arrived, is that which the considerate long ago descried, namely, that *a superior race of human beings is requisite to constitute a superior human society.* This is the one thing needful. The good arrangements may fairly and safely be left to them."

The position, then, is fully conceded that Men must become good—must have a "new spirit breathed into them;" must undergo a "moral transformation," *before* they can carry into effect the scheme of Association. This is essential as a preliminary step. How is it to be effected? The Tribune says, by Association! "I know also," says the Editor, "that its organism tends strongly to correct the faults inimical to its existence." This seems to us a gross absurdity. Association is thus expected to make its own indispensable conditions. It is to create its own creator—to produce its own cause—to effect that personal reform in which it must originate. The very statement of the case demonstrates it absurdity. Cause and effect are not thus to be confounded. The blunder is exactly that of the man who should expect a water-wheel, by turning, to produce the water which is from the first to turn it ;—who should look to the motion of a watch for the creation of the main-spring, which alone can give it motion. It is precisely the error which the would-be inventors of Perpetual Motion have constantly committed. Can any thing be more palpably impossible? And is not this defect *fatal* to the whole system? Does it not strike at its very root? The personal reform of individual men must precede Association. That reform must be effected by some other agency than that which Association offers. That agency is Christianity. We have a right, therefore, to insist that Reformers shall *commence* their labors by making individual men *Christians* : by seeking their personal, moral transformation. When that is accomplished, all needed Social Reform will either have been effected or rendered inevitable.

Now to all this the Tribune replies simply, that "Association will demonstrate its own practicability, in spite of all your (our) *cavils* ;" and points us to the Rapp and other communities, which, it is alledged, have succeeded. We shall not enter upon this point now, farther than to say, that the Tribune must not mistake its own assertions for arguments: that we know of no communities which have proved successful; and that if they had done so, their success would have afforded no conclusive proof of the practicability of Association as a new and universal Social Form, since they have been composed of picked men, and not of men as they exist in general. We may recur to this hereafter. At present we turn our attention to the provisions of Association for the EDUCATION OF CHILDREN, and to their effect upon the FAMILY Relation.

In our last article, we asked several queries concerning the system of Education and Religion in an Association. The Tribune gives to these queries, and to the objections which we suggested, the following answer :—

"Your mistaken assumptions [with regard to eating] evince a sad unacquaintance with a system which you have for years been denouncing as abominable, and imploring every body to understand and execrate as you did. So with regard to Labor, to *Education, Religion, &c. Had you but read attentively any of the writings of the Associationists, you would have seen how your obstacles are surmounted.*"

The Tribune thus refers us for its answers to our queries, to the "*writings of the Associationists,*" at the same time taunting us with ignorance of them. We forgive the sneer, because we mean to show that it is not deserved. We have gone to the source which the Tribune indicates, and have, as the Tribune predicted we should, found there the answers to our inquiries. The most authentic of the "writings of the Associationists" yet published in this country, is Mr. Brisbane's book on Association, published in 1840, which was used by the Editor of the Tribune as a text-book while learning, under the personal instruction of its author, the rudiments of the social theory of which he is now the distinguished advocate. In chapters 30, 31, 32 of that work, we find set forth fully and explicitly the system of Education in Association. Our first inquiry was, whether all the parents in Association would be required to submit their children to the same educational system, or whether each could educate his own children in his own way; the answer is explicit:—

"If there were in the combined order different systems of education, incompatibility of classes and duplicity of manners would take place. Such an effect would produce *general discord*; it is, consequently, the first defect which the policy of Association should avoid; it will do so *by a System of Education which will be ONE AND THE SAME* for the entire Phalanx, as well as for the entire globe." P. 394.

It seems, then, that all the parents, under this new form of Society, will be required to submit their children to the same system of education, and to the direction of that Council, to be chosen by the adult members, which, according to the Tribune, "will have charge of the whole matter." It becomes important, therefore, to know what that universal system is to be—by what successive steps it will conduct children from infancy to maturity. These details we find in the source to which we were directed by the Tribune, and we extract from that work, mainly in its own language, the following outline of the system:—

There is to be a *series* of nurses, divided into *groups*, and of nursery rooms. Infants under two years old are to be divided into *two* classes, called *Sucklings* and *Weaned*, each class having its own nursery, and being subdivided into *three* divisions: 1. the *quiet*; 2. the *noisy*; 3. the *turbulent*. Each nursery is to be divided into *three* rooms for these three divisions, with side rooms for the doctors. P. 396

The groups of nurses are relieved every two hours; and a nurse has only to attend while her *group* is on duty. The nurses receive not only a large share of the general product, but high honors, and a high rank in all festivities, being considered as common mothers. Pp. 397, 398.

Cradles for the children are so built that 20 can be rocked at once. Beside the cradles, Association, whose system is compound, furnishes elastic mats, suspended about four feet high, upon which the children can lie and roll, being separated by silken nets, so that they can see but not touch one another. P. 398.

The most noisy will cease their cries when placed with a dozen others as perverse as themselves. They will silence each other by their screams. P. 400.

In Association the most opulent mother would never think of bringing up her child isolatedly in her own apartments (p. 399), though, as perfect liberty in all relations will exist, she can, if she chooses, have her child with her (p. 397.) Nature demands the education of children in masses (p. 402).

This is a faithful outline sketch of the system of Education provided for children under two years old, which is to be "*one and the same* for the entire phalanx and the entire globe." When the children reach the age of two years they enter the class of *Little Commencers*; and the leading principle of the education they are then to receive is thus set forth:

Our present systems wish, first, to instil in the child principles of *virtue* and *morality*; whereas, *following the primary tendency of Association, the child should first be directed to compound riches.* P. 429.

This is to be done by making little tools and little workshops for them; by teaching them to imitate other workmen; by seating five or six children of different ages at a table to shell peas,

the smallest child taking the smallest peas, the second taking those a little larger, and so on; by giving them badges of distinction for success; by showing them older boys "wearing their little ornaments and uniforms, which inspire with *profound respect* the young beginner;" and by choosing as their guides children a little older than themselves. This is to go on until they are *four* years old, the age at which they "know how to *make money.*" When they reach the age of *five* years they are induced to learn to read; and to accomplish this "resort will not be had to paternal authority," but to the following "stratagem:"

Their teacher, or mentor, is to show them pictures of birds, violets, and other objects in which they are interested, and is to explain two or three of them. When they ask for more explanations, "it is understood that all those to whom they apply shall say they have *not time* to explain them;" and "they are told that if they wish to know so many things they have only to learn how to read." They communicate their disappointments to each other, and "form the noble plot of learning to read." (P. 433.) The same system is to be applied to all branches of study, such as writing, grammar, geography, &c. "A double inducement, like concerted refusals and innocent stratagems, which awaken emulation, will always be resorted to." P. 435.

This is the system of education laid down in those "*writings of the Associationists,*" to which the Tribune referred us for an answer to our inquiries, and a reply to our "*cavils.*" We have been minute, in order to be accurate. We have omitted nothing requisite to an understanding of the system. This is the scheme of EDUCATION in Association—a scheme which is to be universally "*one and the same;*" and from which, therefore, there will be no liberty for parents to depart. Its details, taken by themselves, are too absurd for grave comment. The utter ignorance which they display of the nature of the young; the gross credulity which pervades them; the glowing enthusiasm with which they are urged; and the comical contrast between the noble end and the ludicrous means proposed, stamp the whole thing as the ingenious dream of a lively but lunatic fancy. Ridicule would be the only fitting comment, but for the fact that this scheme, so elaborately prepared and so ingeniously urged, involves moral principles of the gravest importance, and for which, in justice, its advocates must be held strictly responsible. It can not have escaped attention, that the system discards and ridicules the notion that principles of *virtue* and *morality* are to be instilled into the minds of the young; and it is equally clear that intentional *deception* forms an essential part of its plan, since we are expressly told, that these "concerted refusals and innocent stratagems will *always* be resorted to."

But the main feature of this system of EDUCATION in Association, and that to which we ask attention is, that *the authority and control of* PARENTS *over their children* is not only neglected, but is formally *disavowed and annulled.* Until children are two years old, the mothers may have them in their own rooms if they choose, though they would "never think" of exercising the privilege. After that age, however, they are to be handed over, entirely and exclusively, to the teachers provided by Association, free from any interference of their parents. And this result is not accidental; it is an essential feature of the system—necessary to its success, and distinctly set forth in those "*writings of the Associationists*" to which the Tribune referred us. Thus we are assured, in the volume already quoted, that the child will enjoy

"*Perfect independence, or exemption from obedience to superiors, whom it has not chosen from inclination.*" P. 411.

And still more explicitly is this point enforced in the following extract:—

"All authors of systems of education have fallen into the great error of considering *the father*, or a tutor under his direction, as the natural instructor of the child. Nature judges differently, and for a threefold reason: 1st. The father seeks to communicate his tastes to the child. * * The whole mechanism of the passional series would be destroyed, if the son inherited the tastes of the father. 2d. The father is disposed to praise and flatter to excess in the child the little merit it may possess. 3d. The father excuses in it want of skill and dexterity. *Nature, to counteract all these defects of paternal education, gives to the child a* REPUGNANCE *for the lessons of the father and the tutor; the child wishes to* COMMAND *and not to obey the father.* * * The natural instructors of children of each age are those a little superior in age." P. 414.

Setting aside the cold-blooded inhumanity of this sentiment, its utter ignorance of the nature and strength of parental feelings, and its palpable falsity in point of fact, could the authority of Parents over their children be more explicitly disavowed or its rightfulness more distinctly denied, in any other way or by any other language than that of the extract given above? Most certainly the system of Association, if carried into full effect, would completely destroy all such authority and guidance. Parents, it is perfectly clear, would cease to be the natural governors and instructors of their children.

Reverting, then, to the other branch of the FAMILY, and drawing our information from those "writings of the Associationists" to which the Tribune has referred us, let us see what now form the CONJUGAL relation is to receive under this new Social System. We are told (p 298) that the "pecuniary dependency" of the wife upon the husband must be destroyed;—that "woman in her union with man becomes a secondary being;"—that she loses her name; the "liberty of her heart, with its sympathies and affections"—her right of independent action;—and that her dependence is "very unfavorable to the full and noble development of the delicate and romantic passion of love." These relations are termed *abasements*, and in Association it is asserted, that

"Woman can develop her faculties and powers, and acquire fortune, distinction, and renown, by her own efforts and talents. She will then no longer ask support at his hands; she will have no longer to barter sympathies and feelings for physical wants. Invested in Association with her liberty and independence, she will scorn to live upon his industry, and will soon know how to set bounds to his exactions and pretensions to superiority." P. 300.

To go no farther, it is sufficiently evident from these passages that the relation of Husband and Wife, whatever it may be in Association, will *not* be the relation which now exists. A wife, if the term be then retained, will keep her own name, retain her liberty of heart and of action, and be in short entirely independent of her husband in all respects. Will that be the relation recognized as that of husband and wife in the Word of God? Will it be any thing more than a copartnership for certain purposes between the two? A great variety of questions naturally arise in this connection, as to the practical operations of the scheme proposed; and all of them are distinctly answered in those "writings of the Associationists" to which we have been referred by the Tribune for a solution of our difficulties. The system is perfect in all its parts, and all its details have been fully elaborated by its original author. But this branch of the subject we shall leave for the present, insisting simply upon the conclusive evidence we have now presented that in Association the FAMILY, even if it should exist in name, *would be virtually and essentially destroyed*. Its vital elements, its essential character, would be blotted out forever. Even if the *form* of the Family should remain, it would retain none of those features which make it a sacred and peculiar institution, the foundation of the State, and the source of all that is good in social life. Nor would this be an incidental result. It is part, and a most essential part, of the system — distinctly contemplated and aimed at by its propounders and advocates. Thus, to revert to the "Writings of the Associationists" cited by the Tribune, we are expressly told in Mr Brisbane's work, that

"Short-sighted politicians have fallen into error in bringing into action the FAMILY SPIRIT, *which, tending to selfishness, should be* ABSORBED *by corporative ties.*" P. 18.

And so in almost every page of these writings, as well as in the Tribune, the "isolated household" is constantly assailed, and we are told that Association must *absorb it*. *The* FAMILY *is to be replaced by these joint-stock Companies*. We do not intend now to argue against the propriety of such a radical change in society as this, but simply to make clear and plain the *fact*, that such a result is sought, and if Association succeeds, will be reached. THE SUCCESS OF ASSOCIATION WILL INVOLVE THE DESTRUCTION OF THE FAMILY.

The length to which this article has already extended, precludes a reference to other points which we meant to notice. There is nothing, however, in the Tribune's article which needs further reply. It sets forth for the fiftieth time, the existing evils of Society, to which nothing need be said except that Association would increase them tenfold; and repeats the argument drawn from the joint-stock associations and benevolent societies of the present day—which was fully answered in our last article upon this subject. The Tribune also makes another catalogue of the alleged blessings of Association, and adds that "the enumeration might be extended." Of course it might, and that *ad libitum*. Nothing is needed for its extension, but an active fancy and a ready pen. Dreaming, when one's common sense is but half awake, is the simplest thing in the world, and is usually as pleasant as it is easy. There are, however, comparatively few people out of Bedlam who habitually mistake their dreams for the sober realities of common life.

From the Tribune, Jan. 13.
### LETTER VII.

"Oh, moralists, who treat of happiness and self-respect in every sphere of life, go into the squalid depths of deepest ignorance, the uttermost abyss of Man's neglect, and say, *Can any hopeful plant spring up in air so foul that it extinguishes the Soul's bright torch as soon as kindled?*"—CHARLES DICKENS.

*To the Editor of the Courier and Enquirer:*

I INTEND in this article to discuss directly and sufficiently the doctrine of Circumstances, and their influence on Human Character and Destiny. It seems to be your chief difficulty in regard to "Association" that it requires good dispositions in its members, which dispositions it is obvious that a large portion of the Human Family now lack, and under existing circumstances are little likely to attain. Hence you argue, in the spirit of the Caliph who burned the Alexandrian Library, that, since the ignorant and squalid are now confessedly unfit for Association, they can only become so by an intrinsic melioration, which, if effected, would render Association unnecessary. Let us consider this:

Here is a community—say the people of Paterson, N. J., or of some Ward of this City—comprising every grade of fortune from boundless wealth to extreme indigence and emaciation. Some enjoy incomes of $50,000 per annum, with little labor or care on their own part; others, by the most strenuous industry, can not earn $200 per annum, yet from this must pay the rent, food, and fuel of a family. Many, in the greatest need, can find no way to earn a penny for weeks,—but are compelled to subsist at all events. And is not this necessity calculated to degrade them in spirit and in morals? Take two men of equal and medium qualities, and secure to one ample, unfailing, remunerated employment, enlightened associates, daily opportunities to perfect himself in industrial, scientific, and historical knowledge, with the moral certainty of an enduring home and a generous subsistence, while you leave the other to struggle with the wants, temptations, alternations of excessive labor and involuntary idleness of a mere Laborer in this City at present, and who can doubt that the former would naturally grow wiser and better, increasing in self-respect and the respect of his associates, while the latter would steadily gravitate toward the grog-shop and the Alms-House? Not that every individual circumstanced like the former would become wise and good, nor that every hod-carrier and street-sweeper of our City is doomed to end his days intemperate and probably in the Alms-House, but that the *tendency* in each case is to the result I have indicated.

Take another illustration: My religion teaches me, as I think yours does you, that your son and mine are no better than the children of equally tender years now growing up in the cellars of Cross-street and the garrets of Republican-alley. Yet you know, as I know, that the chance of these latter coming to what is called "a bad end" is immensely the greater. The class of News-boys, for example, is mainly recruited from the cellars and garrets tenanted by our City's crowded wretchedness. They are by nature no better and no worse than other boys just outgrowing infancy. And yet few years pass before a large proportion of those who commence as newsboys find themselves tenants of the House of Refuge, Blackwell's Island, &c., &c. How is this? These same boys, if early trained to habits of industry and good conduct, would mainly have been virtuous and useful members of Society. But a mere child of ten or twelve years is driven forth by the intemperance or destitution of his parents—perhaps by the loss of them—to try to earn a living by his own exertions; and almost the only business upon which he can enter without preparation, without permission, and without capital, is that of selling newspapers. A shilling will start it, and the gains are in hand every evening. But this very facility overstocks the calling, and renders its proceeds meager and precarious. Thus evening often falls upon the lad trudging wearily, hungrily home, his pockets empty, his papers unsold. He is morally certain of abuse, if not blows, should he thus seek the shelter of the miserable hovel which his parents inhabit. One desperate chance remains to him: he raises the cry, "Ere's the Hextra 'Erald, (Tribune or Sun) got the news of another great battle in Mexico—Santa Anna defeated, 5000 killed." At once his stock of papers is snapped up at double prices, and he turns the first corner and scuds home, with a full pocket and a light heart. He takes his oyster supper and a glass of grog with a chuckle at his own adroitness, and jots down in his mental note-book, that "Honesty is the best policy"—sometimes;—at others a little jocular roguery does better. To be sure, he has damaged his line of business, somewhat; but he has reaped all the benefit of that, while all but a thousandth part of the damage falls on others. Those who curse the trick and resolve never to believe a newsboy again will not identify him should they meet next day. So he has taken a degree in his education, and is ready for some more daring resort in his next fit of desperation or temptation. So with Hack-driving about our City, and scores of other callings which our existing Society creates and sustains after a fashion. Hundreds all around are making a livelihood in vocations which require no personal integrity on their part—many in ways which integrity would rather obstruct. The young man who deals out silks gracefully in a fashionable Broadway store, or mixes juleps dexterously in a genteel Broadway bar, may keep a mistress in the next street or spend his nights in the gambling-dens of Park-place; yet those by whom he lives know nothing of this; his current reputation is not affected by it. It is but a little while since a man intrusted with the responsible and lucrative business of collecting rents on a large City property was exposed and compelled to fly, after having for months, if not years, been engaged in decoying young women into his den under pretense of employing them as servants, and then accomplishing their ruin by violence when blandishments, threats, and drugs would not effect it. How many are now pursuing like nefarious courses can only be guessed, but all can see that our present Social arrangements afford the amplest facilities and impunity to such crimes. There is (or recently was) in the State Prison at Sing-Sing at least one poor servant girl who was sent there on a trumped-up charge of stealing, because she had been seduced by the son of her employer, and no other means occurred to the family of preventing an unpleasant expense and scandal. But I will not multiply examples. Briefly, it seems to me that if some malignant spirit had undertaken to contrive a Social framework which should subject the poor, the humble, the ignorant, to the greatest possible amount and variety of temptations—which should virtually constrain many and irresistibly draw far more to the ways of dissipation and sin—he could hardly, in the light of Christianity and such Civilization as we have, devise any thing more admirably adapted to his purpose than the Social System under which we now live.

What, then, do we propose and hope ultimately to accomplish? Granted that the mass of the destitute and squalid are incapable of rising by their own efforts to a level with the requirements of a just and beneficent Social Order—are unable even to appreciate such an Order, or to desire its establishment, what then? The good work must be done, nevertheless. I say let those who *are* capable of conceiving a true Society proceed at once to actualize it, as an example and encouragement to others. Let the Wealthy contribute of their wealth, the Wise of their wisdom, the Learned of their science, the Good of their piety and charity, to construct a Social Organization wherein no honest and industrious man can become a pauper or a serf, and no widow and orphans be driven out from their home into a cold and cheerless world because the husband and father has been snatched from them by death. I know all men are not now capable of doing what is needed, but I know *some* men who are, and I am confident that these, by affording Example and Opportunity, could speedily work a vast change in others. Give but one hundred of the right men and women as the nucleus of a true Social Organism, and hundreds of inferior or indifferent qualities might be rapidly molded into conformity with them. I believe there are few of the young and plastic who might not be rendered agreeable and useful members of an Association under the genial influences of Affection, Opportunity, Instruction, and Hope. I see many now hurrying down to death-beds of drunkenness and pauperism whom I am sure might have been, would have been retained in life, vigor, usefulness, and honor, had these influences surrounded them from childhood, and I trust that some of the thousands preparing to follow in the downward road will yet be arrested and preserved. Who ever heard of a drunken or begging Shaker?

When you persist in saying to me "That Reform must be effected by some other agency than that which Association offers—that agency is Christianity," you compel me to regret that I can not render myself intelligible to you. To my mind, Association is the palpable dictate of Christianity—the body whereof True Religion is the soul. I can not doubt that if Christ were here in New York to-day, and could gain access to the dwelling of our Astor, Lenox, Whitney, &c, He would say to them in terms, as He has already done in substance, "Cease amassing wealth for yourselves or your descendants; cease building sumptuous palaces from which your brethren are expressly, and splendid churches whence they are virtually, shut out; cease isolating yourselves in heart and life from the masses who need to be benefited by your superior intelligence, wisdom, morality, refinement, if such you have; cease to make a gain of the wretched hovels in which Famine and Despair are now festering into Sin and Crime; employ your vast wealth in drawing forth from these dens of darkness and misery their crowded, shivering inmates, and placing them where they will have pure air to breathe, ample space to occupy, bread to eat, unfailing and fairly remunerated work to do, with all those refining influences of elevated Social Intercourse, judicious Counsel, ample Instruction, an enduring Home and a horizon of Hope, which you can so well appreciate and of which most of them know nothing.' That, it seems very plain to me, is just what Christianity would have done, and which it is now urgently calling on the wise and wealthy to combine their efforts and their means to accomplish. To say that the needed agency is not Association but Christianity, is to me like saying that a field does not need culture to insure a harvest but sunshine. I beg you to consider in this connection a passage I recently quoted from the leading Editorial of the *London Times* of Nov. 27th, of which I will here quote but the following. The Editor is treating of the Education of the Poor, and forcibly asks:

"What, then, can be done by churches built on the most genuine models, and arranged on the most orthodox plan, or by schools conducted on the most scientific principles, *when the whole teaching of the village, which is the laborer's little world, pulls the other way?* Excessive penury, precarious employment, the denial of common charity in the hour of visitation, *the frequent spectacle of calamity unfriended and crime unreproved, habitations that preclude habits of decency and cleanliness*, and a system of public relief which confounds all the distinctions of morality, constitute a giant whole compared with which the Sunday service and the national school are impotent and ridiculous. * * * *

"'It is impossible to be decent!' is the common language of the poor, cooped as they are, male and female, old and young, married and single, innocent and fallen, a dozen in a few cubic yards of physical and moral infection. 'It is impossible to be decent!' and the result almost too uniformly shows how true the assertion, or how ready the excuse. What avails it that educational and ecclesiastic commissioners are measuring with the nicest care the quantity of atmospheric space to be assigned to the human unit in the school, and the church, when whole families are sleeping, winter and summer, almost in contact and within two or three feet of the slanting roof?"

Can any one doubt what Christianity must dictate with regard to such hovels as these? Can any fail to see that to fill them with Bibles and Tracts, while Bread is scanty, wholesome

Air a rarity, and Decency impossible, must be unavailing! "Christianity," say you! Alas! many a poor Christian mother within a mile of us is now covering her little ones with rags in the absence of fuel, and vainly endeavoring to make sleep induce a temporary intermission of the craving for that food which no one will give her opportunity to earn! And yet our City is full of wealth, and of benevolence also. Hundreds give liberally, and would give more if they could be secured against the abuse of their bounty. There is benevolence enough in our City to relieve all the destitution it contains, were it but unimpeded and rightly directed. And yet thousands after thousands are sinking down through Despair to premature Death, because the Social Anarchy in which we live darkens the vision and arrests the arm of Philanthropy, so that two-thirds of what is given by Charity is intercepted by Prodigality and Knavery, and the residue so applied as to keep alive the evils from which we suffer rather than help to cure them.

A few paragraphs must suffice for the bulk of your unreasonably, oppressively long article.

Your citation of Charles Lane as "one of those who have hitherto been most zealous in support of Association," is grossly erroneous. Mr. Lane, though an Apostle of Social Reform, has ever until recently been hostile to Association. He was here for years an apostle of the Isolated Family as the Divinely appointed form of intimate relationship, and purchased a farm in Massachusetts whereon to give a practical exposition of his idea. All that has been urged by others in favor of the sacredness and supremacy of the Family Relation, I have heard quite as forcibly urged by him. He finally gave up his farm and lived a while with the Shakers, attracted mainly by their devotion to Celibacy, of which he is an apostle; but he was soon repelled by some of their usages and left them From first to last, I never heard of his uniting with or favoring any attempt at Association His concessions, therefore, are not from *my* ground but from *yours*, and his late letter, fairly quoted, is a strong testimony to the necessity and advantages of Association.

I give you the full benefit of your citations from Mr. Brisbane's book, and of your excuse for them. Every fair mind will judge how likely your quotations are to give an impartial idea of your author's views, and how material they are to the great question at issue. I know no two Associationists who agree with Brisbane or Fourier with regard to every matter of speculation or detail, yet these make no difficulty among us, and will make none. I have no doubt myself that infants may with great advantage be trained for a part of the time in common nurseries, combining every facility for their care and nurture, and that this arrangement would be greatly beneficial to them as well as a relief to their mothers. So I doubt not that a substantially uniform system of Education would in time be agreed upon in most if not all Associations, upon a careful comparison of practices and results; and I believe the true way to make children moral and virtuous is to commence at a very early age to imbue them with the love and practice of Industry, to lead them to seek and delight in improvement and excellence in its various processes, and to press on eagerly from one attainment in the useful arts to another. Neither do I doubt that children could and should be induced to *solicit* instruction in letters, from a desire to avail themselves of the practical advantages thence resulting. They may very often and very well be *truly* told that those to whom they apply "have not time" just then to instruct them, though one objcet of the refusal is to incite them to eagerness in the pursuit of knowledge. But all that we Associationists are at all committed to in this is to "Prove all things; Hold fast that which is good." If any suggestion of Fourier or any one else prove on trial erroneous or pernicious, it will be promptly discarded. And if Mr. Brisbane, in urging that the proper instructors of children in most things are those but little their seniors, has erringly transcended the maxims of Raikes and Lancaster, Experience will very soon set right those who attempt to obey his dictum. That there is truth at the bottom of his suggestions, nearly all our Popular Education, Religious and otherwise, conspires to attest. Very few are the children wholly or mainly educated by their parents, or even under their personal supervision.

As to the position of Women, your quarrel is not more with Associationists than with at least half the world around us, and by no means the less intelligent half. From every side protests are finding voice against the practical slavery of the Wife to the Husband, under the laws and usages which have thus far prevailed. A great step toward securing the pecuniary independence of Women was taken in our recent Constitutional Convention, though finally receded from by a close vote, on grounds apart from its intrinsic righteousness. This step has since been decisively taken in Wisconsin, and a renewed effort in its behalf has already been commenced in our Legislature. I know of but one "Fourierite" in the Wisconsin Convention, none at all in ours. Unless you make haste to direct your bolts against the attempt now making at Albany, I have but little doubt that it will succeed, and the property and earnings of the Wife be legally shielded from dissipation through the recklessness or depravity of her Husband. Whether the "vital elements" and and "essential character" of the Family "will be blotted out forever" by such an act, every one will of course judge for himself. My own opinion is, that no man will love his wife and children less, while many will treat them better, because of such legislation; and so of Association. That you are guilty of a gross fraud in effect, though perhaps not in intent, when you quote Mr. Brisbane as saying that "the Family *spirit*,[*] tending to selfishness, should be absorbed by corporative ties," and proceed thereupon to assert that "the Family is to be *replaced* by these joint-stock companies... The success of Association will involve the *destruction* of the Family," &c., in defiance of Mr. B.'s repeated and emphatic disclaimers of any such purpose or thought, I surely need but indicate. Every candid mind will see it at a glance. No man is worthy to advocate a true Reform who is not prepared and willing to be subjected to just such unfair citations and garbled represent-

---

[*] See "Dombey and Son" throughout.

ations as make up the bulk of your article. I leave them with pity for those they may delude, and with sorrow for talents so perverted.

H. G.

#### From the Courier and Enquirer, Jan. 20.
### REPLY TO LETTER VII.

In its reply to our last article, the Tribune professes to "discuss sufficiently the doctrine of Circumstances, and their influence on human character." By a strange oversight, however, it omits to state what that doctrine is. The omission is remarkable, because the question is important. If circumstances, or that arrangement of them which constitutes Society, be the actual *cause* of existing evils, then those evils may possibly be removed by changing that arrangement. But if evil has another and a far different origin, then it must clearly have another and a far different remedy: for the remedy in any case must not only modify the conditions, but remove the essential cause, of the evil it is designed to cure. We regret, therefore, that the Tribune does not tell us which of those opposite views it entertains.

We find in its article expressions which might warrant the inference, that the Tribune's "doctrine" regards circumstances as the *cause* of existing evil. But the only points distinctly stated are, that the ignorance, squalor, and general wretchedness of the degraded poor, subject them to temptations from which others are comparatively free: and that a change in their condition is very desirable, on moral as well as on physical grounds. We can not understand why the Tribune should labor so hard to prove what we expressly conceded at the very outset of this discussion, unless its object be to excite odium, instead of answering argument. The existence of misery, and the necessity of relieving it, are not in controversy, for we have never doubted either. It is only upon the *remedy to be applied*, that the Tribune and ourselves are at variance. That paper insists that Association is the only agency by which the poor can be relieved: that the ignorant, the vicious, and the degraded, can not be reclaimed, unless the virtuous, the wise, and the rich establish with them a community of interests and of life; that to benefit a part, the whole must be changed; that to furnish some with good dwellings, all must abandon their houses and dwell together under a common roof; that the whole fabric of existing institutions, with all its habits of action and of thought, must be swept away, and a new Society take its place, in which all must be subject to common customs, a common education, common labor, and common modes of life, in all respects. This, its fundamental position, we deny. We deny the necessity, the wisdom, and the possibility of removing existing evil, by such a process. We would not thus destroy the good in order possibly to amend the bad. It is not the method of wisdom, or benevolence: it finds no support in common sense or sober judgment. The Tribune promised to prove that it is not only the best, but the only means of relieving the poor; but thus far it has not even attempted to fulfill its promise. It has asserted and illustrated in every possible variety of forms the existence of evils, and the necessity of removing them, and has drawn fancy pictures of the state of things when that removal shall have been effected. But its proof that Association, and nothing but that, can accomplish it, is to come hereafter, if it come at all.

We, on the contrary, have sought to show, 1. That Association can never be established: 2. That if established, it could never endure: and 3. That if it were permanently established, it would *increase* tenfold the evils it is designed to cure. In our last article we urged, that

"The inherent vices and weaknesses of human nature would render impossible such a community of interest and of life as the Tribune advocates. While men continue vicious or imperfect, while they are governed or influenced by prejudice, passion, or self-seeking in any of its forms, they can not combine to carry forward such a community as that proposed."

Now, in regard to this point, the Tribune has expressly admitted, that an

"Association of indolent or of covetous persons *could not endure without a moral transformation of its members.* They must have a *new spirit* breathed into them, BEFORE they can comprehend and act upon the vital principles of social unity."

Now this is a distinct and emphatic admission on the part of the Tribune, that individual reformation must *precede,* and lay the foundation for, Social reform;—that individual men must become virtuous, before Association can become possible;—that just so fast as men become unselfish, virtuous, "morally transformed," Association may become possible, but no faster;—and that when all men have thus been transformed and made virtuous, then Association may become general, but not before. Now this most evidently makes Association the *result* of virtue, not its means or producing *cause.* Association may possibly *follow,* but it can not possibly *precede,* the individual reform of those who are to be its members. The argument, starting from the Tribune's own premises, seems to us cogent and conclusive; and it completely demonstrates the utter worthlessness of Association, regarded as a *means for removing existing evils.*

What is the Tribune's reply? Simply this:—

"When you persist in telling me 'that reform must be effected by some other agency than that which Association offers; that agency is Christianity;'—you compel me to regret that I can not render myself intelligible to you. To my mind, Association is the palpable dictate of Christianity—the body whereof True Religion is the Soul."

Now here is a distinct equivocation; an evasion of our point—effected by an adroit change in the meaning of the word *reform,* as we had used it. Our position was thus set forth in our last article :—

"The personal reform of individual men must [as is explicitly admitted by the Tribune] *precede* Association. THAT reform [viz., *of individual men,*] must be effected by some other agency than that which Association offers. That agency is Christianity."

The Tribune quotes it thus:—

"When you persist in telling me 'that *reform* must be effected by some other agency,'" &c.

This is a quibble upon the word, nothing more or less. We used it, and defined it, as meaning the "personal reformation of individuals;" the Tribune quotes it as meaning *Social* reform. The exposure of the trick of course destroys its effect, and the argument loses none of its force. It still remains true, that personal reform must *precede* social reform; and that Association must follow and depend upon, not precede and produce, the "moral transformation" of its individual members. Then, of course, it follows also that this "transformation" must be produced by some *outside* agency—something *out of* Association. The Tribune intimates that the "example and opportunity" afforded by those who are fitted for Association, would mould others into the same conformity. Nothing known of human character, nothing witnessed in the world around us, warrants the ascription of such a renovating power to "example and opportunity." Some yield to them, it is true, when they second other agencies; but far more reject them and follow their own inclinations. It is not because they belong to a Shaker establishment, that Shakers are virtuous, but because they have within them virtuous principles;—and *their* virtue gives to the establishment whatever success it has. So with Association. Something out of Association must produce that personal reform essential to its success. When *that* reform has been effected in all men, all men may combine in Association, but not before. Or, in other words, when Christianity shall have brought about the *Millenium*, then Association may possibly become general;—but not till then.

But, says the Tribune, Christianity commands the rich to relieve the poor; Association proposes to do that work; therefore "Association is the palpable *dictate* of Christianity;" and men if they be Christians, must be Associationists. Now here the premises are true, but they do not warrant the conclusion. The argument illustrates the Tribune's habitual assumption of the very point in dispute, namely, that Association is the only means by which the poor can be relieved. It assumes that no man can befriend the poor, unless he espouse Association. The best test of true benevolence is practice, not precept; let us look for what it *does*, not what it professes. And, bringing the matter to this standard, we have no hesitation in asserting, that the members of any one of our City Churches do more every year for the practical relief of poverty and suffering, than any Phalanx that ever existed. There are in our midst hundreds of female "sewing societies," each of which clothes more nakedness, and feeds more hunger, than any "Association" that was ever formed. There are individuals in every ward, poor, pious, humble men and women, who never dreamed of setting themselves up as professional philanthropists, who do more in visiting the sick, in seeking out and relieving the poor, in encouraging the despondent, and in meliorating the condition of the degraded and the destitute, than ever have done by any Associationist, from its first apostle down to the humblest of his deluded followers. And one of those three individuals, vilified by name in the Tribune's article as the selfish, grasping despisers of the poor, has expended more money, and accomplished more actual good in aiding the poor, in providing for them food, clothing, education, and sound instruction, moral and religious, and all the blessings of which they stand in need, than has been effected by the advocates of Association in half a century, throughout the world. Hundreds of thousands of dollars have been expended by the Associationists, in propagating their *theories* of benevolence, and in making benevolent "experiments;" yet where is the practical good they have accomplished? Where are the starving whom they have fed, the naked they have clothed, the degraded they have raised, the vicious they have reclaimed, the poor whom, in any way, they have assisted and blessed? The Tribune sneers at practical Christianity as "filling wretched hovels with *Bibles* and *Tracts*," while bread, and clothing, and health are needed. Does the taunt come with good grace from a system which theorizes over starvation, but does not feed it; which scorns to give bread and clothing to the hungry and naked, except it can first have the privilege of reconstructing Society? And is not the taunt proved to be false, by the fact that all the relief which poverty gets comes from Christianity, either directly from its hand, or indirectly from the spirit of Charity which it has infused into every department of social life? All may not be done that should be done, for the poor, the wretched and the sinful; but of all that is done, how small is the share which the Social Reformers of the day contribute!

The Tribune complains that the existing system of society

"Darkens the vision and arrests the arm of Philanthropy;" and that "hundreds who give liberally would give more, if they could be secured against the abuse of their bounty."

Why, then, does not the Tribune cöoperate with those who seek to give them this security? Others have seen and felt this evil; and, like true Christian men, have sought to provide a remedy; one which should be simple and practical—easily employed and efficacious. In this city the "*Association for improving the condition of the Poor*" has been organized for this specific purpose, and has proved entirely adequate to the service required. Here, then, the Tribune has a "security against the abuse of its bounty;" why not employ it, and place in its hands the thousands of dollars it has wasted on Association? It is not the Social System which "abuses the bounty" of the benevolent; it is, simply, the dishonesty and indolence of individuals; and they would do the same under any system, and especially in Association. It is not the Social System which creates crime and gives vigor to villainy. News-boys and hackmen may be exposed to temptation, but they would not commit a crime unless the *impulse* existed within them; and until that impulse be removed or overruled, vice and suffering will exist under any form of Society that can be devised. Nothing else does half so much to "darken the vision, and arrest the arm" of true philanthropy, as the Tribune's constant proclamation that, under the existing System of Society, money given in charity is worse than wasted; that Society is responsible for all existing evils; and that the whole social framework must be reconstructed, before the poor can be relieved  Its constant effect is to draw away the attention from what is practical and true, to that which is visionary and false.

The Tribune's reply to what we said of the inevitable and direct effect of Association upon the FAMILY RELATION, amounts to nothing. It accuses us broadly, but with most cautious vagueness, of gross "misrepresentations," "fraud," unfair quotations, &c.; but it does not, and it can not, specify an *instance in* which these charges are not utterly unfounded. We quoted exactly and fairly in every case; we proved clearly that the system of EDUCATION, which is to be "one and the same" in all Associations, withdraws children from the control of their parents; denies the rightfulness of parental authority, as well as the duty of filial obedience; and thus strikes at the very root of the FAMILY, so far as the relation of Parents and Children is concerned. Our evidence against Association, upon this point, was precise, authentic, and conclusive. It is not impeached, in any particular, by the Tribune. But that paper, in its usual style, attempts to *smoothe over* the matter, to *dilute* these several distinct and explicit statements, and then give to them its own assent. Thus Mr. Brisbane asserted that

"Nature gives to the Child a *repugnance* for the lessons of the Father;" that "the Child wishes to *command*, and *not obey* the Father;" and that "the Child should be EXEMPT *from obedience to superiors whom it has not chosen from inclination.*"

This is distinct, explicit, and imperative. The Tribune refers to it as a "suggestion,"

"That the proper instructors of children, in *most* things, are those but little their seniors;"

And, in *this* form, gives it a qualified endorsement. It deals, in the same way, with each of the specific provisions of Association; and, after all, it puts in the general plea, that if any of these specific provisions prove "erroneous or pernicious," "experience will set right those who attempt to obey them," and "they will be promptly discarded" Precisely the same plea might, of course, be extended to the whole scheme. If the whole theory of Association should prove to be "erroneous," and its practice "pernicious," it would probably be "promptly discarded;" but does that relieve from responsibility those who contend that it is both just and true, and that it ought to be adopted? These details are essential parts of the general system; and just so far as they are set aside, the system itself is discarded also. The Word of God constantly and explicitly commands children to obey their parents, and commands parents to instruct their children. Association rejects and repudiates all this, and substitutes a new theory and new laws of its own.

So also of its effects upon the Marriage relation; the law of nature and the law of God combine to require that the Husband and Wife should be one; that their interest, their sympathies, their affections and their life, should be identical. Association proposes to make them, in all respects, *independent* of each other, to divide their interests, sunder their attachments, and make each entirely independent of the other, in action, affection, possessions, and power. If this be not to destroy the "*essential character*" of the marriage relation, then words have lost their meaning. And if this, in connection with the annihilation of Parental authority and Filial obedience, do not involve the DESTRUCTION OF THE FAMILY, then words *have* no meaning whatever. Yet the Tribune charges us with "gross *fraud*" for quoting the evidence of this fact, and for founding upon it the *inference* we have drawn. Now an "inference" may be wrong, but it can scarcely be fraudulent; and as to our quotation, the Tribune will not assert that it was incorrect. Mr. Brisbane's disclaimer of the *purpose* is entirely irrelevant; we have proved upon the system the *result* specified, and that is all with which we have any concern.

The Tribune reminds us that under the pressure of social reform, several of our States are carrying into effect these principles concerning the conjugal relation. The fact only affords new evidence of the mischief which the Socialists of the day, and the Socialism of the Tribune, are steadily and adroitly effecting. Few persons, probably, are in danger of becoming Associationists *eo nomine*. But the *principles* of Association are daily acquiring influence and dominion over the bodies which make our laws, and the public sentiment which gives them authority. Their crafty and zealous dissemination has already aroused a strong spirit of radicalism in the community, which shows itself in denunciations of the rich, in wanton contempt of authority, and in the bold proclamation of sentiments in regard to the rights of property which, ten years since, would have been, and indeed were, received with alarm in every section of the country. The legislation upon the relation of Husband and Wife, to which the Tribune refers, has grown out of the same spirit. Its tendency and direct effect are, to separate the two, to "put asunder," in interest, in action, and in sympathy, "what God has joined together." Its results can not be witnessed in a single age, or a single generation; but it would eventually work an entire reorganization of domestic life. It makes the interests of the wife *separate* from those of the husband, and it gives her the power to make them hostile. Instead of being *one* with him, she may become his rival in business, and his worst and most fatal enemy in all respects. The law is urged to screen the property of wives from the dissipation of worthless husbands. For that purpose it is not needed, as such cases of hardship are already provided for. And beside, what are we to think of legislation which makes possible villainy the excuse for punishing and enslaving the good? Just as wise would it be, to impose hand-cuffs upon all mankind, lest a few should steal. The law is speciously urged on grounds of kindness to Woman; yet it would prove her worst enemy, for it would create new causes of strife and of suffering, and aggravate all those that now exist. Such legislation is false in principle, and would prove most baneful in practice. We regret, quite as sincerely as the Tribune exults, that it finds so much favor with the public. We regard it as the *entering wedge*, by which Fourierism and Socialism will, if they can, rend asunder the closest relations of life, and in the end prostrate and annihilate the essential character, and the highest worth of the FAMILY RELATION. It is one of the first steps of the downward road, into which the unreasoning and fanatical Innovation of the day is cunningly beguiling the legislation and the public sentiment of portions of our country. In this evil work, the Tribune is the most dangerous agency now in existence; and that, too, mainly because it professes to sail under another flag.

---

From the Tribune, Jan. 29th, 1846

## LETTER VIII.

*To the Editor of the Courier and Enquirer:*

As PROGRESS is my watchword and the appointed limit of this controversy approaches, I will endeavor to resist the strong temptation to follow you into an infinity of irrelevant discussions. It seems to me that the Doctrine of Circumstances—namely, That Circumstances of position, opportunity, encouragement, instruction, temptation, &c., exert a vast and often vital influence, whether for good or evil, over the formation and quality of the Human Character—has already been sufficiently set forth and illustrated. The deduction therefrom that we should systematically endeavor to secure to all, as nearly as may be, education and training under such circumstances as will tend to incline them to Industry, Temperance, Virtue, Self-Respect, instead of those which naturally tempt to Idleness, Dissipation, Vice, and Debasement, seems too obvious to need more explicit assertion. I pass, then, to another branch of the general arrangement.

You say that I have not *attempted* to prove Association the best means of relieving the Poor—how truly the reader must judge. Most surely, if I have not *attempted* this, I have attempted nothing whatever. All my articles have had this single aim. True, I have not wished to assail nor undervalue other means or agencies of philanthropic effort; yet I deeply feel that other plans contemplate, mainly, a mitigation of the woes and degradations which are the *consequences* of extreme poverty, while Association proposes a way—in my judgment rational and feasible—of reaching the *causes* of these calamities, and absolutely *abolishing* Pauperism, Ignorance, and the resulting Vices. I need not, surely, recapitulate my statements of what Association is, and how it will do what it promises. You yourself seem to admit that the evils of Caste, Pauperism, constrained Idleness, Intemperance, &c., *have been* abolished by the Shakers, under an organization far less favorable (it seems to me) than that of Association. I know you say "the Shakers are virtuous, not because they belong to a Shaker establishment, but because they have within them virtuous principles;" but I ask you to consider the fact that these same Shakers are in the habit of taking gladly any such infants as they can get—foundlings, illegitimates, destitute orphans, &c.—the very material from which our Houses of Refuge, Penitentiaries, and Prisons, are mainly recruited, and training them up, with scarcely a failure, into these same industrious, moral, sober, virtuous adults. Does any one believe that the difference between the children trained about the Five Points and those educated by the Shakers, or under virtuous and comfort-giving auspices elsewhere, is intrinsic, and not superinduced by the force of circumstances?

Let me here make one more effort to show you *why* I believe ours the true practical remedy for our existing Social Evils. Keeping in mind what Association is, and how it will certainly (for I believe I take judgment by default on these points) secure to every member Opportunity to labor and produce at all times, with the fair and just Recompense of such labor,—that it will secure to each who will work an unfailing Home, the use of a portion of the Soil on just terms, and insure immense Economies in Production, Distribution, and Consumption, so that ten hours' faithful daily labor will procure to the Laborer far more than twice the necessaries and comforts of life he now in the average enjoys—I beg you to consider with me, briefly, a poor man's present relation to Land and Capital, see what are its innate evils, and say whether they do not suggest appropriate remedies.

Man was ordained to live by Labor; some evade this doom by Riches; more by Roguery and Beggary; but every evasion provokes and insures an appropriate penalty. Some—saddest case of all!—would gladly labor for a livelihood, yet can find no opportunity. I personally know scores of this latter class now in our City; I have not a doubt, from data in my possession, that there are *Thirty Thousand* in our City this day, vainly seeking or famishingly awaiting some chance to earn a bare subsistence. And this cruel wrong must continue and be aggravated so long as our present Social Order endures. Winter insures a great contraction of business in this and other Cities, throwing out of employment thousands upon thousands who found work of some kind during the greater part of the milder seasons. These, I need not urge, are precisely those whose earnings have been smallest while they had work—hod-carriers, stevedores, and mere day-laborers of all kinds, whose weekly earnings can not exceed $5 for the 40 weeks in the year when they can find work—say $200 in all for the support of a family, in a City where fire-wood costs from $6 to $10 per cord, and the rent of a very poor and mean house is oftener $300 than $200. Need I urge that it is very hard for one of these poor men, even if strictly temperate and wisely frugal, to lay up any thing during their better season for the twelve hard weeks of Winter! And how are they to live through those weeks? The Alms-House can not hold a tenth of them; the City will not aid a fourth of them; the Association for the Relief of the Poor does nobly, yet can scarcely do enough to provide them with fuel alone. Yet the Rent must be paid and the Food obtained—how! And do not all agree that Alms-giving, though laudable and vitally necessary, does not tend to remove the evils which it palliates, but the contrary! Does any one believe that there will be fewer paupers here next Winter for all that Public and Private Charity is so nobly doing this Winter! Is it not rather probable that there will be more?

But to the other point. In Oregon, where all the land not actually in occupancy is free to whoever wants it, I have not heard that any provision for Pauperism has been found necessary, though probably some infirm, decrepit, crippled, or idiotic persons are charges upon their relatives. But a vigorous, willing male or female beggar is, I presume, an extreme rarity on the waters tributary to the Columbia. In Iowa and Wisconsin the case is not much different, for there wild land is abundant at $1¼ per acre, and eighty acres, with a rude dwelling and twenty acres in fence, may often be bought for the cost of making the improvements, very nearly. Of course, Labor is in demand, and will command very nearly the value of its product. If we suppose improved farming land in Wisconsin worth $10 per acre, the yearly rental which the landless cultivator must pay for the use of it will be less than $1 per acre—say two bushels of Wheat, three of Rye, or four of Indian Corn; and this mainly or entirely for the use of the improvements made thereon by human labor. And this rent will govern the price of Hired Labor in that community.

But years pass; the population of Wisconsin has swelled to One Million, and, though Products are not increased in average price nor Land in fertility, yet the improved acre is worth in the average some thirty dollars. Now the lack-lander, who must buy or rent a portion of the soil, must pay for it at this rate; that is, the price of six bushels of Wheat, nine of Rye, or twelve of Corn for the annual use of an acre, and in proportion if he buys it. So if he sells his labor to some owner of land, that owner will only pay him for that labor a price which will leave him a share of the products equivalent to the rent aforesaid. Can any fail to see that the market value of Labor (the poor man's only capital) has been depressed—that the mere increase of population from 200,000 to 1,000,000 has diminished the facilities for obtaining a livelihood although much land may yet remain unimproved? But a century afterward the population of Wisconsin will have increased to 3,000,000, and now the arable acre of land will be worth not less than $60, and its annual rent, or the tribute levied by Capital upon Labor for the naked use of the elements which God created for the use of His human creatures, will have been doubled once more. I need not pursue the illustration. Europe in 1847 is its impressive example. At this moment, the Labor of Great Britain employed in Agriculture does not receive one-third of its product as its reward, and while the day's work produces probably twice as much now as it would two centuries ago, the producers are worse fed, lodged, and subsisted every way than they were then. I can not doubt that the root of this injustice is the fact that the few own and enjoy the Soil, while the many must compete with each other for the privilege of cultivating it. Is it not clear that this competition must become more and more intense as population increases, and that Labor must continue bidding higher and higher for land until they reach that point at which existence with strength to labor can barely be maintained? I see clearly that this is the goal whereto Labor in our present Social Order is constantly tending. If it were worth while, it would be easy to quote abundantly from the most eminent writers on Political Economy in confirmation of this melancholy truth.

Now Association is based on the principle of securing to the Laborer the full recompense of his toil. Capital buys the land, and receives an annual dividend proportioned to its investment; but the annual increase in the actual (not nominal) value of the Land, being the fruit of Labor, is passed to the credit of Labor, and gradually forms for it a capital. For instance, an Association commences with a capital of $100,000, and with five hundred resident members, or one hundred families; and goes steadily onward until, at the expiration of twenty years, its lands, edifices, granaries, fences, orchards, factories, machinery, &c., &c., are worth $1,000,000. During the interim, Labor has drawn from the aggregate products its subsistence merely, while the fair dividends of Capital and superior Skill have steadily been invested or allowed to remain in the concern. Now at the twenty years' end, the original Capital will probably have about trebled its investment, while the balance of the increased value will have been from year to year distributed to Labor and Skill, so that the original Capital will have been swelled by annual reïnvestments of income to $300,000, while the other $700,000 will have been distributed to Labor, or an average of $7,000 to each family, according to the efficiency and frugality of each. But no suppositious value will have been given to the land—no advance in price not based upon increased fertility and productiveness; and now the young man commencing with nothing will be on just as good a footing as one of the original associates. Each will have the full and fair recompense of his own Labor, Skill, and Capital; none will receive that which justly belongs to another. But under our present Social Order nearly the whole $1,000,000 worth of property would, at the twenty years' end, belong to the original capitalists and half a dozen of the more scheming among the laborers.

And now a few words on some points raised in your last article:

"*Relieving* Social Evils" is very well; we think eradicating and preventing them still better, and equally feasible if those who have power will adopt the right means, and give them a fair trial. But we do not ask, we have never wished, all to "abandon their houses and dwell together under a common roof," &c., &c. What we ask is that the wealthy and the philanthropic shall furnish the means of making one or more full and fair experiments of Associated Life and Labor, with such human materials as will gladly enter upon the experiment. $400,000 would amply suffice for this purpose, three-fourths of which would be invested in Lands, Buildings, &c, which would be worth very nearly their cost, even should our hopes be utterly blasted. These could be secured by mortgage or otherwise to the Capitalists, to be given up to the resident associates whenever they shall have fairly worked out their own temporal emancipation, repaying or amply securing to Capital the amount of its investment. Meantime, all existing Social Life may remain as it is, not one dwelling be abandoned, nor one person adventure personally in Association who does not choose it. Not one particle of what you call "the good" need be destroyed, until it shall be fairly proved that the bad can really be amended by our plan. An enemy of the steam boat in 1808 might as fairly have argued that Fulton required the abolition of all sail vessels to make room for his steamboat.

I do not consider "Association the palpable dictate of Christianity" simply because it proposes to "relieve the wants of the Poor," but because it promises to every man Social Justice and Opportunity to labor and live. I think if every man had full Justice not very many would long need Charity.

I do not see why you should attempt to array against Association the various organizations and efforts to relieve the destitute in our City and elsewhere. I regard all these as laudable and even indispensable, while I hold that they are not adequate to the work of putting an end to the calamities they labor to mitigate —as, indeed, they do not pretend to be. I believe those most zealous for the relief of present suffering from want will be, as they surely should be, most rejoiced at the success of any effort to remove or vanquish the causes of a great part of this suffering. Prejudice and clamor may for a time delude many of the most benevolent, but I have faith that all will ultimately work clear. If you mean (as your language plainly imports) that the advocates of Association, in proportion to their numbers and means, are not as ready and as active as others in the good work of feeding the hungry and relieving the distressed, I most earnestly repel the accusation, and wait your resort to facts and figures to support it. You are welcome to render the investigation as searching and to bring it as close home as you think proper. If you really mean that we who are Associationists refuse to aid in feeding the hungry, clothing the naked, raising the degraded, and assisting the poor, until we shall first have reconstructed Society, I challenge you to justify your accusation; and if you do not intend this, I should be glad to know what you *do* mean.

Whether the "Association for Improving the Condition of the Poor" has "proved *entirely adequate* to the service required," I will not here discuss. I freely acknowledge my obligation to give in outright alms to the needy according to the measure of my ability, and to employ every dollar I can honestly earn in doing good according to my own best judgment of the mode in which most good may be done. If you maintain that I ought to be governed by *your* judgment rather, we will consider that proposition. My appeals to the benevolent in behalf of the "Association for Improving the Condition of the Poor" have been earnest and repeated; I intend to continue them. But I do not think *all* the means which Benevolence may contribute should be devoted to the relief of existing distress; I think something is needed, and can be advantageously applied to arousing public attention to the *causes* of such distress and to the necessity of devising and applying effectual *remedies* therefor. If the Tribune has been influential to "darken the vision and arrest the arm of Philanthropy," then this community, and especially the readers of the Tribune, must be less generous and charitable than formerly. They must answer this charge for themselves; you may answer it on behalf of the community.

As to "Family Relations," fraud, unfairness, &c., I will make a plain statement, and our readers shall judge between us. They know that I at first proposed, and throughout insisted that we should discuss "*Association as I understand it*," and not as you might see fit to present it by clipping a sentence here and there from the writings of this or that advocate. You long stood out against this, but finally and unreservedly assented. So the discussion commenced and proceeded, until you saw fit to make the unqualified assertion that in Association all would be required to eat at one common table. As this is directly contradicted by every writer on Association of whom I know any thing, as well as by the whole spirit of the Reform, whose object is Freedom and Opportunity, not constraint and a narrow uniformity, I corrected your assertion, remarking that it argued gross ignorance on your part of the writings and views of Associationists. This remark was seized by you as a pretext for violating our express and fundamental agreement. You hasten thereupon to quote, from the earliest and crudest book ever issued in this country by an Associationist sundry passages not at all sustaining your original assertion, nor having the remotest bearing thereupon, but in regard to Education, the Training of Infants, the pecuniary Independence of Women, &c. The design clearly was to excite prejudice against what I *had* proposed by blending it in the reader's mind with what I *had not*, and holding me responsible for the whole. The fairness of this I will not characterize as it deserves.

How far I might agree with all that Fourier and Brisbane have advanced with regard to the points embraced in your citations, is immaterial; most certainly, as *you* represent them, I should dissent from them; and there are some things laid down by Fourier which I object to when fairly quoted. The ground maintained with regard to his writings by the Associationists was fairly and fully stated by us at our first general Convention, held in this City in April, 1844, in the following resolution, unanimously adopted, never departed from, and expressing our sentiments as thoroughly to-day as ever, viz:

"*Resolved, 6th,* That the name which, in this first Annual Convention of the Friends of Association, based upon the *Truths of Social Science discovered by Charles Fourier,* we adopt for ourselves, recommend to those who throughout the country would co-operate with us, and by which we desire to be always publicly designated, is THE ASSOCIATIONISTS OF THE UNITED STATES OF AMERICA. We do not call ourselves *Fourierists,* for the two following reasons: 1st. Charles Fourier often and earnestly protested in advance against giving the name of any individual man to the *Social Science,* which he humbly believed to be, and reverently taught as, a discovery of *Eternal Laws of Divine Justice,* established and made known by the CREATOR. 2d. While we honor the magnanimity, consummate ability, and devotedness of this good and wise man, and gratefully acknowledge our belief that he has been the means, under Providence, of giving to his fellow-men a clue which may lead us out from our actual Scientific and Social labyrinth, yet *we do not receive all the parts of his theories*, which in the publications of the Fourier School are denominated "Conjectural:" because Fourier gives them as speculations; because we do not in all respects understand his meaning; and because there are parts which *individually* we REJECT; and we hold ourselves not only free, but in duty bound, to seek and obey TRUTH *wherever revealed in the Word of God, the Reason of Humanity, and the order of Nature*."

If you can induce any one to believe that the parents in Association will submit their children to any other Education or exercise of authority than they find by experience to contribute most thoroughly to their healthful development—or that a uniform System of Education will be attained to otherwise than by "proving all things" and "holding fast that which is good"—you are welcome to what you can make out of it. Mr. Brisbane says he meant by a uniform system, one affording equal and thorough opportunities to the children of Rich and Poor—not one in which each child should be taught exactly like all the others. But I am in no wise responsible for what he meant nor what he said. You can not make one rational being believe that there is any necessary connection between Association and the suggestion that children should be instructed and directed by superiors a little older than themselves rather than by their parents.

As to the Marriage relation, you quoted Mr B as holding in 1840 that "the Family *spirit*, tending to selfishness, should be absorbed by corporative ties;" and you thereupon asserted that "the *Family* is to be *replaced* by these joint-stock companies"—that "such a result *is sought*," &c. Now you had before you Mr. B's express and emphatic disclaimers of any such thought—his repeated assertions that Association would purify and exalt the basis of the Family Relation, remove many causes of discord and unhappiness, &c., &c. That you should disagree with him on this point is matter of course; but had you any moral right to say that he *seeks* to *destroy* the Family and substitute the Association therefor? Your opinion of the *tendency* of his suggestion is one thing; what he *seeks* to compass by it is quite another. I trust no one will ever represent you as unfairly—nay, as unjustifiably—as you have represented him.

So, again, you say in your last:

"The Tribune reminds us that *under the pressure of social reform* several of our States are carrying into effect these principles concerning the conjugal relation."

Now what I *did* say was very far from this: namely, that laws shielding the property inherited or acquired by the Wife from dissipation by a profligate or reckless Husband, are being advocated and carried, *not* "under the pressure of Social Reform," but by the enlightened and generous who utterly disagree with me respecting Social Reform. I made this statement very broadly and plainly, remarking that I knew of but *one* Associationist in the Wisconsin Convention which has just passed, none at all in *our* Convention, which once passed, but finally receded from, a clause giving the Wife the legal control of her own property. By what right did you transform this into an assertion of the Tribune that Social Reform was at the bottom of this movement?

That the law on this subject will be changed, far sooner than public attention can be aroused to a radical cure of our Social Ills, I do confidently hope, and that we shall wait several generations before we realize the evils of such change, I have no doubt. Let the Wife transfer to her Husband so much of her property as she sees fit, if that be the whole; but do not let the Law step in and confiscate her hard earnings, past and future, to the pampering of a villain's debaucheries because she has been deceived into marrying that villain. It is not right to do it. Your application of the text "Whom God hath joined let no man put asunder," would justify a Hindoo Suttee quite as well as this.

With this, however, Association has nothing to do. What it proposes, and I trust will accomplish, is the providing for each man, woman, and child an unfailing sphere of Industry and Usefulness, so that, though the Husband may die, the Wife and Children shall not therefore be turned out of house and home, and scattered like a lot of slaves set up at auction, but enabled to go on earning an honest livelihood and enjoying each other's society as before. That the day of this and many kindred meliorations of the miseries of human life is not very distant is the ardent hope of

H. G.

---

From the Courier, Feb. 10th, 1847.

## REPLY TO LETTER VIII.

WE acknowledge, at the outset, the sincerity and success of the Tribune's "endeavor" to "resist the strong temptation" to follow the course of our last argument upon this subject. It is barely possible, to be sure, that the temptation was not so "strong" as the Editor would have his readers suppose, and that the struggle to resist it was, therefore, less severe than they might infer. But, at all events, the "endeavor" was successful. The temptation was resisted, and our entire argument remains untouched, except by the general plea that it was all irrelevant. Whether that plea be well founded or not, our readers can easily determine.

Association is urged by its advocates as a *substitute* for the Social System which now exists. It is presented as a plan for "reaching the *causes* of social evil"—for "*abolishing* pauperism, ignorance, and the resulting vices." It is intended, of course, for universal adoption —as a substitute for the present form of Society. Of course, therefore, its merits can be canvassed fully and fairly only by supposing it to have attained the universal dominion at which it aims. We may, it is true, discuss the principles on which it rests, and bring them to the test of established truth, without reference to the manner in which they are to be carried out. But if we seek to investigate the practical workings of the new system, it must he relieved from all the influences of the existing form. We must suppose Association to be universal. Suppose that all men were living, not as they now do, but as Association would have them: What would then be the tendency of things? What would then be the prevailing influences upon human character and human life? And what the results which, so far as reason can decide, those influences would produce? These are the questions involved in this discussion; and upon no other hypothesis can they find an answer.

This simple statement, it will be seen, sweeps away at once most of the Tribune's attempted arguments in defense of the system. It destroys, for example, the pertinence of the Tribune's references to the Shaker, Rapp, Moravian, and other communities which, it is assumed, have fully succeeded. The cases are not analogous. These little communities exist in the very heart of the old Society. They are surrounded on every side by its laws, its habits, and its atmosphere. They find in that Society markets for their produce; laws for the repression of crime; penalties for attempted fraud; a constant pressure which keeps them together; and a place into which they may expel all troublesome members. In Association, of course, when universally established, this could not be so. There could be no such thing as conditions of membership, or expulsion for misconduct. All classes, the wise and the stupid, the industrious and the lazy, the virtuous and the profligate, must then exist together; and must be entirely free from the laws, restraints, habits, and influences of the old Society. The Association could not avail itself of any of the aids or resources of the old form. It must exist alone, and furnish its own restraints, its own methods of education, of worship, and of promoting general order. And when all Society, moreover, had assumed that shape; when all the towns and cities in the land had been converted into phalanxes—each producing all the varieties of needed products—where would any of them find a market for their surplus? There would then be no world of "outside barbarians" to be supplied; but each would produce all it would need—and something more, as is affirmed. Here is a fatal difference between the two cases.

All these little communities, moreover, are under the complete control of some one or more persons. They are absolute monarchies on a small scale. They are held together, furthermore, by the bond of a common religious faith, which is different from that of the rest of the world. Their manner of life is a part of that religious faith; and their faith renders them passively subservient to the will of their leader. In Association there is to be no such head, and no such bond. There is to be no supreme power, clothed with authority, and with the means of enforcing it. While the new phalanxes exist in the bosom of the present Society; so long as they enjoy the defense and shelter of its laws and its influences, they may possibly hold together. But remove this support from them, make the system universal, and it would fall to pieces. At all events, the assumed success of the Shakers, Rappites, &c. (which, moreover, is not real), affords not even the shadow of a presumption to the contrary.

The fundamental element of the present Social System is the FAMILY, or, as the Associationists term it, the *Isolated Household*. It lies at the basis of all Social institutions. The division of mankind into families is the first law of nature—the natural growth of humanity. It seems, therefore, fitting and proper that all Social forms should rest upon that as their necessary foundation; that they should seek its preservation and full developement; and that the effect of any institution upon the Family should be regarded as a just measure of its merit. Association proceeds upon the opposite principle. It regards the Family spirit —that spirit which binds the members of the Family together, which prompts them to seek a home, property, happiness, and general wellbeing for themselves—as a narrow and selfish spirit; and it seeks, therefore, by its organization, not to cherish and promote its growth, but to *absorb* it in other relations. It seeks to bring men together under other forms, and to bind them together by another spirit. It does not leave the Family in its integrity; but aims directly to modify and change its character. Instead, for example, of leaving the families of a township to dwell each in its own house, to cultivate its own farm, educate its own children, and control its own affairs according to its own convictions of what is right, Association would bring them all into a common dwelling; set them at work upon a common farm; have their cooking and other domestic concerns performed in common; submit their children to a common training; and so substitute, in all the details of their daily life, this *Community* of feeling and of action for that *Family* spirit which it seeks to absorb. This is a vast and momentous change. It involves, of course, the complete subversion of all existing institutions, the overthrow of the present Social System, and the entire demolition of the existing fabric of social and of civil life. We are aware that the Tribune attempts to deny this. It says:

"We do not ask, we have never wished, all to abandon their houses and dwell together under a common roof. What we ask is, that the wealthy and philanthropic shall furnish the means of making one or more full and fair *experiments* of Associated Life and Labor," for which "$400,000 would amply suffice."

This language at first sounds like a denial of our assertion; but it amounts to nothing. It means simply that every thing is not expected *at once*; that Association is not to be "built in a day;" that *all* "we ask" is—$400,000 to make a *beginning*. If the wealthy will but furnish this, Association, it is thought, will then be able to go alone. The "experiment" will prove and establish the system—just as Fulton's experimental steam-boat demonstrated the practicability of his theories. The Tribune should bear in mind that the *theory* is the theme of discussion. We do not oppose any experiment the Tribune may make, except as we oppose the *System* it is intended to introduce; for, of course, something more than *example* is expected from a large, wealthy, and successful Association. Composed of picked men qualified for the service, animated by a common purpose, and feeling a common inter est in attaining their end, such an engine would be so used as to make still further encroachment on the existing System of Society, and carry Association, by a large stride forward, toward the universal dominion at which it aims Suppose one such Association, composed of 500 persons, with a capital of $400,000, conducted by the most skilful and determined men, and embracing none but the most zealous foes of the existing order of things, to be planted in the midst of a farming section. The means by which it might extend itself are laid down very precisely in the following extracts from Mr. BRISBANE's treatise:

"Let us examine some of the details of the system which should be followed in the organization of these Associations. The contrast between the industrial organization of the Associated farms and the present mode of farming would favorably impress the rural population around them, and condemn in their eyes the present system of isolated households. The Association with its 500 inhabitants, equal to about 100 families, would not have a hundred kitchens or a hundred fires. One large kitchen would take their place. Various branches of manufactures should be established so as to afford occupation during the winter months. * * The most important operation would be the establishing of a Loaning Fund or Bank in the Association, which would *lend on bond and mortgage to land-owners in the vicinity.* This would give the establishment popularity in their eyes, and reduce greatly the number of money-lenders on a small scale, who are now so numerous in the country. *A bank established on this plan would be the commencement of a gradual but* CERTAIN ABSORPTION OF THE SOIL OR LANDED PROPERTY. Each Association would gradually ABSORB *the little farms and pieces of land around on which it held mortgages, and the lands of persons already involved. Their owners could join the Association if they wished,* which should offer the laborer more liberty and enjoyment than he finds in his isolated house. The Association would also do its own commercial business, and would have its agents in large market-towns, who would sell its products and purchase at wholesale all articles wanted by the establishment. *This operation would cut off the retail country merchants.*" (P. 320, et seq.)

Here is certainly a very clear chart for the conduct of the Tribune's "experimental Association." It was laid down originally to show how what the author calls the "*fourth phasis*" of civilization might be introduced; but its method, of course, is equally adapted to the objects of the "Experiment," which the Tribune calls upon the rich to establish. Such an "experiment" would prove an admirable beginning for the new enterprise, and would enable the System to make rapid strides over the "little farms" that might lie adjacent, and the lands of "persons already involved," toward a still wider dominion. We object to this experiment, because we object to the System it is intended thus to introduce. That System seeks, as we have already stated, to take the place of the existing Society: to substitute other relations, other influences, other motives, and other objects than those which now exist, and which give its distinctive character to the present Social System The Tribune, we are aware, constantly insists that the only change proposed is a *reorganization of Labor,* and the same statement has been repeatedly made by other writers on Association. The first half of the Tribune's reply to our last article is devoted to this point; and sets forth, at unnecessary length, the positions, 1. That in a new Country, where labor is abundant and laborers few, the price of labor is *high*; 2 That in an old Country, where labor is scarce and laborers numerous, the price of labor *falls*; and, 3 That Association seeks to remedy this evil by giving to labor a *fixed proportion* of its product Now the first two propositions simply repeat the familiar principle that *the Price of Labor, like that of every other commodity, is regulated by the ratio of Supply and Demand;* and Association could not possibly alter that law. For in Association, as well as out of it, this ratio would vacillate; sometimes Labor would be abundant and Laborers few, while at others Laborers would be numerous and the work to be done comparatively small The proportion of product which each Laborer would receive would thus be subject to constant change; or, in other words, the price of Labor would rise and fall, in strict conformity to the present law, which is founded in the nature of the case, and can not, therefore, be essentially changed.

But the assertion, that Association proposes nothing but a "reorganization of Labor," is deceptive: quite as much so as the Tribune's similar assertion that *all* it asks is $400,000 for the trial of an "experiment." Mr. GODWIN, who has written, perhaps, the most clear and explicit work on this subject yet issued in this country, says, also, that "the School of FOURIER proposes but one thing—*the organization of Labor in the Township.*" But he has the candor to add that,

"Let a *Township* be once organized according to our principles, and the reform *will soon spread over the whole nation;*" and that "Law, Government, Manners, and Religion would all be more or less affected by a unitary *regime* of Industry."

In fact, the very means by which Association proposes to "organize Labor," involve and require an entire and radical change in all the relations of Social Life. Men, women, and children are to be brought together, to work together, and to live together under new relations; to be held together by new bonds; and to live in an entirely different state of things from that which now exists. Thus we have shown very clearly that this new Social Form requires that Parental Authority and Filial Obedience shall be abolished; that the Husband and Wife, instead of being *one,* as the laws of God have decreed, shall be entirely independent of each other in name and in property, and that each shall have perfect liberty of action and *affection;* that the Education of all the Children shall be committed to a council, chosen by the aggregate members; and that various regulations of a similar character shall be introduced, in order to preserve that *harmony* of action and of life, which could alone prevent Association from falling back into the "discord" and "anarchy" of existing Society. The Tribune assures us that we "can not make one rational being believe that there is any necessary connection" between Association and these requirements; and charges us, in the following language, with having unfairly made quotations in support of that position:

"You saw fit to make the unqualified assertion that in Association all would be required to eat at one common table. I corrected your assertion, remarking that it argued gross ignorance on your part of the writings and views of the Associationists. *This remark* was seized by you as a pretext for violating our express and fundamental agreement. You hasten *thereupon* to quote sundry passages not at all sustaining your original assertion, *but in regard to education, the training of infants, the independence of women,*" &c.

A few words we doubt not, will convince the Editor, that his memory is entirely at fault. In our fourth article of this discussion (Dec. 14th,) we inquired " what provision would be made in Association *for education,*" and " how the principle would be carried into the various departments of domestic life," the conjugal relation, the training of infants, &c. The Tribune replied that

"Education would be the special charge of counsellors elected by all the adult members," and that "as to the definite arrangement of details, it would require columns to state it fully."

In our reply (Dec. 24th) we spoke of this response as unsatisfactory, and mentioned several obstacles to the system of education, worship, and domestic life, so far as it had been set forth, at the same time asking for more definite information. The Tribune's reply, (Dec. 28th) was in these words:

" Your mistaken assumptions [with regard to eating] evince a sad unacquaintance with a system which you have for years been denouncing as abominable, and imploring every body to understand and execrate as you did. *So with regard to Labor, to Education, to Religion,* &c. *Had you but read attentively any of the writings of the Associationists,* YOU WOULD HAVE SEEN HOW YOUR OBSTACLES ARE SURMOUNTED."

Here, then, the Tribune referred us, in the most explicit language, to the "*writings of the Associationists*" for the information we had asked as to " how our obstacles are to be surmounted." We were told that it would "require columns" to give the answer, and that it would be found in the " writings of the Associationists." And to this day the Tribune has given us no *other* answer, and yet it abuses us for using that one! We are still compelled to follow those directions, and have endeavored, as we were advised, to "read attentively the writings of the Associationists," in order to learn what Association proposes to do, and *how* it proposes to do it. The Tribune does not charge us with having misquoted the " writings' to which it referred us; but simply disavows personal responsibility for what they may contain. The Editor apparently forgets that we are discussing the merits of a *system.* We are examining "Association as the Tribune understands it," and as it is set forth in those " writings of the Associationists" to which the Tribune referred us for its understanding of it. In the course of this inquiry we have shown, very clearly, that *the System* seeks to " absorb the Family spirit;" seeks to abolish Parental Authority; seeks to annul the duty of Filial Obedience; seeks to destroy the essential character of the Marriage relation; and we shall hereafter show that it *seeks* to do many other things equally abhorrent to the moral sense and the direct inculcations of the Word of God. Now Mr. BRISBANE may, or may not, disclaim such an intention for himself personally;—so may Mr Godwin, so may Fourier, and so may the Editor of the Tribune.—Disclaimers of this kind do not meet the point. The controversy can not be made a personal one, nor can personal disavowals relieve *the System* from the principles and results which can be proved upon it. Paine repelled the charge of being an infidel, and declared himself to be a Christian;—but this did not in the least change the character of his writings upon the subject. It is needless to add that the Tribune fabricates a quotation, when it makes us say that " *Mr. Brisbane* seeks to destroy the Family." We charge that purpose upon *the System:* and those who uphold it must share the responsibility, although they may disclaim the intention.

To sustain its attempted disavowal of responsibility for the doctrines referred to, the Tribune quotes a resolution passed in 1844 by the " Associationists of the United States of North America" in Convention assembled. That resolution says that those who passed it "do not receive all the parts of Fourier's theories which are termed *conjectural.*" The disclaimer, to whatever weight it may be entitled, includes no other parts of Fourier's theories than those specified. *But the parts we have quoted are not among those which are termed conjectural.* They do not come within the sphere of this disclaimer. They are not set forth as " speculations," but are given as essential portions of that " Social Science," which, in the language of this resolution,

" FOURIER humbly believed to be, and reverently taught as, a discovery of *Eternal Laws of Divine Justice,* established and made known by the CREATOR."

The disavowal, therefore, does not reach the case. And as for saying that " there are parts of the System" which " *individually* they reject," what is that but saying that *the System* does *not* reject them, though individuals may! And the same thing may be said of any system ever promulgated. The American Government may just as well disclaim responsibility for a Republican System, because individuals reject some of its features.

We repeat, therefore, the statement with which we set out, that Association comes before the public as a new SOCIAL SYSTEM, based upon distinctive principles of moral and social philosophy, proposing certain definite results, and seeking their attainment by a definite organization. It is offered as a *substitute* for the present Society, and seeks to replace it in all its departments. It is presented, not as an experiment, not as a scheme of conjectural speculation, but as a " SOCIAL SCIENCE," as *the true,* and the only true, Social System, created by God, its principles implanted in human nature, and first discovered, set forth, and imbodied in a definite organization by Fourier. Thus, Mr. Godwin, in the preface to his "Popular View" of this subject, says :—

"We wish to rest the claims of the Social Science of Fourier upon precisely the same grounds on which Herschel rests the Science of Astronomy. Fourier and his disciples hold that *his social principles are entitled to rank as a Science,* being capable of that rigorous demonstration which only willful prejudice rejects."

Now the *principles* of such a science, if true, must be of universal application—just as the laws of Astronomy are universal. They must reach, and shape, and control all Social forms and all Social life, just as the law of gravitation controls the material universe. It is absurd to restrict their operations to the "organization of labor," or to any one branch of social existence. If they are, as is claimed, the principles of a true Social Science, they must control all departments of Social Life. And this is fully conceded, and indeed is distinctly claimed, by all the writers upon Association. In our next article upon this subject we shall set forth, more directly than we have done hitherto, what these fundamental principles are, and how they "surmount the obstacles" which seem to us likely to prove fatal to the success of the system proposed. In doing this, we shall, of course, follow the directions of the Tribune, and consult, "attentively, the writings of the Associationists." One or two points of the Tribune's last article, which we do not notice now, will then be considered.

---

From the Tribune, Feb. 17.
LETTER IX.
*To the Editor of the Courier and Enquirer:*

WHOEVER comes before the public as the advocate of any momentous change in the habits, customs, or relations of men, is fairly bound to demonstrate two things—first, the *necessity* of change, and, secondly, the expediency and practicability of *such* change as he proposes. In other words, he is properly required to prove that an evil exists, and that the change he advocates will provide the appropriate remedy or remedies. His argument naturally arranges itself under three heads—treating of the needful *work* to be done, the *mode* or means of doing it, and the *end* to be accomplished or attained These distinctions I have endeavored to keep in mind in the progress of this discussion. I have endeavored first to show that are radical defects or vices in our Social institutes and usages, demanding radical remedies; secondly, that these defects are curable; thirdly, that their remedy is to be found in ASSOCIATION. The controversial form has not permitted me, without seeming disrepect to my opponent and inattention to his statements, to keep this distinction always before the reader and pursue my argument with the logical sequence of an essay; but I trust the reader will have made the necessary allowance. It seems to me that the first proposition—namely, the *necessity* of a radical reform—is the essential matter, and that if I could really convince you of this, all the rest would follow of course. Concede to me that Society needs literally to be re-formed, and you are welcome to black-ball Fourier, Brisbane, &c. to your heart's content. I am solicitous for results only, not names nor parties. And as I understand you still to maintain that there are no evils in the constitution and laws of Society, I will devote this one more article mainly to that branch of the question.

Permit me once more, then, to call your attention to these facts:—That while the essential or productive value of Human Labor in civilized Society is rapidly increasing, its market value is steadily diminishing; That while, through the rapid multiplication and improvement of Labor-saving Inventions, the Laboring Classes of to-day produce ten times as much as they did four centuries ago, their reward is more scanty and their living more precarious than that of their ancestors in the days of Columbus; That while Production and Wealth have been immensely increased, Want and consequent Wretchedness have increased along with them; That while, through the inventions of Watt, Arkwright, Hargraves, &c, the labor of one person in spinning produces more yarn than that of *two hundred* did even a century since, so that warehouses groan and the markets of the world are glutted with every variety of fabrics, yet there are this day more naked backs, more suffering for want of adequate and comfortable clothing, than there were in the fourteenth century; That while on all hands there is manifest need of the limitless application of Labor—Lands to be cleared and subdued, Marshes to be drained, exhausted, or inferior Soils to be made fertile, Railroads, Canals and Buildings to be constructed, &c., &c.—there are at this moment and at all times great numbers of Laborers vainly seeking employment, and suffering for the want of it, while vastly many more are driven by hard necessity to work for wages utterly inadequate either to reward their exertions or to procure a comfortable subsistence; and, finally, that this enforced Idleness, and the consequent Destitution and Misery, are among the most potent causes of the Ignorance, Intemperance, Vice, Degradation, and Wretchedness so generally prevailing. For these fundamental facts there are appropriate and adequate causes, the root of which is found in that Isolation of Efforts and Antagonism of Interests on which our present Social Order is based. In that order the Owners of Property form one class, the Producers of Wealth mainly another; and it is the apparent and eagerly-pursued interest of the Owning class to procure the Labor of the Working class at the cheapest possible rate. To accomplish this end, there are different modes—direct Slavery, Hiring for Wages, Rent or Purchase of Lands, Usury, &c.—not equally objectionable or pernicious, but all tending to the same end. Every year brings upon the stage of life its millions, each of whom must have food, shelter, implements, &c., before he can earn for himself as well as afterward; and the great mass must have the use of the Earth and its natural products to give scope to their labor and render it available But here they find themselves confronted with a smaller but more powerful class, who *own* this same Earth, and these its needful products, and who are authorized to exact, and *do* exact, for the use thereof, prices graduated by the number and consequent necessities of those requiring them. Suppose a township six miles square, located in a new country, and having as yet but 500 inhabitants: here those who need land will usually buy it wild, at one to three dollars per acre, or cleared at five to fifteen dollars. Now let this population increase to 2,000, and that same wild land will be worth three or ten dollars and the improved twenty to fifty dollars per acre. But in time the population swells to 5,000, and now (all other things being equal, and no large tracts of vacant land so situated as to draw off its population) the primitive forest as well as the improved soil will command fifty to one hundred dollars per acre, and even more. But even at 5,000 to the township of six miles square the limits of Population are not reached, if human existence can be maintained, and the race perpetuated upon the wages, direct or indirect, which Labor will still command. What is the remedy for this evil? What shall arrest the palpable tendency of increasing Population to depress Labor and diminish the means of subsistence for the great mass of mankind? The Free-Trade Economists answer, *The poor must not "increase their numbers*—it is a crime in them to do so—they must marry late in life, and have few children, on pain of starvation." The Tribune answers, "Society must be so re-formed that Population may be increased without depressing the condition of the mass, diminishing the reward of their Labor, or depriving them of constant opportunity to earn and live in comfort: all these conditions are clearly attainable through Association" The Courier answers—what? Our readers will determine.

But let me here stop to correct your error of assertion in regard to what Association will do in the premises. You say it will make no change at all—that the price of Labor will vacillate with the proportion of Supply and Demand—that in Association " the price of Labor would rise and fall in strict conformity to the present law." This shows that you do not yet understand what it is you are opposing; and at the risk of being tedious to many a reader, I will again explain the relation of Labor to Capital in Association

We have seen that, as a township increases its population, the price or rental of Land rapidly increases and the wages of Labor proportionally diminish. This is the result of a tendency or law inherent in civilized society, with the earth monopolized by a part, while the larger number own little or nothing. It may for a season be counteracted and checked by the introduction of new branches of industry or the rapid extension and diversification of those which do not require much land for their advantageous prosecution; but the snake is "scotched, not killed;" Labor flows in from all sides to profit by the newly-created demand for it, and wages are soon pressed down to their former minimum, pushed to the brink of a farther fall, and then over it. Meantime Land, Houses, and nearly all fixed Property have been vastly increased in price or rental by this very influx of Population, so that the surplus earnings of labor have been swallowed in an ever-yawning abyss. A multitude has been rapidly drawn together, and *because* they are thus assembled they are obliged to pay exorbitantly for ground to stand upon and the roofs that shelter them. The tailor, shoemaker, &c, pay each a double rent; one on the cost of the buildings they severally occupy, and the other (termed "ground-rent") for the privilege of being convenient to their respective customers, though those customers pay likewise for the privilege of being near *them*. These two premiums above a fair interest on the cost of the buildings are paid to Capital, not because they *should* be, but because they *must*. It simply holds up its dish and catches the golden shower. But in Association these various artisans and customers are brought together and *not* subjected to any such inroad upon their earnings. They pay a fair rent on the cost of their several shops and dwellings, but nothing answering to ground-rent beyond the five to twenty dollars per acre that the naked ground actually cost the Phalanx. Here, then, is *one* law vitally and balefully affecting the price of Labor in existing Society which would be entirely set aside in Association.

But again the laborer is a partner in the Association, and is recompensed as a partner. Suppose there are one hundred effective adult male laborers at the outset; these would divide the products or proceeds among them according to a prearranged scale, giving to Capital its stipulated interest or proportion. But the number of laborers gradually increases to five hundred: what then? Is the recompense of Labor consequently diminished? Do they pay more per head for shelter, more per acre for land, and so retain a smaller share of the products for themselves? By no means — rather the contrary. The original capitalists own and receive dividends upon so much stock, as before, unless they have actually invested more capital in the improvements or additions since made; if they have, they receive dividends on this likewise; all beyond this which has been added to the value of the property by peopling it, building, draining, fencing, fertilizing, planting trees, orchards. &c , has been regularly awarded to Labor, and stock issued accordingly. The laborer is his own employer; his Father in Heaven is his paymaster, and the amount of his dividend is mainly determined by his efficiency and subordinately by the prices which such surplus products as he may have to sell will bring in the market. As a general rule, his labor will become, through experience and improved processes, more and more effective as the number of his associates increases, up to the limit at which land can be advantageously cultivated from one center or dwelling.

But again: Society as it is presents the constant spectacle of Labor vainly seeking employment, and this becomes more frequent and general as population increases. In Ireland it is calculated that the permanent surplus of Labor —that is, the Labor which can not find employment—is *one-fifth* of the whole amount, equal to Three Hundred Thousand able men, at all times idle, because they can get nothing to do at any price. Suppose the labor of these men to be actually worth fifty cents each per day, and that they would willingly work three hundred days in each year, the positive loss to the world, by their lack of employment, is no less than *Forty-five Millions of Dollars*. Say that the labor of women and minors, doomed to idleness, is worth but one-third so much, and we have an aggregate of *Sixty Millions of Dollars*, absolutely wasted every year on one little island, because of the anarchical relation of Labor to Capital under our present Social regime. Wasted, did I say? No; far worse than wasted—employed to lure millions every year into habits of dissipation, indolence, and depravity. An old proverb asserts that the Evil One finds work for those who have no other. Is it advisable to leave such an important function in such hands? I think not.

Now, let any man who doubts inquire, and satisfy himself that Labor has found full employment in every attempt at Association, no matter how rude and imperfect—I think I need not except even that Clarkson abortion, destitute of capital, leading, and every requisite to give even a chance of success which has recently been dug out of its early and well-grassed grave, and paraded through journals of your stamp, to deepen the prejudice of Ignorance against any Social Reform. In the only examples we have of Communities—the Moravians, Rappites, Shakers, Zoarites, &c, I am confident that no man, for many a year, has stood idle a single day for want of work to do. Go to the Township most thickly populated, where most Labor stands idly in the market-place, waiting, till "hope deferred maketh the heart sick," for some one to hire it, and inquire if there be not even there work enough needing to be done, and you will find it abundant. The Land needs Labor to render it in the highest degree salubrious and fertile; Labor extensively and urgently needs employment and recompense; but an evil genius has built up a wall of iron between these two necessities, which ought to flow into and satisfy each other. The Laborer eagerly seeks employment, and would gladly accept even an inadequate reward; the Land would richly reward an immense addition of labor, but it belongs to persons who are either unable to improve it thoroughly, or deem it inadvisable to do so—is held on leases by those who apprehend that a high state of cultivation would increase the prices at which they must ultimately buy or again hire it—is in law or in chancery, or in the hands of executors or guardians, who do not feel authorized to improve it, or in some one of a hundred other ways its improvement is forbidden. But in Association the Laborers of the Phalanx or Township are, at all times, directors of their own efforts, with full power to improve where and when they think proper, and be fairly recompensed for the additional value their Labor shall have created. The owners of two-thirds of the Capital may die without at all arresting or interfering with the regular routine of Industry or Education. The settlement of an estate will require simply the division among, and transfer to, the heirs of so many shares of stock as belonged to the deceased, with the adjustment of his running account for labor, subsistence, &c, with the Association.

But again: It will be the palpable *interest* of Capital and Talent in Association to have the entire Labor at all times fully employed. Suppose this City of New York were now in some plain way a gigantic Association or Joint-Stock Community, in which each individual who would work was guaranteed a minimum of subsistence—does any man believe that the hod-carriers, bricklayers, stone-masons, &c., &c., whom the approach of winter throws out of their accustomed employment, would be suffered mainly to spend the three cold months in unwilling idleness and penury? No, sir; nothing like it. The very first winter would witness meetings at the Exchange and in the Bank parlors to devise ways and means of setting at work all those thus doomed to idleness and pauperism. Money in thousands would be subscribed to establish new Manufactures, &c., if only for the winter months, wherein men, women and children should find ample and unfailing employment at some rate which would enable them to earn a livelihood. I trust that, in the obvious though irregular progress of Society to a state of general guarantyism, this will soon be effected at any rate. But in Association the impulse to provide work for all would be instant and irresistible.

Allow me to call your attention to a few striking facts, showing that, as Civilization advances and Population increases, the reward of Labor grows more and more meager and the condition of the Laboring Class more depressed and hopeless. I trust you will not have any difficulty in perceiving their bearing on the question now in controversy between us.

Five centuries ago* (A.D. 1350) a British statute (23d of Edward III) fixed the prices of Labor in England as follow:—For common labor on a farm per day, *three pence halfpenny;* reaping per day, *fourpence;* mowing an acre of grass, *sixpence;* threshing a quarter of wheat (eight bushels), *fourpence;* and other labor in proportion. In Bishop Fleetwood's "Chronicon Preciosum," a work of repute, are found various accounts kept by bursars of convents. From one of these dated in the fourteenth century the following items are taken:—A pair of shoes, *fourpence;* russet broadcloth, per yard, *thirteen pence;* a stall-fed ox, *twenty-five shillings;* a fat goose, *twopence half-penny;* wheat per quarter (eight bushels), *three shillings fourpence* Sir John Cullum (quoted by Hallam), substantially corroborates these statements, quoting the price of wheat in the fourteenth century at four shillings per quarter, or sixpence per bushel. Fleta, who wrote about 1330. likewise gives four shillings per quarter as the average price of wheat in his day; so that the week's wages of a common farm laborer in England would purchase *three and a half bushels of wheat,* or five pairs of shoes, or over a yard and a half of broadcloath, or over eight fat geese, while fourteen weeks' work would buy a fat ox, and so on. In harvest-time, his wages were an eighth higher, and the price of mowing an acre of grass would buy a bushel of wheat. For threshing twelve bushels of wheat the laborer received the price of a bushel.

In 1444 (act of 23d Henry VII.), the wages of a reaper were fixed at *fivepence* per day, and other labor in proportion. The account-book of a convent of a little earlier date, quoted by Sir F. Eden. gives these prices: Wheat (average) *five shillings per quarter;* Oxen, *twelve to fifteen shillings each;* Sheep, from *fourteen to sixteenpence;* butter, *three farthings per pound;* cheese, *a halfpenny;* eggs, *twenty-five for a penny.* Hallam states the average price of butchers' meat in the next century at *a farthing*

---

* Most of the following facts respecting the ancient and modern recompense of labor in Great Britain are taken from an article, entitled "One of the Problems of the Age," in an old Democratic Review.

and *a half per pound.* In the next century (act of 24th of Henry VIII), it was decreed that no person shall take for beef or pork above *a halfpenny,* nor for mutton or veal above *three farthings* per pound, and less in those places where "*y* are now sold for less." Thus it appears that through the fourteenth, fifteenth, and sixteenth centuries, the week's wages of an English farm laborer would purchase an average of four bushels of wheat, or half-a-quarter of beef, or one and a half fat sheep, or ten fat geese, or six pair of shoes, or nearly broadcloth enough for a coat. Compare these with the present prices of Labor and Food in Great Britain (I do not refer to the famine prices of this season, but those which have ruled for the last ten or more years), wherein the average wages of farm labor have been eight shillings per week,' just the average retail price of *one bushel* of wheat or fifteen pounds of beef! The British laborer of our day works harder and produces far more than did his ancestors four centuries ago, yet receives in the average no more for a month's work than that ancestor did for a week! The balance of his product is absorbed by the profits of Capital, including the enormous rental or valuation of Land

That the British laborer four centuries ago enjoyed a degree of comfort unknown to his living descendants, need hardly be added. Fortescue, Chancellor of England, writing in the fifteenth century, says the common people of his day are "rich in all the comforts and necessaries of life," and that "they drink no water except at certain times, upon a religious score, and by way of doing penance," and adds:

"They are fed in great abundance with all sorts of flesh and fish, of which they have abundance everywhere. They are clothed throughout in good woolens; their bedding and other furniture in their houses are of wool, and that in great store. They are well provided with all sorts of household goods and necessary implements of husbandry. Every one according to his rank hath all things which conduce to make life easy and happy."

We may readily admit that this picture is rose-colored, but what Chancellor or Editor could possibly assert any thing like this in *our* day? That the above is substantially true is confirmed by a variety of testimony. White, of Selborne, the naturalist, in his history of his native village, mentions incidentally, a record, dated 1380, that certain men, for disorderly conduct, were punished by being "compelled to *fast* on bread and beer." Cobbett, who quotes the above anecdote, has also dragged to light a statute of 1533, the preamble of which, after naming four sorts of meat, "beef, pork, mutton, and veal," adds, "these being the food of the *poorer* sort."

That, in those ages of rude implements and unskillful husbandry, there were sometimes famines after bad harvests or the desolations of war, is quite true; so there are now. These do not affect the general and appalling truth that during the last five centuries there has been a complete and disastrous revolution in the ordinary condition of the Toiling Millions of Civilized Europe (for the same is true of other countries as well as England, in proportion to their increase in population and individual wealth)—a revolution which has depressed them from comfort to wretchedness, from careless ease to incessant anxiety and struggle for the bare means of existence. They have reached that point where, in the words of the Westminster Review, "there is not a step but merely a hand's-breath between the condition of the agricultural laborer and pauperism." Instead of the fare of his ancestors described above, his family are scantily subsisted on potatoes and salt, bread and lard, with a little intensely-skimmed milk as an occasional luxury His weekly wages will barely procure this diet and pay the rent of his cot, and when sickness or a failure of employment overtakes him, he is driven to beggary or the union workhouse.

Will any say, You are talking of *British* distresses: what do they prove as to *us?* Ah, sirs! the same general causes which have produced this fearful change in Europe are now at work here. Population is rapidly increasing; Wealth is concentrating; the Public Lands are rapidly passing into private ownership, often by tens of thousands of acres to a single individual. And as our population becomes compact, and land costly as in England, the evils now experienced by the Many in Europe, will gradually fasten upon their brethren here. Our Political institutions may do something to mitigate this; but how much? The masterevil in the condition of the English and Irish is the monopoly by the few of the God-given elements of production, which are necessary to all. Abolish Monarchy, Titles of Nobility, Church Establishment, National Debt, and whatever else you please, so long as the Land shall remain the exclusive property of a small and isolated class, competition for the use of it as active as now, and rents consequently as high, so long will nothing have been accomplished beyond clearing away some of the elementary obstacles to the real and essential Reform.

But in our own country the footsteps of advancing Destitution and abject Dependence for the Many, already sound ominously near. In our journals are advertisements to let out some hundreds of robust men from the Immigrant alms-houses to work through the winter for their board, while tens of thousands in our City would gladly have been so disposed of from December to April. Nor is this lack of employment by any means confined to immigrants with those displaced by them. Thousands of American-born Women are at this moment working long days in our City, for less than the cost of one good meal of victuals per day (say twenty-five cents); and it was but yesterday that a friend, living in the country, casually informed me that he could hire as much farm labor in winter as he wanted, for the laborer's own board, or for 37½ cents per day without board. And these laborers are not foreigners, but the descendants of those who won our liberties on the battle-fields of the Revolution.

I rest here my argument on the point that THERE MUST BE A SOCIAL REFORM—a reform which shall secure to Labor unfailing Employment and adequate Recompense; to Children and Youth, universally, ample and thorough Education, moral, intellectual and physical; and to the Poor as well as Rich comfortable, abiding Homes, the largest Opportunities for Social and Mental Elevation, with freedom from incessant anxiety for Work and Bread. We have the confessions of the best thinkers and ablest journals in the Old World (see London Times, also Morning Chronicle) that the old order of things has proved a failure—that new principles must be invoked, and new and profounder remedies for Social Evils be resorted to. (See also the Queen's late Speech.) "Let us alone" and "Every man for himself" have gone to the end of their tether; we must now try the opposite principle of "Each for All," and seek Individual only through Universal Good. This is in essence what I understand by Association—whatever appears to me essential to this, I advocate; to nothing farther in this relation am I committed, no matter who is its author or commender. "*The System*" of Association is no man's formula, but whatever experience shall prove needful or helpful to give effect to the Principles above set forth, and to attain the Ends herein stated. Whoever has written on this subject as an advocate of Association I listen to with respect; his suggestion of means to obviate practical difficulties, I welcome; but to nothing am I committed beyond what is involved in the fundamental idea of Associated Industry, Education and Life. All this you very well understand; and I but waste words in repeating it. If you can make any one believe that one model Phalanx will lead to the formation of others, unless it demonstrates immense advantages in the Associated over the Isolated sphere; or if you can induce any one to think that Association will be more difficult when it becomes general than in its first experiments, I can only say that argument from me would be lost on *such* readers. Whoever will imagine an article from a Courier and Enquirer of 1606, demonstrating from experience the impossibility of colonizing the Atlantic coast of North America, or at least the certainty that there can be no *general* colonization of that coast, though one or two of the first settlements may do well enough, will realize the light in which your argument presents itself to    H. G.

---

From the Courier and Enquirer of March 5th, 1847.

### REPLY TO LETTER IX.

The Tribune has now devoted nine articles almost entirely to the proof of an assertion, the truth of which we expressly conceded at the very outset of this discussion; namely, that great social evils exist, and demand a remedy In its last article, which we have copied above, the Tribune expresses the opinion that if this position be once established, "the rest will follow of course." If this be so, the controversy ought long since to have been closed: for the position in question has never been denied. We have taken unusual pains to admit, from the very beginning, that the condition of a large part of society is not what it should be; and that the great law of Christian charity, as well as the dictates of common humanity, enjoins the most zealous, constant, and intelligent efforts for the relief of existing misery and the removal of the causes which give it birth. We dispute only the assertions of the Tribune concerning the *causes* and the *cure* of these evils. Far from denying their existence, we insist that they are deeper and more fundamental in their origin, and demand a more thorough and radical remedy, than the Tribune supposes. That paper charges them to the prevailing *forms* of society: we attribute them to the selfishness and depravity of human nature, which pervade all social forms and depend upon none. The Tribune demands a new form of social life, as the only remedy for them: we insist that, as they do not originate in any form, so no change of form could cure them: that, as they spring from an inherent and dominant principle of sinful selfishness in the heart, so they can only be cured by a radical change in individual character: and that, moreover, the form of society proposed by Association is impracticable, and certain to produce, if carried out, greater evils than it seeks to cure. Our arguments upon these several points, as well as upon others which have sprung up in the course of this discussion, remain as yet unanswered: and we do not intend, therefore, to repeat them here.

The Tribune devotes nearly the whole of its last article to the assertion of the principle upon which, half a century ago, Mr. Malthus based his famous and exploded theory, viz: that as the population of any country increases, the condition of its laboring classes becomes worse and worse. This position is laid down by the Tribune in every possible variety of forms: and the effort is made to sustain it by some statistical statements of the relative prices of *labor* and of *food* in England during the last five centuries. The point is stated thus: that five centuries ago the condition of the laboring classes in England was better than it is now: that they enjoyed, as the fruits of their labor then, *a better living and more comfort*, than the same labor will command now: that, while the aggregate wealth of the *whole mass* has increased, the wealth of the laboring class has constantly diminished: and that this is the natural, and inevitable tendency of society everywhere We regret that the Tribune should have copied its statistics upon this subject so blindly "from an article in an old Democratic Review," and adopted so hastily the "foregone conclusions" which that article was compiled to establish. It quotes, for instance, the rates of labor fixed by a British Statute in 1350, as the regular, average prices of labor in that age; whereas, if it had taken the pains to examine even the preamble to that statute, it would have found that it was based upon the express averment,

"That a *great part* of the people, and especially of the wor*kmen and servants, had lately died of the pestilence;*" and that "many, seeing the necessity of masters, and the great *scarcity* of servants, will not serve unless they may receive *excessive wages*; and some are willing to beg in idleness rather than by labor to get their living," &c.

Just at that period, moreover, the great body of the laboring class in England, who had before been *villains* or serfs, had thrown off their chains of service and become free laborers; and it is a matter of history that, under the exhilaration of this change in their condition, they refused to work except at exorbitant rates. In view of these facts, it is easy to see that the prices of labor, quoted by the Tribune, are very likely to be deceptive. And to a still greater extent is this true in regard to the prices of food, clothing, &c.; as is clearly stated, by one of the writers quoted by the Review upon this very point, Bishop Fleetwood, in his "Chronicon Preciosum," or prices current of that early day. It is said expressly that

"The accounts of the prices of grain are usually the prices in dearths, or in *years of very extraordinary cheapness*, and are no very accurate criterion of the mean or *ordinary price*."

And another writer has remarked that the value of money, in those days, may be

"Made to bear any proportion to its value in the present day that the fancy of the calculator might prefer, or that it *might best suit his particular object to fix upon*."

These statistics, therefore, on which the Tribune relies, are by no means conclusive. That paper, moreover, neglects entirely the fact that new and cheaper kinds of food and clothing have been substituted, by the advance of civilization, for those that were used in that early day. An immense increase, in the means of subsistence, has taken place; and although certain kinds of food and clothing may have increased in price, the average cost of living has greatly diminished. It can not be necessary, however, to pursue these details in order to disprove the Tribune's assertion, that "the British laborer, four centuries ago, enjoyed a degree of comfort unknown to his living descendants;" and that the laboring classes have been "depressed, during the last five centuries, from comfort to wretchedness." It has been repeatedly refuted since it was first propounded by Malthus, and is now almost universally abandoned by the soundest writers on political economy. The rose-colored pictures of the condition of England three or four centuries since, quoted by the Tribune, are simply the *best side* which officials and placemen proverbially put outward, and are entitled to much less weight than would be due to sketches of the condition of Southern slaves, by Mr. M'Duffie or Governor Hammond. They are, indeed, contradicted by the most disinterested and reliable writers Erasmus, in the reign of Henry VIII, describes the condition of the ordinary dwelling of the English laborer in terms which would be grossly exaggerated if applied to the Five Points, in our city. Dr. Heberden, who has written fully and ably upon the subject, ascribes the plague of 1665 to the universal and constant "filthiness of the streets and houses," and the wretched diet and clothing of the mass of the people. Sir Thomas More, as quoted by Lord Russell, in his recent speech upon Ireland, draws a picture of society in England, as it was in his day, of the most appalling darkness. And the accurate and pains-taking M'Culloch, gives the following, as the result of his investigations upon this very point: it is so direct and emphatic, that it needs no comment:

"Let any one compare the state of this or any other European country five hundred or one hundred years ago, with its present state, and he will be satisfied that prodigious advances have been made, that the means of subsistence have increased much more rapidly than the population, and that *the labor-*

*ing classes are now generally in the possession of conveniences and luxuries that were formerly not enjoyed even by the richest lords.*"

These considerations, it seems to us, show conclusively that the Tribune's theory is groundless. It is not true that the increase of population of necessity renders more wretched and hopeless the condition of the laboring classes. The increase of population is necessarily subordinate to the increase in the means of subsistence, and will not, because it can not, in the long run, outstrip it. And, especially, is its theory untrue as applied, by the Tribune, to the United States. It is not true that "wealth is concentrating" in this country, or that any such "causes, as have produced the present state of things in Europe," are operating here. All estates there go to the eldest son; here they are divided among all the children. The prices of all the necessaries of life are there raised to an artificial standard, by the enormous taxes levied upon them; no such causes are in operation here. Our public lands are, indeed, "passing into private ownership;" but it is the very step necessary to secure their cultivation, and through that, an increase of the means of subsistence. The constant tendency of things with us is, to divide among many the large estates which may have accumulated in the hands of individuals. And, as a general rule, in this country, no man who is able and willing to work need ever suffer any lack of the food and clothing essential to his comfortable subsistence. In large cities, and especially in this city, exceptions may be found to this general rule: but they are far less numerous than they are represented, and are the result of temporary and accidental causes. Cities, moreover, never offer a just standard for estimating the condition of a people, since extraneous causes there prevent the fair operation of the general laws which govern society; and the condition of the great body of the population of the United States, of the farmers everywhere, is one upon which the most zealous philanthropist, if he have no pet theory to support, may look with unalloyed satisfaction The population, it is true, is increasing with great rapidity; but this is owing to the immense and rapid increase in the means of subsistence; and it is a settled principle of political economy, that the latter must not only keep pace with the former, but take the lead.

Leaving this view of the case for the present, let us consider another portion of the Tribune's argument. That paper reiterates its complaints that the *wages of labor constantly fluctuate*, as population increases and the work to be done diminishes; and demands that labor should receive a *fixed proportion* of its product. Our reply to this is, that *the price of labor*, like that of every other marketable commodity, *is of necessity regulated by the ratio of Supply and Demand;* and the scheme of Association can not possibly alter that law, or evade its operation. *When laborers increase faster than the capital that employs them*, labor MUST FALL: *when the increase is in favor of capital*, labor WILL RISE. And this law would operate in Association, precisely as it does in society now. The Tribune answers this point thus:—

"Suppose there are 100 effective adult male laborers at the outset: these would divide the products or proceeds among them according to a prearranged scale, giving to capital its stipulated interest or proportion. But the number of laborers gradually increases to 500; what then? *Is the recompense of labor consequently diminished?*"

Most assuredly it must be, unless the *demand* for laborers, and the *capital* to employ them, have increased in the same ratio. Suppose, for example, that the net product of an Association of 100 laborers at the end of the year is $10,000, after paying the interest on capital, &c. It is clear that each one would receive as his share $100. But when the laborers increase to 500, it is clear that in order to give to each the same sum as before, the aggregate profits must become $50,000 instead of $10,000 as before. The demand for labor must be increased as rapidly as the number of laborers: or in other words, *the ratio of Supply and Demand must be maintained.* If the former predominates, wages will *fall*: if the latter they will *rise*, in Association, just as they now do in the existing order. "As a general rule," says the Tribune, "labor will become more and more effective, as the number of associates increases, *up to the limit* at which land can be advantageously cultivated." Of course: and so it is now, and wages remain fixed so long as that proportion holds good. But when that "limit" is reached, what then? The surplus members of the Association, the Tribune will say, must then emigrate. True: but how does that differ from the present order? If the surplus laborers of this city, that is, those who are not needed to supply the existing demand, would emigrate, the remainder would do well enough. The state of things in Association must of necessity be the same.

Now the Tribune answers all this, by assuming and insisting that Association would overrule and set aside these laws: that if the market price of labor was low, Association would *pay more*, &c. This could only be done, it is clear, by lessening the profits of Capital. The products of Labor must of necessity be sold at the market rates. If then the owners pay their laborers *more* than their neighbors do, their profits must be less. Capitalists will not do this, in the first place, because they are governed mainly by self-interest: and next because in the end, such unequal competition would ruin them. The owner of the Tribune, for example, pays his laborers the market price for their work; and clears say $20,000 per annum, or *thirty* per cent on the capital invested. If he were to *double* or *quadruple* their wages, his own profits must fall: and his neighbors would outstrip him in the race. The owner of the Tribune, therefore, will not do this: he will not make the laborers he employs partners in the concern, nor increase their wages above the market price; because for such a step something more is requisite than a belief in the *theory of Association*: the *self-seeking* tendency, the principle of selfishness, must first be rooted out, before any man, before even the owner of the Tribune, will thus carry into full and thorough operation these principles of disinterested benevolence. The *individual character* must first be radically changed, before Association can become possible.

We have thus answered, at greater length than we intended, the Tribune's plea in behalf of Association, so far as it sets at defiance established principles of Political Economy. But we do not intend to lose sight of the higher, moral interests involved in the scheme, nor to overlook other and more important departments of its operation.

In our last article we proved conclusively that Association claims to be a SOCIAL SYSTEM, based upon distinctive, universal, and immutable laws, and intended to embrace, not only the organization of Labor, but all departments of domestic, social, and civil life. In its last article the Tribune asserts that all the evils which afflict humanity "have their *root* in that *Isolation of efforts* and antagonism of interests on which our present Social Order is based," and of which, in domestic life, the Isolated Household is the type. Association proposes to remedy these evils by destroying their supposed root,—to "destroy their *causes*," to "*abolish* pauperism, ignorance, and the resulting vices," in the language of the Tribune, by getting rid of this *Isolation*, and substituting for it a COMMUNITY, of interests and of life. Men are no longer to labor for themselves and their families mainly or primarily "We must now try the opposite principle," says the Tribune, "of each for all, and seek individual *only through* universal good." The first step to be taken in carrying this theory into practice is, to bring men together under this new relation—to have them live, not in isolated households, but in a common dwelling; to labor upon a common farm and for a common profit; to conduct all their affairs, domestic, social, educational, industrial, political, and religious, not as individuals nor as separate families, but as a COMMUNITY. Now to accomplish this vast result, to bring to pass so momentous a change in men's habits of thought and of life, as this implies, there must be an elaborate, well-defined SYSTEM of MEANS, *adapted carefully and exactly to the ends to be attained, and the obstacles to be surmounted.* We have endeavored, throughout this discussion, to obtain from the Tribune a distinct statement of that System and its provisions: and have detailed very many obstacles to its practical operation. The answer of the Tribune is embraced in the following passage:

"*With regard to Labor, to Education, to Religion, &c., had you read attentively any of the writings of the Associationists, you would have seen how your obstacles are surmounted.*"

We have found in the sources indicated the information required. Our objections had been fully anticipated, and every supposable emergency had been provided for, in the SYSTEM of Association. It is our present purpose to examine these specific provisions, and to set forth, on the authority of these "Writings of the Associationists" the *fundamental principle* from which they grow. We have objected to the practical operation of the scheme, that Parental Authority might interfere with the supreme authority of the Association;—we are told in reply, in the "writings of Associationists," that parental authority will be *abolished*. We have urged that the duty of Filial Obedience may conflict with obedience to the Association;—we are told in reply, by the same authority, that the duty of Filial Obedience will be *annulled*. We have said that the essential character of the Conjugal relation, the *unity of Husband and Wife*, the dependence of the latter upon the former, &c., might clash with the principles and purposes of the Community;—we learn from the "Writings of the Associationists" that the Husband and Wife are to be one no longer: that each is to be entirely independent of the other in name and in property; and that each would have, in Association, "*full LIBERTY of action and AFFECTION.*" In short all those obstacles to the success of Association which spring from the Family Spirit, and from the Family Relation, are to be "*surmounted*" by "*absorbing*" that spirit, and destroying the essential character of the relation itself. This, however, is only one department of social life; and we have accordingly suggested obstacles likely to arise from other quarters. Thus we have urged that some of the members of an Association might refuse to work; that others would not like the special service assigned to them; that differences of opinion would grow into causes of enmity:—that individual convictions, prejudices, passions and selfish aspirations would disturb the harmony of the new Society; —and that there was no bond provided, strong enough to control all these jarring elements and preserve to the Association that *unity of action*, of purpose, and of feeling, without which it must inevitably fall in pieces. The question then arises, what principle is there to bind men thus together? The family spirit binds the family together;—what similar bond will bind together the members of an Association? What *fundamental law* will control their choice of occupations, their relations to each other, and the subjection of their private wills to the general objects of the community. The "Writings of the Associationists," cited by the Tribune, furnish the answer. We learn from them that the law of PASSIONAL ATTRACTION will be the controlling power in Association. That law, they maintain, was created by God, implanted by him in human nature, discovered by Fourier, and intended to be universal in its operation upon the arrangements of Society, just as the law of gravitation is upon all the relations of the material universe.

"Attraction," says Godwin. "is the general law. Written on the heart of all, it reveals perpetually and unitarily the *Will of God*; *it acts at all times and in all places.* It impels each being on his way, it *indicates to him his Destiny,* and it remains forever incompressible."

The law is this: that *the Passions, feelings, free impulses of Man point out to him the path in which he should walk, the relations he should form, the labor he should do, the functions he should discharge, and, generally, the whole course of life which he ought to pursue.* That this is the exact meaning of the law, and that it is also the fundamental principle of Association considered as a Social System, may be made perfectly certain whenever it shall be disputed. Nearly all the Associationists who have ever written upon the subject, either in Europe or in this country, have more or less distinctly asserted it. It is claimed that when this Law shall have been universally established, and this new form of Society shall have been perfected, in order that it may have free and full effect, all existing causes of dissension and of evil will have been removed; a perfect bond will have been provided to keep mankind in harmony; isolation of effort and of life will be unknown: and we shall have, in the words of Mr. Godwin, a "Social System in which order will be produced *by the free action of the passions;*" a "Social System devised by God and reserved for the discovery of Man." Then, to quote the same writer,

"Reason and Passion will be in perfect accord; duty and pleasure will have the same meaning; without inconvenience or calculation, *man will follow his bent;* hearing only of Attraction, he will never act from necessity, and *never curb himself by restraints.*"

Thus we have reached the fundamental principle, the supreme, controlling law of this new Social System. We do not stop now to insist upon the palpable fact, that this principle is in the most direct and unmistakable hostility to the uniform inculcations of the Gospel. No injunction of the New Testament is more express, or more constant, than that of *self-denial*; of subjecting the passions, the impulses of the heart to the law of conscience. We may hereafter present this point more fully to public notice. But for the present we wish to follow the necessary operation of this fundamental law, upon some of the details of industrial and domestic life. How will it guide and control the arrangements of labor, the relations of the sexes, &c., &c.? The Associationists urge that the passions of men will impel or attract them, to form certain assemblages called *groups*, with their fellows. Thus if a man has an impulse, or a decided liking, for plowing, for gardening, or for any other branch of industry, he will enter into the group devoted to it; and in this way he will become a member of as many groups as he has special and definite impulses In the same way are formed other groups, in other departments, and created by the free operation of other impulses. Every "passional attraction" must find its proper object, and be fully carried out. In this way provision is made for the following various groups; as we learn from the "Writings of the Associationists," to which the Tribune has referred us:—

"Group of FRIENDSHIP,
All attracted to each other in confusion.
Group of AMBITION,
Superiors attracting Inferiors.
Group of LOVE,
Women attracting the Men.
Group of FAMILY,
Inferiors attracting Superiors."

Now we shall take the third group named in this schedule, and inquire into the operation of the law of *Passional Attraction* upon the mutual relations of the two sexes. In an Association the passional attraction of *love* will prompt men to form certain relations. This is provided for by the system. In forming these relations, "each party would consult the dictates of the heart;" "the choice thus made would be declared a *marriage*;" and the parties would pass from the Vestalate to some other Corporation composed exclusively of the married. Now suppose the passional attraction which led to that connection should lose its force and take another direction. Suppose the same man should be attracted by other women. What then? How does the fundamental law operate in this case? How shall these instances (and it is certain that they will occur) of changing impulses and new attractions be controlled and guided? What does the theory of the System require? When a man has a special passion for a dozen kinds of work, he joins a dozen groups. When he has a special passion for a dozen kinds of study, he joins a dozen groups. So, if the System be carried out, if its fundamental principle be not repudiated, if the whole scheme be not abandoned as a System —if a man comes to have a *passion for a dozen women, there must be a dozen different groups for its full development and gratification.* We insist upon this as a necessary, logical, *inevitable,* deduction from the fundamental principles of the System of Association. If we are wrong, show the fallacy of our argument. It seems to us invincible; the conclusion can not be evaded. There *must be,* if the theory be maintained, *groups* in this department of life, as in others; and those whose *passional attractions* impel them to form various connections, *must* have liberty to do so. "Man will *follow his bent,* and never *curb himself by restraints."*

We insist upon this as a logical necessity. And we shall proceed now to show that the "Writers on Association," referred to by the Tribune, recognize this necessity, and have made their arrangements accordingly. Those who have given most attention to the study of the System, those who have made it the subject of closest and most constant thought, have seen, and have said, that this result is rendered *imperative* by the fundamental principles of Association. We quote the following passage, upon this very point, from Mr. Godwin's "Popular View," to which we have before referred:

"But suppose this arrangement [Marriage] should have been entered into unwisely, that the parties subsequently find that they are not fitted to each other, or that one or the other should be *inconstant in passion:* does Fourier regard the tie as indissoluble? He answers *No!* He thinks that Love is too sacred a passion to be forced, except in those incoherent and imperfect Societies where the rights and liberty of the individual are of necessity sacrificed to the general order.

"We should be unfaithful to the task we have undertaken were we to conceal that Fourier was decidedly of the conviction that, while a part of mankind were formed for *constancy* in love, *there are some who are formed for change.* * * * *The various relations of the Sexes will lead, like all other passional relations, to an organization into groups and series.* Departing from the Vestalate, each one will enter some corporation having constancy for its rule. *Many will stop there; but others are so peculiarly formed that they will join themselves to other Corporations, more or less severe, as may be agreeable to their inclinations and temperaments.* * * * * In this way no one will have any inducement to dissimulate, *being always free to follow another rule,* simply declaring it by joining another Corporation. * * * The Affective Passions, Fourier continues, as well as the sensitive and intellectual, are susceptible of scientific education and progress. The passion of Love, he argues, before it can yield all the results of which it is capable, *must undergo an organization by series, to meet all the wants of all the natures that God sends into existence.* The first organization is that of the Vestalic Corporation; another would be a Corporation of Constancy, as we have said, at which the most part of men and women stop: while others again, named Bacchantes, Bayaderes, &c., *would pass into other Corporations not so strict in their requirements.* Such characters as Aspasia, Ninon De L'Enclos, &c., Fourier regards as essential parts in the variety of the human race."

Here, then, we have distinctly set forth, as parts of the *System,* the precise arrangements which, as we have proved above, the fundamental *principle* of the System requires. It is by the operation of that principle of *passional attraction,* that all the confusions and collisions of life are to be harmonized. This is the great principle which Fourier discovered, and upon it are based the whole theory and practice of Association. All the passions of Man, it is held, are divine in their origin, and good in themselves. Evil flows only from their repression or subversion. Give them full scope, free play, a perfect and complete development, and universal happiness must be the result. They are the true revelation of God's designs within the soul. Their promptings are the true utterances of Nature. Listen to them; obey them; follow the path which they indicate; create a new form of Society in which this shall be possible; let *attraction,* or in common language, the impulses of the heart, become its only law; and then you will have a perfect Society; then will you have "the Kingdom of Heaven that comes to us in this terrestrial world."

We must, for the present, leave this statement of the fundamental and essential principles of Association with our readers. These are the principles which according to the "Writings of the Associationists," are to "surmount the obstacles" we have suggested: and this is the method in which that result is to be reached. We shall hereafter consider some other departments of their operation, and if need be, fortify our demonstration of their character and tendency, by farther citations from the authorities to which the Tribune has referred us.

From the Tribune, March 12th, 1846.
### LETTER X.
*To the Editor of the Courier and Enquirer:*

WHEN I assume to have demonstrated that "there are *radical* defects or vices *in our Social institutes* and usages, demanding *radical* remedies," what do you propose to gain by saying that you concede the truth of my assertion that "great Social evils exist and demand a remedy!" Can you suppose a single reader of this controversy so obtuse as not to perceive the wide difference between my proposition and your very gratuitous concession! Nay; do you imagine that a single candid reader has failed to discern which is proved by my facts, my proposition or yours! You may seem to put out your eyes by your ostrich-like burrowing in the sand, but the world will see, notwithstanding.

Let us suppose the Dukes of Sutherland and Newcastle, the Archbishop of Canterbury, the Bishop of London, &c., could be induced to meet and consider earnestly the woes which afflict the millions around and beneath them, and to devise or adopt comprehensive measures for relief. Before them appear the Courier and the Tribune, as advocates of their respective theories. The Courier, by right of seniority, opens: "Please your Lordships, the fundamental evil in the premises, is the selfishness and depravity of Human Nature, and the only remedy is a radical change of each individual character. I counsel you, therefore, to give liberally in charity to relieve the distresses of the destitute; to endow a Church in each village, and distribute a Bible and Tracts to each family, and, thus laboring for, await such mitigation of the practical woes afflicting Humanity as the essential Depravity of Man's Nature will permit." The speaker pauses; the rubicund visages of the Christian Peers and Prelates are lighted up with a glow of satisfaction, and a thrill of self-complacent delight courses from the brain to the toes even of the goutiest.

"Men and brethren!" the Tribune strikes in, "I am constrained to say to each of you, as Nathan said to David, 'THOU ART THE MAN!' All that the preceding speaker has counseled you to do is very well; Do it, and more such if you will. But he has not touched the heart of the disease, so far as it affects *your* opportunities and your duties. These Millions are famishing, Messrs. Dukes and Prelates! because *you* grind their faces by merciless exactions of rents and tithes which it is not just that they should pay—which they are yet compelled to pay because the robber ancestors of some of you acquired titles, by violence or fraud, to vast portions of the Soil which God made for the sustenance of all His children. They could tolerably live, in the little cottages they have built, on the narrow patches you permit them to cultivate, did *you* not rack them of five to twenty-five dollars per acre rent for their little holdings, to swell the enormous incomes which you annually squander in useless pomp and baleful luxury. And you, Reverend Prelates! I grieve to say, make yourselves parties to this robbery, and clutch your thirty pieces of the spoil. Instead of admonishing the titled monopolists to 'let the People go,' you are the bulwarks of the system which crushes them. Your enormous revenues could never be realized by preaching and practicing the Religion of Him of Nazareth whom you call Master. It is the price of blood!

"What I would have you do, sirs, is this: First, Recognize the Right of all men to Labor—consequently, to the use of such portion of the Soil as may be essential to their subsistence on such terms as Justice, not Necessity, shall dictate. Secondly, Recognize and fulfill the duty devolved upon you, by reason of your superior advantages, mental culture, and general resources, to live in truly fraternal relations with your poorer and less fortunate fellow-beings, and to minister to their needs, moral or physical, according to your best ability. Nature and Revelation concur in enjoining this upon you; dare not to neglect it, and then charge the consequences upon the heads of your victims!

"You say the Poor are improvident: I reply that *your* wrongs have made them so! Robbed by you of one half their just earnings, to pander to your over-gorged lusts, what wonder if they would make sure of the remnant by consuming it before your rapacity and craft should grasp that also? You say they are often idle, and seldom steadily industrious: Can you wonder at this when they are not enabled to work steadily, but only as the avarice or necessities of others shall have occasion for them? You say they are grossly ignorant: So they are, as their fathers have been before them for many generations. How could Ignorance, encrusted by Poverty and Social degradation, ever lift itself out of the mire in which it has groveled until its nature became thereto assimilated? *You* and your kin have enjoyed Knowledge, Leisure, ample Means—why have you not improved and diffused them? Have you even habitually set the Poor examples of the Frugality, Industry, Temperance, Morality, you require of them? You say they are brutish and vicious: So they are: And what have you done to improve and refine them? Look at the wretched hovels in which they exist, feeding like dogs and sleeping like hogs, without a chance to observe the requirements of modesty and decency. Consider what are the hopes animating, the environments surrounding, the influences depressing them, and say whether their general character is not substantially such as these are naturally calculated to produce. Are they intemperate and grossly sensual? Think of their frames bowed, their sinews strained by excessive, meagerly-rewarded toil; think of their lack of education, of good example, of elevating associates, of wholesome recreations, and say whether this too is not just what was to be expected. In short, do *you* what is incumbent on you, by ceasing to be oppressors and becoming true guides and brotherly helpers of these your poor, depressed brethren. I bid you do them JUSTICE and they will not long stand in need of alms—

"'Justice for the young and old;—
Give them *that*—not rich men's gold. * * *
Justice, and no man is poor,
Though another owneth more.'"

Here is the essence and the substance of ASSOCIATION. I doubt not that the dukes and archbishops I have instanced would consider the Tribune's talk Agrarian, Jacobinic, Infidel, and a great deal more of the same sort. Perhaps the classes who most nearly approach them in position in this country will so regard it, at first blush; yet if they will but calmly consider—if they will but *feel* that they are the brethren of the Millions now famishing throughout Ireland, Europe—alas! throughout the civilized world—they could not fail to realize that the laws and usages which allow one man to monopolize a portion of the Earth from which hundreds of thousands must gain a subsistence, leaving these hundreds of thousands destitute of any home or means of support save at the sufferance of others—that such laws, and the whole system of clutch-and-hold of which they are a part, are primary and potent causes of the miseries which all now witness, and most profess to deplore.

I will not waste many words on your treatment of my array of facts intended to prove that the condition of the Laboring Class in

Great Britain is worse now than it was five centuries since. If the Statutes, the Prices Current, Village Registers, the Convent Account-Books, &c., of bygone centuries may not be quoted, where they substantially agree, to prove in a rough, general way, the relative prices of Labor and of Food in their times, then I despair of fixing the truth by any means whatever. Many of the facts I quoted (not mainly from "officials and placemen") come out in that incidental, unconscious fashion, which adds greatly to their weight with me. What British legislator, for example, in 1847, or at any time these twenty years, would have named in the preamble of a statute "beef, pork, mutton, and veal," and added, "these being the food of the *poorer* sort!" I don't believe there is a hereditary blockhead in the House of Lords who could blunder so grossly.

Your M'Culloch and other "soundest writers on Political Economy," are the very men whom I have been battling these twenty years, as I understand you to have been for the last four or five years. I deem them most *unsound*—mistaken in their premises, and of course wrong in their conclusions. I am sure they are wrong in assuming that the condition of the mass of British laborers in our day is better than was that of their forefathers five centuries ago. That there has been some improvement in the dwellings they occupy is probably true, though I see not how human beings could manage to exist in dwellings much more miserable or filthy than many now thickly tenanted even here. That many materials of their clothing are cheaper now than formerly is true. True, also, the progress of invention and improvement have placed some conveniencies and luxuries within the reach of common people which were formerly beyond the reach of the richest, because they had no existence. That "new and cheaper kinds of food"—such as watery Potatoes and decayed Turnips—have taken the place of the Wheat, Mutton, Beef, Pork, which our laboring ancestors ate when a day's wages at plowing or reaping would buy four times as much Wheat or Beef in England as now, I fully understand. Whether the prevailing tendency here is to the aggregation or to a more equal diffusion of Wealth, is a point which must remain in dispute between us. Let every reader look thoughtfully around him, and decide for himself. Whether, in view of the landless condition of such multitudes, the causes which confessedly deprive many of constant employment are indeed "accidental and temporary" or otherwise, he will also judge. To me it seems that, to the landless and portionless millions, being without work is the natural condition, and obtaining it is the accident, even though it be admitted that those who have work at any time considerably outnumber those who are unwillingly idle.

I have thus looked through your argument on the past and present condition of the Laboring Class, to see whether you propose or contemplate any remedy for the master-evil, the Monopoly of Land, to which I have endeavored to win your attention. You do indeed deny that the reward of Labor grows more and more scanty and precarious as Population increases, but is it not manifest that such must be the result? Supposing there are 1000 inhabitants to a township six miles square, the average price of fair land will not exceed ten dollars per acre, and the rental of the arable portion will perhaps average one dollar an acre. But the population increases to 10,000, and now, other things remaining as before, the soil is worth fifty to one hundred dollars per acre, and will rent for five to ten dollars. In other words, the actual cultivators must now give one-half to three-fourths of the usual product of the soil to landlords, for the privilege of working it. Now let the population swell to 15,000 or 20,000, and what is the natural effect on those who are born landless? But why do I ask? Do I not hear you say, "It is a settled principle of Political Economy that Subsistence must not only *keep pace* with Population, but take the lead?" We are all familiar with this sort of logic in the "sound Political Economists," and sometimes are permitted to know what it means. The Edinburgh Review tells us frankly that the Poor who find themselves shut out from the soil, and have no assured means of maintaining a family have no right to marry—that it is a crime in such to obey God's command to "Be fruitful and multiply," for which an after-life of privation and famine is the appropriate penalty. To repress the sentiment of Love in enduring celibacy or drown it in a career of debauchery is the course pointed out by the "sound Political Economists" to those who have the misfortune to be born and continue landless and portionless.

I demur altogether to your doctrine, though quite aware that it is laid down as an axiom by your "sound Political Economists," that "When Laborers increase faster than the Capital that employs them, Labor must fall; when the increase is in favor of Capital, Labor will *rise*." There is no soundness in it, using Capital to imply Wealth owned by individuals. If the Real Estate of this City had never obtained one-half of its actual valuation, the "Capital" of New York would be vastly less than it is, but I do not think its Labor would be less generously rewarded—rather the contrary. There have been rapidly-succeeding duplications of the Labor in Oregon and California, with no corresponding increase of the Capital; but I do not hear that the Labor is depressed or likely to "fall" in consequence. Suppose a lake or a river to yield $1,200,000 worth of fish every year, of which some patroon or landlord claiming to be seignior exacts one-third for permission to fish, giving him a snug item of income of $400,000 per annum. But the fishermen at length grow weary of paying; they doubt the rightfulness of the exaction; and, putting the matter properly at issue before the legal tribunals, they obtain a verdict, and are at liberty to fish rent-free evermore. "Awful destruction of Property!" groans some Courierite; "a Capital of $6,000,000 demolished at a blow by an Anti-Rent decision—how *will* the Poor survive it?" "Tolerably well, thank you!" reply the fishermen; "we don't find it materially harder to get a living now than formerly." And so vanishes the whole fog-bank about the reciprocal influences of the increase and diminution of Capital and Labor.

But, suppose we admit the evils the Tribune insists on, answers the Courier, how will Association remedy them? Why, sir, I have explained this twice already. Association will secure to every member employment at all times, and the fair reward of his labor. It will give every mechanic a comfortable and convenient home, warmed, lighted, &c., for a fraction of the rent he now pays. He pays one price for his tenement, and another for its proximity to the consumers of his products: in Association, he will pay the former only, while enjoying in unexampled perfection the latter. The immense Economies of Association in regard to buildings, fences, fuel, schooling, traffic, teams, waste ground, &c., will render one thousand acres of land fully adequate to the subsistence of a number for whom three or four thousand acres are required under our present system. Of course, "the pressure of competition for Land," which the Queen's Speech so deplores in reference to Ireland, will be quietly, gradually abated. And the fundamental law that Capital shall receive as its dividend a fixed *proportion* of the general product, based upon its actual contributions, and not upon arbitrary valuations — a proportion which can never be increased because of the increased value given by Labor to the common property—renders morally certain the Emancipation of honest Toil from the privations, anxieties, sufferings, it is now too generally doomed to endure; and the immense Economies of Association, which are so obvious that even the Courier can not deny them, will secure to Labor double the comforts and advantages it now enjoys, without diminishing the average income of Capital—possibly increasing it.

I thank you for your reference to "the Tribune for example," though its motive is apparent. It is not true that "the owners pay their laborers *the market price* for their work:" we pay one-fourth *more* than the average "market price" of similar labor in our city, and one-third more than the lowest price at which we could obtain it, which is the price the "sound Political Economists" say we ought to pay. It is not true that we clear $20,000 per annum or any thing like it; but, on the other hand, our "unequal competition" with those who obtain labor cheaper than we do, has not seriously threatened to "ruin" us yet. Whether Association dictates that the Tribune Establishment should be parceled out to those who encounter no risk, and expended no capital, to create it; and if so, whether it should be shared among those who worked on it, and were paid therefor the first year, the last, or some intermediate, it would probably require some one better acquainted with the doctrine than him of the Courier to determine. As to "self-seeking" and "selfishness"—but let such imputations await their answer. If, on a full and final review, my life and practice shall be found unworthy my principles, let due infamy be heaped on my memory, but let none be thereby led to distrust the principles to which I proved recreant, nor yet the ability of some to adorn them by a suitable life and conversation. To unerring time be all this committed.

I approach that part of your last article in which you assume to set forth from "the writings of Associationists" what is the belief of the school with regard to Love, Marriage, Conjugal Duty, &c., and I will endeavor to repress the indignation I feel, and speak of it with entire calmness. How utterly all this violates the fundamental condition on which I agreed to debate this subject with you, how paltry is the pretext on which you have assumed to set aside your own solemn compact, our readers already know. But those who are not familiar with Mr Godwin's "Popular View of the Doctrines of Charles Fourier," can not realize, and will not readily believe, how grossly you have misrepresented him. You had before you his book, in which the broadest line is drawn between those speculations of Fourier, which the Associative School do and those they do not accept, forming two distinct, broadly-defined portions of his work. You have read and had your attention called to his "Intermediate" chapter on the "Essential Distinction between the Two Parts of this Work," in which he protests, in advance, against such perversions as you are guilty of, indignantly denies the charge that we who have adopted Fourier's constructive principles of township organization have any design to abolish Property, the Family Relation, or Religion, and proceeds:

"Whoever, then, undertakes to criticise or accuse the Phalansterian School, must, to be honest, do so on other grounds than these. He must take up directly and only the project they present, and prove that it is in itself worthless or impracticable. Random charges against opinions which we repel and plans we do not propose, can only expose the authors of them to the contempt of all fair-minded people.

"*The School of Fourier proposes but one thing*: THE ORGANIZATION OF LABOR IN THE TOWNSHIP. It has no other *object*, no other *faith*, as a School. Individuals are, of course, always at liberty to promulgate whatever opinions they may see fit.

"Let a township be once organized according to our principles, and the reform will soon spread over the whole nation.

"Slavery, direct and indirect, will then be abolished, because labor will have become attractive; savages and barbarians will more readily adopt the manners of refined and cultivated life; science, art, and industry, will be largely developed, and the most perfect order will reign along with the most perfect liberty.

"This is our conviction: this is ALL we teach."

Again, as if determined not to be misrepresented, except by those who deem nothing unfair nor unjust so that it assails Association, Mr. Godwin expressly reiterates:

"We feel the necessity of repeating once more that the Social School, which professes to teach the positive doctrines of Fourier, have but a *single and exclusive aim*— *The Organization of Labor.* * * * We are not so senseless as to desire the suppression of all coercive means, and the full play of the Passions, before a long and satisfactory experience of the reformed state of Society shall have shewn, *to future generations*, that it would be unattended with dangerous results.

"So long as the Passions may bring forth Disorder—*so long as Inclination may be in opposition to Duty*—we reprobate as strongly as any class of men, all indulgence of the inclinations and feelings; and where Reason is unable to guide them, have no objection to other means," &c.

I need not quote farther to show how utterly you have perverted Mr. Godwin's book in order to strike through him at the Associationists—

as palpably as he who cited the express words of the Bible to prove that "There is no God."

You say, indeed, that all the results you indicate flow logically from the theory of Passional Attraction; but *I* have propounded no such theory; much less asserted that such Attraction is to be universally followed. I lay slender emphasis on Theories of any sort, save as their truth and utility have been demonstrated by Practice. This thing Association, as I hold and advocate it, is a matter of Practice altogether—the simple actualization of the truth of Universal Human Brotherhood. Christ's Law of Love is palpably outraged and contemned in a world of palaces and mud hovels; of famished Toil and pampered Uselessness; of boundless Wealth uselessly hoarded, and helpless Infancy dying in bitter agony and supplication for "only three grains of corn." Let us redress the palpable wrongs before us by prompt action, and we will consider theories and speculations at our leisure. Fourier's idea that God governs the Universe throughout by Attraction—that this is the law of life and health for all intelligent beings—is a grand and inspiring one: it may possess great practical value when we come fully to understand and apply it. But, when he concedes that there will be human beings truly educated and living in a wisely ordered Social State, who will deliberately abandon a life of purity to wallow in incontinence and sensuality, he proves, not perhaps, that his Law is fictitious, but that he knows not how to apply it. I do not believe that a rightly-trained, truly-developed human being will any more have "a passion for a dozen different women," etc., than he will have a passion to commit a dozen murders, requiring the organization of murdering groups accordingly. "*If a man comes to have a passion*" for doing any act contrary to Morality and General Good, his "passion" must be repressed or punished. Such is *my* "logical, inevitable deduction from the fundamental principles of the system of Association." I know nothing of "Groups and Series" organized, or to be organized, for the perpetration of crimes or the practice of vices.

But why should I be required to interpose a defense against such accusations? Why should I not be permitted to set forth what it is that I advocate, and have that discussed and considered, as was agreed at the outset? Why should I be required to defend not only myself but others against the grossest misrepresentations? Why, indeed, but that every appeal for Justice and Humanity has ever been resisted exactly after this fashion! "He blasphemeth!" "He hath a devil!" "Behold a gluttonous man and a wine-bibber!" "Away with him!" "Crucify him!" Such have been the vociferations with which every newly-asserted truth of any value has been assailed from the foundation of the world. That truth is indestructible by such attacks, and will triumph over them at last, is the unshaken conviction of H. G.

From the Courier and Enquirer of March 19, 1847.

REPLY TO LETTER X.

PHILOSOPHERS tell us that the severe exercise of any one faculty of the mind renders impossible, for the time, the equally active exercise of any other. The Tribune affords an illustration very nearly in point. The Editor's extraordinary effort to "repress the *indignation* he feels, and to speak with entire calmness" of the argument embraced in our last article, developing the principles and showing the tendencies of Association, seems greatly to have impaired his memory of facts. While we *yawn*, it is said, we are *deaf*; and so when the Tribune attempts to be good-natured, it becomes oblivious. The Editor "looks through our argument" to see "what remedy we propose for that *master-evil*, the monopoly of land;" as if *that*, and not *Association*, were the theme of this discussion. We do not believe the "monopoly," that is the ownership, of land, to be an evil. But whether it be or not, is not the legitimate topic of this inquiry. The Tribune asserts that existing evils can only be remedied by substituting for the present social forms its new system of Association, founded upon distinctive principles, aiming at certain results, and proposing for their attainment a specific, elaborate, and well-defined system of means. We deny the feasibility of the system, and assert that it involves essential principles at war with morality, Christianity, and political economy. The Tribune challenged us to a discussion of its merits, upon which we accordingly entered. But now the Tribune asserts that "this thing, Association, *is a matter of practice altogether*," not a theory, not a doctrine, not a system to be discussed, but simply something to be practiced; not a *science* to be examined, but a *machine* to be set a-going. Why, then, did the Tribune challenge us to its discussion? And why has it not sooner made this discovery which, if it be well founded, should long since have ended this controversy? Why does it not set its machine at work, instead of extolling the principles on which it is constructed, and calling upon us to show that it will not succeed? We trust the Tribune, when its wrath shall have subsided, will recover its memory, and see clearly, as it did at first, that Association involves a *theory*, as well as a practice; and that the latter must be impossible, if the former be demonstrably false.

Of the political economy of Association we have but little more to say. The Tribune asserted that "the laboring classes of England during the last five centuries, have been depressed from *comfort* to *wretchedness*," by the natural and necessary operation of the laws of existing society. The "few words" which the Tribune "*wastes*" on our "treatment of its array of facts" intended to prove this statement, require but little notice. The question is purely one of *fact*, though very difficult to be answered; and we have cited on our side, those persons who have given the most thorough, intelligent, and laborious attention to the sources of evidence by which it must be settled. The Tribune answers that these authorities are "the *very men* whom its editor has been battling these twenty years!" They are unfortunate, certainly, and we extend to them our sympathy; and yet we think it possible that their conclusions upon this point are quite as reliable as the assertions quoted by the Tribune from a partisan "article in an old Democratic Review,"

The Tribune declares with oracular emphasis:—

"*I am* SURE they are *wrong*, in *assuming* that the condition of the mass of British laborers in our day is better than was that of their forefathers, five centuries ago."

But even this, to our minds, is not perfectly conclusive; the writers in question do not "assume" their point, as the Tribune asserts, but prove it; and their conclusion seems to be very fully conceded by the Tribune itself, when it confesses that "there have been improvements in the dwellings" of the laboring classes: that "the materials of their clothing are cheaper now than formerly;" that "the progress of invention has placed conveniences and luxuries within the reach of the common people, which were formerly not enjoyed by the richest;" and that "new and cheaper kinds of food" have been introduced. How all these things can be, consistently with the assertion that "the British laborer, four centuries ago, enjoyed a degree of comfort unknown to his living descendants," the Tribune's sophistical ingenuity can alone determine.

With regard to the reward of labor, and its dependence on the ratio of supply and demand, it seems to us, nothing more need be said. We find it impossible, indeed, to reconcile the Tribune's positions, not only with common sense, but with each other. Thus that paper says in one paragraph:

"You deny that the reward of Labor grows more and more scanty and precarious as Population [or the number of those who labor] *increases*: but is it not manifest that *such* MUST *be the result?*"

And in the next paragraph we find this assertion:

"There have been rapidly succeeding *duplications* of Labor in Oregon and California, with no corresponding increase of the Capital: *but I do not hear that the Labor is depressed or likely to fall in consequence.*"

The first paragraph asserts that Labor *must* fall as laborers increase: the second asserts that it *need not!* Both positions can not be true: yet the Tribune uses one or the other, as the exigency of its argument may seem to require. That paper, however, still adheres, as nearly as we can understand its argument, to the doctrine of Malthus, that Population naturally, inevitably, and universally, increases *faster* than its means of subsistence: and that the constant tendency of things, therefore, is toward destitution and misery. The Tribune assumes that this tendency exists; and proposes to check it by Association: the Editor also makes the following assertion as to the means of checking it pointed out by others:—

"To repress the sentiment of Love in enduring celibacy, or drown it in a career of debauchery, is *the course pointed out by the 'sound political economists'* to those who have the misfortune to be born and continue landless and portionless."

Now this imputation is utterly unfounded. Malthus, whose premises the Tribune adopts, is the only original writer on political economy who "points out" any such "*course.*" He says expressly that,

"If any man choose to marry without the prospect of being able to support a family, he should have the most perfect liberty to do so. Though to marry in this case is clearly an *immoral act*, yet it is one which society should not punish. To the punishment of *nature* he should be left, the punishment of want. All parish assistance should be denied him, and he should be left to the uncertain support of private charity."

Here, then, it will be seen that the writer upon whose premises the Tribune builds its new social edifice, himself advocates the policy imputed by the Tribune to his opponents. The "*sound* political economists" whom we have quoted, and whom the Tribune pretends to quote, deny and discard the *premises* of Malthus, which the Tribune accepts. They do not denounce marriage as a *crime* on the part of the poor; but they assert that, as a matter of fact, generally true though not without exceptions, men do not and will not marry until they can support their families; and that *therefore* "subsistence must not only *keep pace* with Population, but take the lead." Thus M'Culloch says:—

"Man is not a mere slave of instinct; his conduct, speaking generally, is influenced by prospective considerations; and when we look at bodies of individuals, we uniformly find that *the period and frequency of marriages and the rate of increase are determined by the increase of food, and that the latter is never outrun by the former.*"

M'Culloch, however, is one of the "very men" whom the Editor of the Tribune "has been battling these twenty years" upon the subject of Free Trade; and therefore his opinions upon all other topics will probably be pronounced unsound and absurd. We will therefore quote another writer upon the subject, against whose authority, perhaps, the Tribune will be less emphatic. William Atkinson, in his "*Principles of Political Economy*," published in 1843, "with an introduction by Horace Greeley," devotes a chapter to the examination of this fundamental proposition of Malthus (which the Tribune now in the main adopts), that Population increases in a *geometrical* ratio, while its means of subsistence increase only in an *arithmetical* ratio. The conclusion he reaches is this:—

"Thus we are necessitated by the facts now collated to *reverse* the geometrical and arithmetical ratios, and to assert that the former is more nearly applicable to the laws of the formation of capital, and the latter to the laws of the increase of population. * * I now submit that I have proved how entirely Mr. Malthus has failed to substantiate either predicate of his two great propositions; and I can not avoid expressing the *utmost astonishment* that these ratios of increase which were promulgated by him as theories, *should have been received with* ANY PORTION OF CREDENCE, *either by statesmen or statisticians.*"

And this excessive "astonishment" on the part of Mr. Atkinson seems to have been shared by his American Editor; for in his introduction to the work Mr. Greeley says:—

"It can not have needed the horrible deductions of Malthus, who declares that those who can not find food without the aid of the community, should be left to starve, to convince this generation of the *radical unsoundness of the* PREMISES *from which such revolting conclusions can be drawn.*"

Having thus disposed (we hope finally) of the crude and absurd positions on which the Political Economy of Association is based, we shall again turn our attention to its MORALITIES, to its fundamental principles and necessary tendencies as a SOCIAL SYSTEM: and we trust the Tribune will renew its effort, and meet with more than its usual success, in "repressing the indignation" which it always feels, or affects to feel, when this department of the subject is approached. We have full confidence that, in spite of the Tribune's efforts "to put out its eyes by an ostrich-like burrowing in the sand, the world will see notwithstanding," the abyss of sensualism into which the principles of this new Social System directly lead. And we must have some more cogent reasoning than the denunciations of the Tribune have yet afforded, before we are convinced that this portion of our argument is not directly in the line of discussion which that paper proposed. At the hazard of some repetition, we shall present the leading points of our argument in a consecutive form.

1 *Association is offered to the world as a new Social System, intended to embrace all departments of Social Life.* The Tribune pretends, whenever such pretence seems to suit its purpose, that *Labor* is the only interest which Association seeks to reorganize: and that all the other interests and relations of life will be left untouched. That this pretence is utterly unfounded, we need not stop to demonstrate. Not a single writer upon the subject gives the slightest support to the assertion; and the Tribune itself contradicts it in nearly every article it has written upon this topic. It uniformly speaks of associated *life* as well as labor, and has distinctly asserted, that Education, domestic habits, religion, and indeed the whole sphere of Social existence, would be modified and controlled by the scheme of Association which it advocates. It quotes also from Mr. Godwin's "Popular View," the declaration that "the School of Fourier proposes but one thing, the *organization of Labor in the Township:*" but the very same paragraph, which, it also quotes, contains this equally explicit assertion:—

"Let a *township* be once organized *according to our principles, and the reform will soon spread over the whole nation:* Slavery will be abolished; Science, art, and industry will be largely developed: and the most perfect order will reign along with the most perfect liberty. This is *all* we teach."

And that embraces all that we have charged. Labor in a township is to be organized, in order that "the reform" may "spread over the whole nation," and bring within its scope all the relations and interests of social life. And if any farther evidence on this point be needed, it may be found in the proof of our next position, namely:—

2. *Association is offered to the world as a Social Science of divine origin, and immutable in its essential principles.* It is not put forward as something to be "demonstrated by practice," as an experiment to be tried, but as a system devised, calculated, and ordered by God In proof of this, we refer to the uniform language of every one who has written upon it. Thus Mr. Godwin declares, in the *preface* to his book, that

" We wish to rest the claims of the Social Science of Fourier upon precisely *the same grounds* on which Herschell rests the *Science of Astronomy.* Fourier and his disciples, hold that his social principles are entitled to rank *as a Science,* being capable of that rigorous demonstration which only willful prejudice rejects."

Still more strongly is the same position laid down by Mr. Brisbane:—

"God, as Supreme Economist," he says, "must have preferred Association, and reserved for its organization, some means, the *Discovery* of which was the task of genius. * * The duty of God, is to compose a Social Code and to reveal it to man: it is evident that he has fulfilled this double duty," &c. &c.

So in a letter which Mr. Brisbane published in the Buffalo Commercial Advertiser of Nov. 25, 1846, he says:—

"The social order which Fourier discovered, was not a scheme of his own discovery, but in his belief, was the social plan, or social code which *the Creator precomposed and predestined for Man before creating and placing him upon Earth.*"

We might multiply these citations to any extent: for all the "writings of the Associationists" are full of the same pretensions. The *Harbinger,* published by the Brook Farm Association, constantly speaks of the System as the "*divine* order of Society." The Address of the North American Phalanx ." to the friends of *Social* Re-organization," asserts that they propose a "form of Society harmonious in all its relations with *Divine* law"—a "fitting embodiment of the spirit of Christianity." Mr. Ripley, in his Lecture of Monday evening last, as reported by the Tribune, spoke of Fourier as "the discoverer of the laws of Social harmony, and the *Scientific* expounder of the principles which govern the destiny of man on earth;" and the Tribune asserts that "he *showed* that Fourier's system was only an exposition of a *divine, social code, ordained by the Deity* for the establishment of social order." And the following quotation from the Tribune of Oct. 4, 1842, is certainly *conclusive* proof of the position we have stated above.

"Fourier proposes no system of his own—r scheme which is the result of his individual reason. He says that God, before creating man and giving him *passions,* must have adapted them to some system of society in which they would produce order, harmony, and justice. Fourier says he has *discovered the divine social order.* The system of Association is based upon the great religious idea that God must have composed for the human race a social system, for the regulation of their *social regulations and passions.* Fourier himself declares, on all occasions, that he gives no system of his own: he says that *he has discovered the laws by which God governs the Universe, that these laws are universal.* His discovery is the practical continuation of Christ's divine doctrine."

This extract in the Tribune is accompanied by the editorial remark that the column in which it appears had been purchased "*by the advocates of Association,* in order to lay *their principles* before the public" These principles are thus distinctly recognized as those of the "advocates of Association." And in addition to this, the Tribune, on the 29th of January last, quoted as *authority,* a resolution passed at what he styles "our first general convention, held in this city in April, 1844," in which it is asserted that they are in favor of the "social science which Fourier humbly believed to be, and reverently taught as, a discovery of *Eternal Laws of Divine Justice, established and made known by the Creator.*" Having thus demonstrated that Associa-

## ASSOCIATION DISCUSSED.

tion is offered to the world as a *social science*, intended to reach all departments of social life, and based upon certain definite, immutable, universal principles, we proceed to show,—

3. *That the law of* PASSIONAL ATTRACTION *is the fundamental and essential principle of Association; that the whole system rests upon that; that if that be abandoned, the whole system falls to the ground; that according to this law, the Passions of Man point out and control his destiny; and that Society is to receive a new form, which shall allow and render easy their perfect development.* In proof of this position, we shall quote freely from the "Writings of the Associationists," because the Tribune has referred us to them for information concerning the system, and because they are the only legitimate source of evidence upon the subject. Mr. Brisbane, in his treatise, after stating that "the *passions* are implanted by the Creator in man, *to direct him rightly in the social order precomposed for him, and to which these passions are adapted,*" goes on to say that

"The special task of the mind, with its faculties, is to discover the law of universal movement, the series which distributes all its harmonies, and apply it to the organization of society, which would *guarantee to the passions* A FREE AND FULL DEVELOPMENT, and to man the attainment of his destiny. This is the great problem to be solved. Fourier, in his discovery of the mechanism of the series of groups, *has accomplished this important task.*"

Mr. Brisbane then proceeds to set forth what the *twelve* passions are, and to show how the system of Association provides for their "full and free development." And he thus states the essential difference between this view of the passions, and that which generally prevails:

"Human science declares war against all these springs of action of the Soul, which it wishes to repress, compress, and suppress. * * * Science wishes to preserve the basis, *change the springs of action*, preserve the present social system, and change the nature of man. It has necessarily failed in every respect. We can not change human nature, *we can only change its developments.*"

And he thus distinctly asserts that the whole theory of Association rests upon this view of the Passions as its basis:

"The science of Association consists *solely* in knowing how to form and develop in full accord a mass or phalanx of Passional series, perfectly free, impelled by attraction alone. * * * The WHOLE PROBLEM *of Association is to give free course and development to the twelve radical passions;* otherwise there will be oppression, not harmony. These twelve passions tend to form a series of groups. * * * All the twelve passions being *developed and satisfied in each individual*, each *one attains to happiness, which consists in a free development of the passions*. This doctrine, opposed to all repressive and civilized theories, is the only one *conformable to the desire of nature*, and the presumable views of the Creator, who would be an unskilful mechanician had he created our passions so that the stronger should smother the weaker, as they do in the civilized system. There is nothing arbitrary in the system we propose: we resort to no laws or regulations of human invention.

"Happiness consists in the *continued satisfaction of the twelve passions* harmonically developed. Moralists having pursued an entirely false route in their studies of Nature, have, of course, arrived at exactly a contrary definition; they declare that happiness is only to be obtained in a continued repression of the passions, and that reason is given to us to control them. But this harmonic development, answer moralists, is incompatible with *virtue*. They think so because they believe the passions are *naturally depraved*," &c.

We might fill our columns with declarations to the same effect, but they can not be necessary. It is universally conceded by the writers on Association, that the *leading principle* of Fourier's System is, "That the Creator distributes passions and attractions to all his creatures *in exact proportion to their Destiny;*" and it is therefore the great Social problem which Fourier has solved, to construct *a Society adapted to these passions*. Thus Mr. Ripley, in his lecture of Monday evening, endorsed and extolled by the Tribune, declared Association to be the "divine form of Society *adapted to the Nature of Man*." So, also, Mr. Godwin, in his Popular View, declares (p. 30) that

"The *inclinations* of men, like natural forces, can produce good only in so far as they act in their fitting sphere. To attempt to *modify* those inclinations because they produce evil, *is to resist a natural law* and strive after an impossibility. To urge man to suppress them is to renounce the use of fire, because it may be the cause of disaster. No; *the duty of man is to study his inclinations in order to arrive at a social form* in which they will yield good results."

In another part of the same work, the same writer says that

"Fourier alone has taken man for the invariable term of the social problem. Seeking a *Social medium in perfect accord with the nature of man*, it was necessary for him to know strictly what man and his passions were."

And he proceeds to set forth the number, nature, and demands of these passions, and then to show how the Social order proposed will be adapted to their full and free development. When this order shall have been established, he declares that

"Reason and Passion will be in perfect accord; duty and pleasure will have the same meaning; without inconvenience or calculation, *man will follow his bent*; hearing only of attraction, he will never act from necessity, and *never curb himself by restraints.*

"Each man carries in his heart the twelve radical passions, and the absolute or relative energy of his passions in the individual determines his character, and consequently his natural position in society. * * * Excesses and vices are not an essential part of the passions, but on the contrary *depend on external circumstances*, which may be removed. All that is necessary is to *discover a society* in which every bad route for the action of the passions will be closed, and in which the path of virtue will be strewn with flowers."

Now let us turn to still another authority, "The Harbinger," published by the Brook Farm Phalanx, the official paper of the advocates of Association in this country. We find in the number for March 13 an exposition of the system, from the French of Laverdant, endorsed by the editors as sound and authentic. This article sets out thus:

"The theory of Association is true, simply because it is true that attractions are proportional to destinies [that is, because the Passions of Man point out his functions and position in society]. What constitutes the supreme science of Fourier is the thorough knowledge of man and his attractions. What constitutes the *discovery* of Fourier is the

*Series*, which is *the mode of distribution of functions adapted to the human soul.*

"This proposition of the necessary unity between the motive-spring and its mode of action, *between the passion and the series,* can cause no question in the School. No one is a Phalansterian in earnest, if he has not penetrated this science of the soul, and *if he does not take it for the basis of his doctrines and of his ideas.* We say further: whoever admits the Phalanstery, *whoever approves simply the industrial organization of the Phalanx,* the SAME ADMITS, by implication, *our psychology,* since the Phalanstery is but a *mechanism essentially adapted to the soul as described by Fourier.*

"There are those, perhaps, *who say they take the Phalanstery, but reject the psychology.* We will wait until it shall be given, by some special grace, to these *indolent* intelligences to ascend back from *effects* to *causes.*

"Others, we are aware, accept the Phalanstery only as an excellent transition. These (we take a pleasure in informing them) *do* accept the psychology of Fourier, *whether they care about it or not, whether they are conscious of it or not.* It is simply another Monsieur Jordain, who spoke prose without knowing it."

We commend this consoling assurance to the Tribune's special attention; and make but one more quotation, from the same source, upon the same point.

"If Attractions are proportioned to Destinies, it is evident that each of the cardinal passions bears in itself a certain type of order. *Since these passions embrace all the mutual relations of men,* it follows, with *rigorous exactness, that they themselves* DETERMINE THE LAW *of these relations;* and, if among the forces of the soul they hold the rank of cardinals, if they are the focus of the social life, if they are the man himself, then it is incontestible that *in their natural requirements we ought first to seek the principal laws, the necessary conditions of essential order.*"

These quotations from writers on Association of acknowledged authority, referred to by the Tribune itself, and all asserting the same thing, *establish,* we submit, beyond a doubt, our position that the law of PASSIONAL ATTRACTION IS THE FUNDAMENTAL AND ESSENTIAL PRINCIPLE OF ASSOCIATION. The organization of Labor, which is only one *branch* of the system, is to be attained *through* this principle. Laborers are to be guided in their work, by their passional attractions. Groups are to be formed of persons attracted, or impelled, toward similar functions. Each man's place in the Phalanx is to be determined by his special passion or impulse. The same principle is to guide and govern all industrial, domestic, and social relations. It is to give shape to the new society. The entire social problem is, *given human passions, to find a form adapted to their free and full development.* And that is exactly the problem which Fourier claims to have solved, and of which Association is the result.

Now how does the Tribune disprove this argument! It says simply:

"*I* have propounded no such theory; much less asserted that such attraction is to be universally followed."

This may be true, for the Tribune has propounded nothing at all, except unconsciously, in this discussion. Its constant effort has been to *evade* every thing, to conceal the principles of the System it challenged us to discuss. But it has referred us for an answer, to our direct inquiries concerning the details of this system, to the "Writings of the Associationists;" and in those writings we have found the theory of PASSIONAL ATTRACTION; and they all, without exception, make it the fundamental law of the entire system. The Tribune may disclaim it, but if it does so it abandons Association. The Tribune may characterize our compliance with its directions as a "paltry pretext," but it cannot deny that the pretext was furnished by itself. But when it charges us with misrepresenting and *perverting* those "writings of the Associationists" to which it referred us, it makes a charge which is utterly without foundation, and which is thoroughly refuted by the very attempt which the Tribune makes to prove it true. The Tribune insinuates, though it does not assert, that the proofs we have drawn from Mr. Godwin's book, of our position, *that the law of Passional Attraction is the fundamental law of Association,* are quoted from a portion of his book, in which he simply sets forth certain "speculations" of Fourier, which the Associative School *do not accept,* in distinction from that which sets forth the principles which they *do* accept. Now it is a sufficient reply to state, that every word we have quoted from Mr. Godwin upon this point is from the *first part* of his book — that in which he lays down those principles only, "which are," to use his own words, "*universally adopted and defended by the whole school of Societary Reformers.*" We established the principle, therefore, upon authority which the Tribune itself admits to be valid. We then applied that principle to one department of social life, and demonstrated that the law of Passional Attraction would overrule and destroy the Family relation, the relation of Marriage, and require the formation of *groups* and *series* for the "full and free development of the passions" in the relations between the sexes, as in every other department of social life. The strict cogency of that argument the Tribune itself does not deny. And to fortify it still further, we quoted from Mr. Godwin the explicit statement that Fourier took precisely the same view of the case; that *he* also insisted that the fundamental law of Association would require such an arrangement; and that *he* did not hesitate to carry his essential principles into full effect *there,* as in every other department of Associated life. He declared explicitly, that,

"*The various relations of the Sexes will lead, like all other passional relations, to an organization into groups and series:*" that "some would stop in a corporation having *constancy* for its rule," while "*others are so peculiarly formed that they will join themselves to other corporations more or less severe, as may be agreeable to their inclinations or temperaments.*"

Now the Tribune will please to observe that we quote this not as *authority* to show that such an arrangement is distinctly enjoined, but as corroborative *evidence* of the necessary requirements of the fundamental principle of Association, which is the law of Passional Attraction. We cite it to show that Fourier had the same view of the necessary operation of this law as that which we have taken. If the law be true, it must operate here as well as elsewhere. If the law be true, Love as well as Labor must be organized according to its requirements. And if the law is *not* true, then the whole fabric of

Association falls to the ground. We leave the Tribune to extricate its system from this dilemma.

But the Tribune proceeds to quote Mr. Godwin's declarations, to show that the school of Associationists "do not desire the suppression of all coercive means, and the *full play of the passions*," before "future generations" shall see that it may be done with safety. And the Tribune says for itself:

"I know nothing of groups and series organized, or to be organized, for the perpetuation of *crimes* or the practice of *vices*."

"*So long* as the Passions may bring forth disorder," says Mr. Godwin, "we reprobate their improper indulgence."

"*If men*," says the Tribune, "come to have a passion for immorality, it must be repressed."

This may seem very plausible, but it begs the whole question, or rather it conceals the real question. *So long* as the passions produce *crime*, say these men, we would repress them. But, as we have shown, they also maintain that crime is *never* produced by the passions themselves, but only by the mode of their development. They are *now* repressed, checked, resisted; *therefore*, say these writers, they produce confusion and crime. But when we have a form of Society *adapted* to them; when we have a Social System shaped by, and of course answering to, their free action, *then* that action will be harmonious, smooth, a source of constant happiness, which consists in the gratification of the passions. *Then*, that is when Association has been established, we can have a "free and full development of the passions," though not now. *Then* what seem *crimes* now, will become *virtues*. Thus Mr. Godwin says:

"How could the passions lead to crime, when every thing should be arranged to *satisfy them* in the most agreeable manner. * * * Thus, *in our present Society*, Fourier says that Freedom in matters of Love would lead to a frightful confusion. But *if men lived in a society where a larger liberty in marriage and divorce* would be *without danger*, then it would not be obnoxious to the peculiar condemnation with which it is *now* necessarily visited.

"These, then, are the views of Fourier on the subject of Love, which will not be satisfactorily adjusted until *after society shall have been brought into a state of organic unity and individual independence.*"

Or, in other words, until Association shall have been established, and Woman made perfectly independent in name, property, person, and affection.

Here, then, is the whole case. The theory of Association, we say, implies and requires *full freedom* in matters of love, just as in all other relations of social life. The Association school reply, *not yet*: in the present form of society it would be dangerous; but that form is *false*; we seek to substitute a *new* one, founded on community instead of isolation; *then*, when this new form has been established, when the fundamental principle of Association shall have wrought out its perfect work, these irregularities will cease to be *crimes*. We can not do every thing at once; we must begin with Labor in the township; "the reform" commenced thus will spread over the whole nation and embrace all departments of life. We can not carry the law of *Passional Attraction* into all relations *now*; we must leave it, therefore, so far as the relation between the *sexes* is concerned, to "future generations:" but "*There's a good time coming*," when the passion of Love, like all other passional attractions of the human soul, "shall undergo an organization by series to meet *all the wants of all the natures* that God sends into existence." This is our clear, necessary, inevitable deduction from the fundamental principle of Association. We are not alone in so regarding it. Fourier himself took exactly this view of the effect of his essential law. His disciples almost universally have conceded its logical necessity. And one of the ablest, as well as most enthusiastic among them,[*] whom we quote not as *authority*, but as corroborative evidence, thus applies the law to the very point under consideration:

"I am by no means *reconciled* to society, and *marriage* I regard as one of the *most odious* institutions. I have no doubt that *it will be abolished when the human race shall have made some further progress toward justice and reason*. But *at present* men are too gross, and women too cowardly, to seek a nobler law than the law of iron which rules them. The improvements of which some generous spirits dream, can not be realized in *such an age as ours*; those spirits seem to forget that they are a hundred years in advance of their cotemporaries."

In thus rehearsing and fortifying our previous argument upon this point, we trust we have aroused no "indignation" on the part of the Tribune which may not be easily "suppressed." If our space would allow, we should follow this demonstration with some remarks upon the direct and open *hostility* of the System of Association to the whole spirit and teachings of CHRISTIANITY. But, in consequence of the nature and extent of the evidence required to substantiate our position, this article has already reached an unusual length: and we must leave this point, as well as others involved, for future inquiry.

---

From the Tribune, March 26th.

LETTER XI.

*To the Editor of the Courier and Enquirer:*

IN opening this Discussion, on terms which I need not restate, but which were expressly though reluctantly agreed to by you, I set forth very plainly the Principles on which I proposed to demonstrate the expediency, justice, and duty of effecting the Social Organization I advocate. From the premises there laid down I deduced the duty of every Christian, every Philanthropist, every one who admits the essential Brotherhood of the Human Family, to labor earnestly and devotedly for a Social Order, which shall *secure* to every human being within its sphere the full and true development of the nature wherewith God has endowed him, Physical, Intellectual and Moral. The absolute, indefeasible Right of every Child to proper nourishment and culture, of every Man to ample Opportunity to Labor and to the fair recompense of his Labor—the Right, in short, truly to Live, to cultivate the Soil and enjoy the product of his Industry—these are the premises on which I now advocate, as I for six years have done, the Organization of Society on the basis of the Associated interests and

---
[*] This extract is from "Jacques," by George Sand, *one of the deadliest enemies of Fourier and his system*.—H. G.

efforts, in contradistinction to that hitherto prevailing. If Humanity, Christianity, Social Justice do not demand this, then you have the better position. If I have not *shown* that they require it, then you have of course the argument with you, and will take a verdict against me from our readers. But if I have *shown* this, what avail all your attacks on "Passional Attraction," the views of Fourier, &c ? Suppose you were to take a verdict by default against them, *my* argument stands unshaken, for it does not rest one feather's weight upon *their* foundations. Until I place myself behind their line of defense, by what right can I be asked to abandon or maintain its alledged positions?

That there is beneficent and inspiriting truth in the theory that Man may be so trained and directed, so circumstanced and incited, that he will be inclined to Good as generally and as thoroughly as he now appears to be to Evil, I do joyfully believe; but my faith in Association is not based on that theory, for I was an ardent Associationist before I had any such conviction. If experience shall conclusively demonstrate that theory, even *you* could not well resist the argument thence resulting. But I take Man as he notoriouly is, and I say, Look at Great Britain, at Ireland, with their wealth and refinement, their civilization and arts, with their famishing tens of thousands and their beggared millions, after fifteen centuries of Christian rule and teaching; then look at any little community of Shakers, so recently commenced in abject poverty, under such a defective organization, with so little intellectual culture or scientific power; see how they have utterly extinguished Pauperism, Servitude, Caste, Physical Want—see how many of the destitute they assimilate, how few (if any) they cast off—see how the earth becomes green and fruitful beneath their steadily advancing footsteps—see the Shakers of New-Lebanon sending of the surp'us products of their healthful, ungrudged toil, a thousand dollars' worth of food and clothing to aid in relieving Irish destitution—and say, if you can, that the superiority of Associated Life and Labor over the isolated, competitive, no-system usually prevailing, rests at all on the soundness of Fourier's teachings with regard to Passional Attraction.

Having satisfied yourself as to the propriety of evading the fundamental basis of our Discussion. I submit that the misnomer of your chosen title has become too glaring. Instead of "The Socialism of The Tribune examined,"* I suggest that your articles would be more justly entitled "The Socialism of everybody else dexterously quoted from, in order to raise a dust of prejudice against that of The Tribune." But no matter. I think those who closely read your citations will be able to discriminate between the Passions intended by Fourier (that is, the impulses, affections, faculties of Man) and those perverted and vicious exhibitions of human infirmity which the term is commonly understood to imply. They will be likely, I think, to mark the difference between your statement—

"The entire Social problem is—given Human Passions, to find a form adapted to their full and free development"—and Mr. Godwin's not exactly equivalent expressions :

* The title given under which Mr. Raymond's articles appeared in the Courier and Tribune throughout.—H. G.

"The duty of Man is to study his inclinations in order to arrive at a Social form *in which they will yield good results*,"—and

"All that is necessary is to discover a society in which *every bad route for the action of the Passions is closed*, and in which *the path of Virtue will be strewn with flowers.*"

You have indulged in a statement which, however unintentionally, will grossly mislead your readers, in saying that

"Every word we have quoted from Mr. Godwin upon this point [Passional Attraction] is from the *first part* of his book—that in which he lays down those principles only, ' which are,' to use his own words, ' universally adopted and defended by the whole school of Societary Reformers.'"

Your readers will suppose this a contradiction of what I had stated on this subject, but you know it is not. My complaint expressly was that "in *that part* of your article in which you assume to set forth, from ' the writings of Associationists,' what is the belief of the School with regard to *Love, Marriage, Conjugal Duty*, &c.," you had shamefully misrepresented us, quoting from that last portion of Mr. Godwin's book which expressly purports to set forth the views of Fourier which *are not*, in contradistinction from those which *are*, generally accepted by Associationists, without a word of intimation of this essential truth. Your readers would never have suspected, from your way of handling the subject, that Mr. Godwin's book was so divided into two Parts, and that between them was an "Intermediate" chapter, on the "Essential Distinction between the two Parts of this Work." It was this concealment and misrepresentation that I protested against, and most justly.

If the matter in controversy could only be shaken free from a film of unfamiliar and misapprehended words and phrases, I am confident I could convince all except the small though powerful class who mortally hate any suggestion of Social Reform, from a natural and instinctive though short-sighted dread that their share of this life's comforts and luxuries would be diminished by a more equal distribution. I am very sure I could, had I half a day's leisure for examining its files, establish, on the testimony even of the Courier and Enquirer, the truth of all the "Passional Attraction" that is essential to my argument. For example, I take up your last issue, and read, in your Editorial column and type, from the Paris letter of "A 'States' Man" on "The State of Europe," as follows :

"The truth is that the Irishman of the lower classes is *in his own land* a poor creature of shift, whatever be the cause and *whatever may be his good qualities and disposition to labor when transplanted to a foreign soil.*"

The truth here suggested is abundant for my purpose. Here are Seven Millions of People branded by History and "Sound Political Economy" as indolent, improvident, "poor creatures of shift," and living from century to century in filthy squalor and horrible destitution in the land of their birth, under the eye of all those whose good opinion they value ; yet transplant them to a different region—a region which might be expected to freeze them into torpor with its atmosphere of sullen countenances and coldly indifferent hearts—and we see them bound forward at once on a career of industrial energy, pecuniary thrift, and soaring ambition. No men are better soldiers or heartier workers out of Ireland than they who in their own land are said to be cruel and cowardly in war and invincibly idle and thriftless in peace. What is the cause of this striking contrast? Why are the Irish so efficient abroad and inefficient at home? I know your correspondent proceeds to say, "the root of the evil is *in the man himself*," and adds, that "Cromwell knew it when he commenced his *cruel but politic* scheme of *wholesale extirpation*;" but I submit that the uniform history of the Irish out of Ireland emphatically contradicts him. Give them but Opportunity and Hope, and they instantly proceed triumphantly to vindicate Irish Character and Human Nature from the calumnies which Rapacity, Tyranny, Robbery, and Bigotry have been heaping upon them for centuries. And the like change, I can not doubt, would lead to like results with regard to the enslaved, the benighted, the down-trodden, the despairing all over the world. Call it the theory of Passional Attraction, or whatever term you choose, I maintain that the wretched, the outcast, the palpably depraved, could be won to Industry, Usefulness, Virtue, if the right means were used in the right spirit. There would be apparent if not real exceptions to this as to all general laws, but in the immense majority of cases the result would vindicate the soundness of the principle which maintains that evil, physical as well as moral, is never inveterate, but may surely be confronted and overcome by good.

Let us briefly review what you have premised on the subject of Political Economy.

I have no sympathy whatever with Malthus, and do not see how you can "understand" me as affirming with him

"that Population naturally, inevitably, and universally, increases faster than its means of subsistence."

So far is this from the truth, that I have been trying hard to show that "the constant tendency of things" ought to be toward abundance and increased comfort for all—toward better recompense for toil, and ampler leisure for physical relaxation and mental improvement, because of the vast and rapid increase of the productive power and efficiency of Human Labor. The average day's work now produces far more of the necessaries and comforts of life than it did in any former period of the world's history—produces more, that is, to the world, infinitely less to the mere laborer alone. He is starving amid the abundance which his rugged, unremitting toil has created. I have admitted that there are some compensating circumstances, but the general fact is thus: "I am *sure*" it is, because the proof comes from many quarters, and really seems irresistible, in spite of M'Culloch and his school. The average price of Agricultural labor in England is not above two dollars per week, which is just about the present price of a bushel of Wheat; out of this sum the laborer is to board, clothe, and lodge himself—to pay his rent and subsist his family, if married. How *can* this be done with decency, not to speak of comfort, on such a pittance? What is the evidence collected by Parliamentary Commissioners with regard to it? Who does not feel that the Westminster Review's statement that "there is not a step, but a mere hand's breath, between the condition of the Agricultural laborer and Pauperism," *must* be true? We have abundant testimony that coarse bread and lard, and far too little of that, forms the habitual food of large masses of those laborers; and that in summer, and especially in harvest time, many thousands have no choice but to sleep in barns or under sheds, scores and hundreds in a flock—men, women, and children indiscriminately huddled together, regardless of every consideration of modesty and morality. I am not speaking of peculiar cases, but of the usual and (by the victims) unavoidable course of things—witnessed and never heeded by the landlords—the money-lords—the great farmers—the dignitaries in Church and State, who are constitutionally shocked with Mr. Bumble in "Oliver Twist," —at "the depravity of the lower classes." Turning again to your own Courier and Enquirer of this day, I read, in your "State of Europe," already quoted from:

"Were it not for the famine which rages in Ireland, slaying its thousands outright, and preparing victims without number for the first disease that may pass by, more would be said of the destitution, if not starvation, which *universally* prevails. Only a few nights since, for example, it was asserted without contradiction, by a member of the House of Commons, 'That in the County of Somerset [England] people are subsisting on a scanty supply of horse-beans and rotten turnips, picked up here and there in the fields;' and a Belgian journal of the 24th ult. says: 'The mortality, already frightful, has not yet reached the horrible acme to which it will quickly rise, and the reports of several physicians prove to us that the detestable food of the people of the country creates diseases, which must inevitably spread death around.' France, Germany, and other countries are alike suffering."

This in the middle of the Nineteenth Century, in the very center of Christian Civilization, glutted with the wealth of a plundered world, and with food enough to subsist amply those whom famine and consequent diseases are sweeping by thousands into their graves. True, the last crop was below an average; but there is food enough yet, if those who need it could obtain it; and, if they could sell their labor at any fair rate, they could buy it even at the prices to which Monopoly and Forestalling have raised it. The great mass throughout the world endure lives of often excessive, irregular, half-requited toil, are scantily fed, poorly clad, and hardly at all taught—not because Production is deficient, but because Distribution is imperfect and unjust. Europe might easily support ten times, America one hundred times, its present population, under a wise and true Social Economy. Secure Opportunity, skillful Direction, and just Recompense to the present population, and their average Production would be quadrupled. And I can not doubt that the progress of Agricultural Science will outstrip the increase of Population for centuries to come.

You wrench from my last article two lines, saying that as Population increases the reward of Labor it must become more scanty and precarious, without noticing the preceding assertion, that this is the result of that "monster evil '*the Monopoly of Land*,'" and then quote, with an air of triumph, my statement, that the population of Oregon and California has been doubled without prejudice to any. Of course, you only needed farther to show that the virgin soil of Oregon and California is monopolized and held at onerous prices, increased as fast as practicable, by those who seek to realize wealth from other men's labor, and you would have made out a case requiring explanation from me As it is, I submit that the facts so triumphantly grouped by you afford a striking confirmation of the truths for which I am contending. In Oregon the settler pays nothing for wild land, which is abundant, and no man is allowed to claim or hold more than a mile square. In California, any settler takes almost any unimproved land, paying nobody therefor; and such land, if allowed to be claimed in large tracts, has as yet attained no considerable price. Had the Land System of our State, from its first settlement, resembled that of Oregon, I believe its population might have more rapidly increased to Ten Millions with far less destitution of Employment and inadequacy of Recompense than has already been experienced among us, though our population has not yet reached Three Millions. I trust you will see that your citation of Atkinson and Greeley as adverse to Malthus's notion of Population naturally outrunning Subsistence, was quite superfluous. They never were any thing else.

That the "Sound Political Economists," so called, *do* commonly denounce Early Marriages among the Poor as not only improvident but culpable, I think all who are accustomed to read the Edinburgh and Westminster Reviews, &c., and especially their articles on Pauperism and the Poor-Laws, will attest My recollection of the fact is distinct and vivid, though I have no time to hunt up authorities on a point so unessential. But it, as you say,

" they assert that, as a matter of fact, generally true though not without exceptions, men do not and will not marry until they can support their families; and that *therefore* ' subsistence must not only *keep pace* with Population, but take the lead,'"

they assert what is not true. The Poor-Law Commission returns and the "Liberal" Reviews are full of complaints that the Poor *will not* and *do* not act rationally and deliberately in this matter; but, finding their condition desperate at best, are too apt to act on the assumption that Marriage may alleviate its miseries, and can not aggravate them. And this is natural. however deprecated and denounced by " Sound Political Economists " Hence you will find that nowhere is Early Marriage so general as among the Irish Poor. The only segment of truth in the statement above quoted is this :—Those who are actually suffering the agonies of famine are not likely to marry, if single, nor to have children if married. "Sound Political Economy" has just two real remedies for its fancied over-population: Starvation and Licentiousness among the Poor. If the latter fails to check the too rapid increase of Laborers, the landless and unskillful drift inevitably toward and are wrecked upon the former.

A few words on the Relations of the Sexes, and I take leave of your last article :

If I believed that God created some men for inconstancy, in any other sense than some are created to steal, forge, and murder, I should hold, as Fourier appears to do, that, in a perfect Society, such as can not be hoped for until after ages of preparation and experience, marriages might be dissoluble without reproach at the mere pleasure of the contracting parties. But, believing most thoroughly that Purity is inseparable from Constancy, and that the physical and moral nature of Man imperatively require them both as vital conditions of healthful existence, I hold that human beings rightly developed and faithfully educated in a true Society will no more desire change in the conjugal relation than to be continually swapping children with their neighbors. If I am right in the premise that Constancy is the dictate of Nature and of Providence, then you are wrong in confounding Freedom with License, and in your whole argument on the subject. Fourier, reared amid the convulsions and license of Revolutionary France, and living a keen observer of the boundless debaucheries of Paris, believed that Inconstancy was natural to a part of the human family, and not the result of false relations and perverse development. Here was his error—not that he taught that Crime, or whatever tends to produce evil and wretchedness, should be tolerated, but rather that in a true Society Inconstancy need not be a crime because it would not produce debasement and woe, as it now notoriously does. He held as firmly as any one that all individual acts and impulses inconsistent with the highest general good must be repressed: he erred in presuming that, in an entirely different Social State, at some period in the indefinite Future, Inconstancy will be no crime, not because men will be impelled to it, as they now are to rob, oppress, and slay their fellows, but because no evil consequences would result from yielding to its impulse. How entirely this differs from " The Socialism of the Tribune" which you profess to " examine" you very well understand

And now, since you insist on extending your articles immoderately, and your mode of discussing what you choose to combat instead of what I propose, has scarcely allowed me a chance to present affirmatively my own propositions, I will go on to demonstrate more fully one important feature of Association. I maintain, then, that

LABOR CAN BE AND OUGHT TO BE SO ORGANIZED AS TO RENDER IT ATTRACTIVE.

I mean by this that industry in general may be so organized that men and women shall cheerfully do their respective proportions of Useful Labor gladly, finding pleasure in the work itself as well as in its results or recompense.

That a small portion of mankind *now* labor in just that capacity wherein they can respectively be most useful, and find their greatest earthly pleasure therein, I presume none will dispute. That Productive Labor, humble as is the estimation in which the mere digger or carver is ordinarily held by the more fortunate classes, is the source of nearly all material comforts, and indispensable to the subsistence of every human being, I need not waste words to establish. That very few now labor with their hands from a hearty love of such labor, or because they take pleasure in so doing, is a deplorable truth. But why do men usually hate, and, if possible, shun Labor? Not, I maintain, because it is necessarily repugnant, but because it is pursued under circumstances and upon conditions which make it practically so. Those who do the *bona fide* work of the world are mainly the hirelings and dependents of others—the time, place, and manner of their working is dictated by others, who, usually doing little or less than themselves, are yet esteemed their social superiors—they must work, if mechanics or artisans, in shops not constructed with a primary view to their comfort, but to others' profit, often noisome, gloomy, unhealthy ("If you don't like it, you can leave—there are plenty more ready to take your place"), and Agricultural labor is subject to similar repulsive conditions. They generally feel, too, that they do not receive the fair and full recompense of their labor, and often are in doubt whether they will or will not be recompensed at all. No pains are usually taken, no outlay incurred, to render the workshops pleasant, cleanly, cheerful; if the capitalist has a library, paintings, statuary, &c., they do not enrich nor ornament his factory, and his workmen are very rarely gratified with the sight of them. So in Agriculture, the Hired Laborer finds no provision in the fields for shelter against sudden showers; for the prevention of offensive exhalations (though they are wasteful as well as offensive and unhealthy); no books convenient for a leisure hour or evening; no planning of grounds, or arrangement of work with a view to *his* improvement, comfort, or convenience. Can any wonder that Labor is repulsive? Were it possible to have a Ball, a Fishing Party, a Concert, under such circumstances, to be enjoyed for twelve or thirteen hours with no cessation but a short one for dinner, who does not realize that it would be even more fatiguing and repulsive than work is?

What Organization may do to render the repulsive attractive is seen in the case of War and Armies. Intrinsically the most revolting employment that can be suggested to a man is that of maiming and butchering his fellow-men by the wholesale, and taking his chance of being maimed or butchered in turn. And yet millions are found to rush into it, take delight in it, spend their lives in it, in preference to peaceful and better rewarded avocations. And why? Because (I speak of the regular soldier, who makes war his life-long profession) rulers have given to war an Organization, which satisfies two of the senses—that of Hearing by Music, that of Sight by glittering uniforms, precision of movement, and beauty of array. In a few, Ambition is also excited, while to the mass the assurance of an unfailing though meager subsistence is proffered. By these simple expedients the imagination is led captive, and millions constantly enlisted to shoot and be shot at for an average of not more than sixpence per day.

O that the governments of the world were wise enough, good enough to bestow one-half the effort and expenses on the Organization of Labor that they have devoted to the Organization of Slaughter! We should have enjoyed, long since, the blessings of an Industry so organized and adjusted that every one who wished could at all times have work, and every one who worked could not fail of the fair recompense of his toil—an arrangement under which Labor, so organized as to secure to each worker associates and directors of his own free choice, instead of those thrust upon him by his dire necessities and other men's avarice—the regulation of his own hours of toil, with frequent alternations from one employment to another, and from workshops ventilated, beautified, and tempered with a primary regard to his own comfort and ease, to the surrounding fields, so planned as to give the richest beauty and diversity to the landscape, and to satisfy and elevate the taste of the cultivator, laboring in joy and pride on a domain which he loves as the secure home of his children and associates, the support and stay of his old age. Here, with ample Education for the Young, Music, Libraries, Paintings, Sculpture, &c., &c., open to all (the few enjoying more than at present, but not shutting up the trophies of Refining Art from the many), with civic crowns and official distinction awarded, not to the destroyers of human lives, but to those who excel in Art, Science, Invention, and useful effort generally, I can not doubt that Labor will be rendered truly Attractive to the great body of our Race, so that each shall joyfully accept and pursue a career of peaceful Industry, and scorn the devices and shifts by which too many now contrive to live uselessly, while others are repelled from attempting the like only by despair of success. Attractive Industry, once generally established, Pauperism and Starvation are at an end. The rich will not grasp; the Poor will not envy; and no man will be impelled to covet that which is his neighbor's. In the faith that Association will beneficently solve this mighty problem of the true Organization of Labor, I remain H. G.

---

From the Courier and Enquirer, April 16th.
## REPLY TO LETTER XI.

THERE is very little in the foregoing article from the Tribune that requires reply. It advances nothing in defense of Association that has not been already answered, nor does it, in any degree, break the force of our demonstration, that the Law of PASSIONAL ATTRACTION is the fundamental principle of the System. We proved conclusively that this Law is the sole foundation of the theory, and would be the supreme rule of practice, in the new Society which the System aims to bring about. The "Harbinger," which is the official exponent of the Associationists of America, declares, as already quoted, that no man can be an Associationist "*in earnest,*" who does not accept this law "as the *basis* of his doctrines and of his ideas:" and that all who advocate the system do in fact accept the law "whether they are *conscious* of it or not." And the truth of this remark is admirably shown by the Tribune itself when, in the article we have copied above, it speaks of Association as a "Social Order which shall secure to every human being within its sphere *the full and true development of the nature* wherewith God has endowed him, physical, intellectual, and moral." Now the nature of man includes, of course, his impulses, appetites, propensities, desires, and passions; and the aim of Association, according to the Tribune, is, to secure to every man, their "full and true development," that is, their constant and complete satisfaction, to the full extent of their demands and in strict conformity to their tendencies. This is exactly the Law of Passional Attraction—in its whole length and breadth. The Tribune, therefore, like the Frenchman, "speaks prose without knowing it." Even while professing to disavow the law, it asserts and proclaims it in the broadest and most explicit terms.

In this principle, then, lies the germ of the whole theory and practice of Association. We have on the one hand Man with his Passions, as active powers; and on the other Society with its forms, as the medium of their activity. That evil, misery, suffering attend upon and result from Man's action in the existing state of things, is a fact universally conceded: as is also the necessity of providing a remedy. But before a cure can be applied or devised, the *cause* of the evil must be ascertained: and here at the very outset, the theory of Association comes in direct collision with the teachings of Christianity. No truth is more distinctly taught in the Word of God than that of the sinfulness of the human heart: the proclivity of Man's *nature* to act in violation of the rule of right. The *origin* of sin must always remain a matter of doubt: but the fact of its existence in the human heart is not only most explicitly asserted in the revelation of God, but lies open to universal observation. Christianity assumes it, and teaches also that from this intrinsic depravity of the heart flows all the evil that afflicts the world. It is solely because malice, covetousness, envy, lust, and selfishness in general exist, as active principles, in the heart of man, that their *fruits* exist in Society. It is solely because the *fountain* is poisoned, that the streams which flow from it are bitter. Here, then, Christianity says, is the *cause* of all social evil, in the sinfulness of the heart of Man. The remedy must reach that cause, or it must prove inefficient. The heart must be changed. The law of Man's *nature* must cease to be the supreme law of his life. He must learn to subject that law to the higher law of righteousness, revealed in his conscience and in the Word of God. All the passions, appetites, affections, propensities, and impulses of his nature, which tend to evil, must be repressed, controlled, and overruled; must become subject to the law of conscience: and that subjugation can only be effected by his own personal will, with the supernatural aids furnished in the Christian Scheme. These are the plain teachings of the Christian faith; and are held to be such by the great body of the Christian world. We, of course, make no appeal upon this point to those by whom they are rejected.

The theory of Association rejects them altogether. Its advocates maintain, in opposition to them, that the heart of man is not depraved: that his passions do not prompt to wrong doing, and do not therefore by their action, produce evil: but that evil results solely from the attempt made to check and control them. This attempt they say, distorts their proper development, and so produces suffering. "Human Science" is denounced by Mr. Brisbane, because it seeks to "suppress, repress, and compress these springs of action in the soul." The evil which exists arises from this *attempted* suppression, and not from the action of the passions themselves. The remedy, therefore, they say consists in *removing* this restraint; in taking off this repressive force: in giving to human faculties, propensities, and impulses their full and free development. They are good in themselves: they lead naturally only to good results: they ought, therefore, to have a constant and complete activity. This suppression, they add, is the work of society: it results directly from the social forms in and through which man lives and acts. "This development of souls and their faculties," says Mr. Brisbane, "is not practicable in civilized relations, in isolated households and incoherent industry." Then, he adds, "Civilization should be *denounced*, and some mechanism *entirely opposed to it* should be sought." We must have a new social form, which shall provide for, and render possible, this full and free development of the nature of man. Now, isolated households, the laws of society, the Family relation, the constraints of Marriage, individual effort, and the prevailing scheme of labor and of life, impose checks and restraints upon the action of man. We demand a Society which shall break this bondage; which shall take its laws from the *nature of man*, and not seek to overrule that by another law; in which labor shall be performed because it is attractive; in which men shall be brought together only according to their mutual likings: in which those only shall work together who like each other and their common labor: in which the Marriage tie shall be binding only while the passional attraction which gave it birth shall continue: in which no law of Society shall overrule the impulse which impels men and women to form new unions: in which children may obey no superiors but those of their own choice: in which, in short, all labor and all life, in all their departments, shall know no other law than that which springs from the tendency of the passions and propensities of individual men. Such a social form, the Associationists contend, is demanded in order "to secure to every human being within its sphere the full and true development of his nature, physical, intellectual, and moral." And that development, it is further held, whenever it can be secured, will lead to universal happiness, because "happiness," in the words of Mr. Brisbane, "consists in the constant satisfaction of the radical passions;" and thus all evil will be forever banished from the world. Then, in the words of the Tribune, "the rich will not *grasp*, the poor will not *envy*;" for a covetous or conceited person could no more exist in Association, than a wicked one could in Heaven. (Tribune, Dec. 18.) Association thus proposes to reform man, to banish evil from the world, and to effect the regeneration of the human race, by changing the circumstances under which men live and act. And the possibility of doing this is repeatedly asserted, and constantly assumed by the Tribune in this discussion.

Now it can not escape attention, that in all this the *Law of Nature* is assumed to be the *highest rule of human conduct*. Man, with his passions and impulses, is regarded, in Mr. Godwin's language, as "the *invariable term* of the social problem;" and a "Social medium is sought in *perfect accord* with his *nature*." So, also, says Mr. Brisbane, "we can not change human nature: we can only change its developments." Whatever, then, accords with, and flows from the *natural impulses and propensities of Man*, it is assumed, will lead to good results, and therefore must be right. The Law of Nature is the Supreme law. If nature prompts man to *any* act, that act is right, provided it does not lead to suffering. If man's passions impel him, for example, to discard his wife and take another, it will be right for him to do so, if the state of Society is such that the act will not occasion trouble. In the *present* state of Society, of course, it can not be done: but under a new social form its evil consequences could be averted, and *then* the act would be right, because it would be in accordance with the nature of man. The Tribune thinks that man's nature would not prompt him to such action; that "in a true Society human beings will no more desire *change* in the *conjugal* relation than to be continually swapping *children* with their neighbors;" but at the same time, the Tribune holds to the general principle that the law of nature must govern human conduct in this as in other respects; and says that if it held that purity and constancy were *not* demanded by man's *nature*, it

"would hold, as Fourier appears to do, that in a perfect Society *marriages might be dissoluble without reproach, at the mere pleasure of the contracting parties*."

Now, as a matter of fact, man's mere *nature* does often impel him to inconstancy. That nature will, of course, be the same in Association as it is now: man's desires, impulses, passions, will remain unchanged. In Association, then, it *is* certain, men *will* desire to "change their wives" far oftener than to "swap their children;" and the Tribune's professed belief to the contrary is preposterous. But this is immaterial: whether it be true or false, the Tribune's adherence to the *principle* is equally explicit. It makes the law of nature *supreme*: if Constancy is the dictate of that law, *then*, and only then, according to the Tribune, it should be the rule of Society. But man's *nature* should be developed, to whatever it may lead—the great law of Passional Attraction should be supreme, whatever may be its requirements. And the first thing necessary is to devise and put in force a *Social form*, which will allow this. Here comes in, as we have already seen, the machinery of *groups* and *series*, to replace the existing relations of the Family, township, &c.

Now all this is clearly in direct hostility to the teachings of the Bible. No doctrine is more distinctly taught there than that of the depravity of man's *nature*. The law of his nature is a law of sin. And it is made the great aim of his being to rise above that law; to become freed from the bondage to evil which his mere nature imposes; and to repress, deny, and subject to the higher law of conscience the passions and appetites of his nature—the "lusts of the flesh which *war against* the soul." No injunction of the Gospel is more definite or reiterated than that of *self-denial*; of "repressing, suppressing, and compressing the passions," in Mr. Brisbane's phrase; and of making the dictates of our depraved *nature* subordinate and subject, in all things, to the law of absolute right, which for all men must be supreme. There can be no mistake in assuming this as the plain commandment of Christianity; nor is there more room for error in asserting its palpable contradiction to the fundamental principle of Association. The latter makes the *law of Nature* supreme: the former makes it subject to a higher law. No such higher law is recognized in this Social Scheme. It never makes allusion to it, but always takes for granted its non-existence. It does not admit the existence of *Sin*, except in the form of suffering. Nothing, in its view, is good or bad, right or wrong, intrinsically, but only as it produces happiness or misery. There is no reference, ever or anywhere, to a *law of right*, to a commandment from God, to an injunction of conscience. The *law of Nature*, in this system, supplies the place of all these moral and spiritual obligations. The institution of Marriage, for example, is not regarded as of divine appointment and permanent in its character. The fact that it was recognized as such by Christ is disregarded. Association considers it a simple *form*, the creature of society, and to be changed, modified, or destroyed, as society may allow. Thus, it is held, a time may come when it will be felt as a needless restraint upon the nature of man. And they have no hesitation in saying that *then* it should give way to new and more liberal forms of intersexual relation. Then Society should be so organized that a man may have a dozen wives, or a woman a dozen husbands, if their passions prompt, without producing suffering and debasement. The intrinsic *right* of the matter is treated as a nullity. Christ's injunctions, the teachings of the Bible, the dictates of Christianity are allowed no weight.

This is a distinguishing feature of the whole system. It has in it nothing religious; nothing that even recognizes the existence of spiritual and moral laws; nothing that takes any, the slightest account of the Bible and its injunctions. The Law of Nature is its supreme commandment, both in theory and in practice. It recognizes nothing higher, and knows no other sanctions. The system, we are aware, pretends to be religious, and even claims to be the only true Christianity. But, as we have seen, it rejects the plainest doctrines of the Bible, nullifies its most imperative commandments, and substitutes for them its own interpretation of the laws of *nature*. Thus the God in whom it professes faith, becomes, in its definition, simply the "*principle* of universal unity." The Trinity in which it pretends to believe, is resolved into a trinity of the "active, passive, and neutral principles of life and order." It gravely declares that by the "Kingdom of Heaven" is meant Association: and the command of our Savior, "seek ye first the Kingdom of God and his righteousness," is interpreted to mean "seek ye the harmony of the Passions in Associative unity!" Thus it believes in Christianity, only when Christianity has been forced into its likeness, only when it reflects *its* image: and then the *image* of itself, and not the substance of Christianity, becomes the object of its faith. Its whole spirit is in the most direct hostility to the doctrines of the Bible. It recognizes no absolute distinction between right and wrong, knows nothing of the law of conscience, ascribes no authority to revelation, seeks no ends and knows no laws above those of mere *nature*, and aims at nothing beyond the "full and true development of the nature of man." To call such a system *religious*, is a gross abuse of language. It is the exact antagonist of Christianity; it starts from opposite fundamental principles and aims at precisely opposite results. It is, in its essential character, *infidel*: its principles, its aims, and its means are all those of infidelity. It is very true, as will probably be urged in its defense, that Association is not alone in thus regarding the law of nature as the supreme rule of human conduct. Phrenology, Mesmerism, and the countless brood of novel "sciences" which have of late years dawned upon the world, all agree in this. They all unite in discarding moral distinctions, in annulling conscience, and in rejecting the idea of spiritual laws and even of spiritual existences. Every thing is identified with the laws of Nature. These laws are revealed sometimes in bumps upon the skull; sometimes in the nerves, and by means of galvanic action; sometimes in the outward forms of life and matter: but *always* in Nature. The law of Nature is to them all the *only* law of God. And in this they occupy precisely the ground of Association: but this coincidence by no means vindicates that theory from the charge of infidelity to the Christian creed. The principle, wherever and whenever it manifests itself, is the antagonist of revelation. The fact that it insinuates itself into, and works through so many forms; that it pervades so many different subjects, and mingles itself with so many diverse opinions, affords new ground to apprehend danger from its prevalence, but it can not in the least change its character. It is in all its forms the same; equally hostile to the Christian faith, and equally fitted to destroy all confidence in the established principles of morals and religion. It may seem to be harmless, because it appears to be merely speculative : but this fact only disguises and thus increases the danger. The scheme of Association is the only one which seeks directly and avowedly to reduce it to practice: to bring society and life, in all their departments, under its power. But, like all other fundamental principles, whether true or false, it creates its own form of manifestation, and will be practiced as fast and as far as it is believed. The Association doctrine concerning Marriage, for example, can not be believed without producing its natural results If men become convinced that the *Law of Nature* alone should regulate intercourse between the sexes; that the bonds of Marriage, as Mr. Godwin contends, have no sanction except in the arbitrary customs and observances of Society; that they ought to have no force beyond the consent of the parties whom they bind; that the passion of *love*, being an impulse of nature, ought, therefore, always to have its "full and free development;" and that this law of passional attraction is the highest law which man can or should obey, they will inevitably act upon that conviction. They will come to consider the restraints of Marriage as unjust and oppressive, whenever they find them in conflict with their own propensities. And those bonds will be cast aside, and made to yield to the law of their nature, just as fast and just as far as the "false forms" and "subversive institutions" of society will permit. A moment's reflection will convince any one that this *must* be the result of faith in such principles. And there are among us witnesses of the *fact*, that in specific instances *these doctrines have produced these, their natural fruits*. Men and women, in this City and elsewhere, have gradually yielded assent to the principle of Association, that passional attraction should be the supreme law · and avowedly under its influence, acting in accordance with it, they have thrown off or disregarded the restraints of Marriage, and formed *other* relations, in more "perfect accord" with the promptings and passions of their nature. Now the advocates of Association, we fully concede, do not aim at such results *now :* they contend that the existing form of society is not *suited* to the "full and free development" of man's nature. But they also maintain that society can and should receive a *new* form, adapted to it, and that *then* the whole theory may be carried into full effect. Fourier himself went no farther than this. He taught that a time would come when inconstancy would be provided for, and that it would then be no crime, because it would cause no suffering, "because no evil consequences would result from yielding to its impulse." The Tribune hesitatingly intimates that he was in error in thinking that it would produce no suffering; but if not, if he was right in so thinking, then the Tribune has no further scruple ; it would then insist upon such forms as would "secure the full development of human nature." Here then, is an entire agreement as to the fundamental principle of the supremacy of the *law of nature*. And both stand in exact hostility to the fundamental doctrine of Christianity, that there is an absolute distinction between right and wrong, by which wrong can *never* become right, whatever may be its consequences. The doctrine of the Bible is, that Marriage is in itself an institution of divine sanctions: Constancy is a law of divine injunction Its violation is *always* wrong, no matter what may be the consequences resulting from it. The moral character of the act does not at all depend upon its results. A "perfect Society" would certainly seem to be that in which the law of God should be most perfectly obeyed; that in which, therefore, marriage should *never* be dissoluble except in those cases for which specific provision has been made. Those cases are those of adultery, those in which impulses of inconstancy have already been allowed "free development." If there had been, however, no inconstancy, if the Society were *perfect*, marriage would be, according to the law of God, absolutely *indissoluble*. But the Tribune's theory of a "perfect Society" is quite the reverse of all this : for in such a society, it says, marriages might be dissoluble "at the *mere pleasure* of the contracting parties."

In this respect the scheme of *Association* agrees entirely with *Owenism*, and all the various schemes of social reform which have, from time to time, been propounded, attempted, and exploded. In some of the minor details of their machinery, there may be an apparent difference between them; but they all agree in making *Nature* the only supreme law-giver; they all reject the scriptural doctrine of man's depravity—the Christian atonement—the reality of spiritual laws and divine sanctions, and the other fundamental doctrines of the Christian faith. They all start from this hypothesis: that evil is the result of *circumstances*, and not the fruit of sin in the heart—and then they all attempt reform in the same direction; namely, by *changing* the circumstances by which men are surrounded. *All these schemes, therefore, in their fundamental principles, are anti-Christian—are infidel in their tendencies.*

The Tribune reiterates its disavowal of responsibility for any thing that is objectionable in Association. This, it asserts, is not the "*Socialism of the Tribune.*" Now we have never understood the Tribune to claim the *authorship* of the system it advocates. It does not pretend to have invented a new system: but simply espouses, advocates, and defends a scheme already discovered by Fourier, and introduced into this country by one of his personal friends and followers. The Tribune, therefore, can not make of that system whatever it pleases. It is not working alone in its behalf, but in conjunction with others. It has no right, therefore, to reject portions of its provisions, and yet claim to advocate the system. And still less can it repudiate the fundamental principle of Association, and yet claim to be an Associationist. We regard it as a most gratifying evidence of the utility of this discussion, that it has *compelled* the Tribune, in form at least, to disavow and abandon some of the most vital and essential elements of the Association theory. It sees clearly that they will not bear inquiry—that when examined and brought to the test of established truth, they are found to be false; and that the natural tendency of their operation would be toward crime and consequent suffering. And, therefore, it seeks to rid itself of all responsibility concerning them. But this can not be done unless the Tribune also abandons Association, as it is held and urged by the body of American Associationists. If it chooses to take down that flag, to leave their ranks, and espouse some new theory of its own, avoiding the obnoxious doctrines of Association, and presenting simply some plan of its own for modifying the relations of Capital and Labor, then it would be entitled to a different kind of consideration. But until it does that, it must in justice be held responsible for the *System* of which it is the most able and efficient advocate in this country. What that System is, upon what principles it is based, and to what results they tend, we have already shown at length, and with a copiousness of evidence that must prove conclusive. Nearly all these facts, as to the nature and tendency of the System, have been drawn from the work of Mr. Brisbane, published first in a volume, and then condensed into a pamphlet. The Tribune seeks now to give the impression that it does not approve of, and is not responsible for, these positions and sentiments of Mr. Brisbane. But the following extract from an *Editorial* article in the Tribune proves this pretense to have been an after-thought; and proves the book to have published with the full sanction, and partly through the agency of the Editor himself:

*From the Tribune, March 25, 1843.*

"We have received a great many letters from almost every part of the Union, asking us all manner of questions with regard to the character, tendencies and progress of the doctrine of Association. *We can not find time to reply privately*, but a large pamphlet of eighty pages will be issued *containing answers to nearly all of the inquiries and objections which have been put to us*. It is prepared by Albert Brisbane, an intimate friend of Fourier in life and *an ardent, intelligent apostle of his doctrine since his death.* This work has been got up in part *by subscription of the friends of the doctrine.*"

We therefore deny entirely the justice of the Tribune's charge, that we are not discussing Association; that we are quoting from "the Socialism of everybody else," in order to excite prejudice against that of the Tribune. We claim to have submitted proof, copious and conclusive, of the fact that the "Socialism of the Tribune" is that of the school of Associationists, of which Fourier was the founder; and that the fundamental principles of that school are those which we have defined them to be. We are quite willing to submit this point, as well as all others involved in the discussion, to the judgment of our common readers.

The Tribune insists upon a distinction between the *passions* of man (meaning his "impulses, affections, faculties,") and "those *perverted and vicious exhibitions of human infirmity* which the term is commonly understood to imply." But is not that very "infirmity" part of man's *nature?* And yet the Tribune demands a "Social Order which shall secure its full *development.*" What occasions these "*vicious* exhibitions?" What causes this infirmity: and why is it that, if all man's impulses are good, they should so often have "perverted and vicious exhibitions?" The Tribune may reply that *Society* perverts and vitiates them? But how came Society to be vicious, if its individual members were not so? Society is simply a form, which active principles of life and character have created; and that form is of necessity determined by the law of its life. An acorn produces an oak, and not a bush, because that is the law of its development. Precisely so, good impulses, right motives, just and righteous principles, in the life and conduct of individual men, can not possibly create a perverted or vicious social form. If that form is bad, it must be because its vital, formative principle is evil. "A good tree can not bring forth evil fruit." The Tribune's distinction, therefore, fails entirely; it only evades, it can not affect, the objections we make to the "full and free development" of man's impulses and passions.

The Tribune reiterates its assertion, that the condition of the mass of the population of England is worse than was that of their ancestors five centuries ago; and repeats its citations in proof of it. But we have already shown that they are not conclusive, and the Tribune offers nothing new. It is perfectly clear that great suffering exists among the common people of Europe at the present time; but that fact by no means proves that there has never been greater. Much of it, moreover, is owing entirely to temporary and fortuitous causes, while the fact is only pertinent to this discussion so far as it can be traced directly to the working of a general principle. If the Tribune, however, will take the trouble to refer to some authentic source of information upon this point, it will find that *the average length of human life in Great Britain*, which is the surest possible test of the physical condition of the people, *is greater now than it has ever been before*. This could not be the case if, as the Tribune contends, the means of sustaining life, within reach of the laborer, had been constantly and rapidly diminishing. More upon this point, though much more might be said, can not be needed. In fact the Tribune abandons the position, when it discards the theory of Mr. Malthus that "Population naturally outruns subsistence." With its usual consistency, however, it immediately proceeds to reiterate and prove what it had just disavowed.

The Tribune's parallel between the condition of Ireland and that of the Shaker Establishment at New Lebanon, is striking enough; but it scarcely warrants the inference which the Tribune would draw from it. If the principles of this Shaker Association could be applied to Ireland—if all private property were abolished there—all marriages annulled, all intercourse of the sexes prevented, and the whole population brought directly under the despotic control of a single person whose will was law, even in the minutest details of life, and if all who violated any of the imperative commandments by which Shakerism rules its subjects, could be at once expelled and removed—it is quite likely the Green Isle would present a different aspect from that which it now exhibits. We doubt, however, whether Mr. Labouchere and the Imperial Parliament will soon be released, by such a substitution, from the cares and duties imposed upon them by the affairs of Ireland. The Tribune's attempt to reason from one instance to the other, lacks the first element essential to the argument, that of *analogy* between the two cases. It would be just as rational to compare the state of Ireland with that of some private family in Ohio or Oregon, and draw inferences *ad libitum* therefrom.

But the Tribune says that "Labor can and ought to be rendered *attractive*" *per se*, and not simply from its rewards or results. And it proceeds to urge that this may be done by decorating workshops, sheltering farmers, and by various other devices, such as are employed in war, music, marches, &c. These things Association proposes to provide: it proposes to have *groups* and *series*, center and wings, companies and battalions, for working as for fighting: it proposes to have men plow, and reap, and work everywhere in full uniform, to the sound of music, &c. Thus, says Mr. Brisbane:

"If music, uniforms, badges, honors, concerts, and rivalries of masses, have made WAR *attractive*, may we not suppose that, applied to production, they would render *industry* attractive?" * * * "But all the stimulants of art, of honors, of ambition, of emulation, are perfectly incompatible with the narrow, civilized, *domestic* organization. Here is the radical defect of our Societies, and here it is that a radical reform must begin. * * * We must combine and associate large masses to develop the harmonies of *human nature*. We must free man from his present embarrassed and prosaic life, and restore him to the liberty of his being. We know how strongly civilized man clings to his isolated household, or *family life*, and what *prejudices* there are to overcome on this point," &c.

But all this is too absurd for argument. Working by music, plowing in uniform, conferring nominal and empty honors, &c., might do for children, but to urge it as a means of making hard labor attractive, is nonsense. The only thing that can make labor attractive to the mass of men is the stimulus of reward, the hope of recompense, and above all, the certainty of possessing and enjoying that recompense, whatever it may be. So far as these motives operate, they make labor attractive. Men now toil first to obtain a subsistence, and then to acquire the means of comfort for themselves and their children. They labor willingly so long as they know that what they thus acquire will be *their own*. They expect to *own* it, to retain possession of it, and have over it the supreme control. They desire and expect to "*monopolize*" it, for themselves and their posterity. One great purpose of Law is to secure to them this right; to secure the safety of property; to confer upon and preserve to them their right of absolute and permanent ownership. Whatever, therefore, perfects and secures this right, renders Labor attractive, in the only sense in which it can become so. But the Tribune denounces the "monopoly of *land*," that is its ownership by individuals, as the "monster evil" of Society: and the premises upon which it bases this assertion, as has been shown in the early part of this discussion, involve a denial of the right of *monopolizing* any thing. Destroy the right of owning property, or of owning land, and no devices of human ingenuity could render labor attractive, in *any* sense.

These remarks, we believe, cover the entire ground of the Tribune's article. To one or two of the topics touched upon, however, we may recur in our next, which will conclude this discussion.

---

From the Tribune, April 28.

## LETTER XII.

*To the Editor of the Courier and Enquirer:*

IN the lately-issued North American Review, for April, 1847, page 280, in the article on the Intellectual Aspect of the Age, you will find the following passage:—

"Let us now cast a cursory glance at the work which remains to be wrought in coming ages, and in which we trust that our own will begin to bear part.

"First, the practical skill, which has almost exhausted its resources in the material world, must apply itself to *the reörganization of human society*. That the social system is out of joint, is only too obvious. Here are the vast masses of superfluous and unproductive wealth; there the crowded ranks of the suffering, the starving, the degraded, the enslaved, for whom no healing or *restoring* influence has ever gone forth. These are the valleys to be exalted; those the mountains to be brought low. War, still the scourge of a guilty world, must be put away, and the principles of peace, forbearance, equity, and good faith brought down to the details of domestic and social life, and thence (for it can be only thence) infused into the machinery of governments and the counsels of nations. Groveling toil, both among the sordid rich and the hunger-driven poor, must be made to relax its demands and to equalize its burdens, so that in all classes of society the mind and heart shall claim their rights, and have their dues—their sufficient space and means for culture and enjoyment."

As the writer proceeds to disparage and denounce *Fourierism* " and a' that," I think it will readily be seen that " speaking prose without knowing it," is a very common occurrence in our day. Again: *Le Semeur* (The Sower), the leading Religious periodical published in Paris of the Calvinistic School, in its leading article of January 27th last, on the Social Discontents and Food Riots of our times, thus discourses :

" The last year, if our memory does not deceive us, the Minister of the Interior jested pleasantly at the ideas of some innovators. 'The Organization of Labor,' asked he, 'what does that mean? Do you understand any thing by the Organization of Labor?' and he descended from the tribune with the applause of the Center. The flippant tone is not, in our judgment, the proper one for subjects so serious.

" We have one or two reflections to submit to the friends of the Gospel as to the task they ought to perform. Let us not be in haste to condemn without reserve the obvious weakening of the spirit of patience and resignation in the bosom of the popular masses. Quite as little let us suppose that *the only remedy for it is to preach the Christian Faith.* The first fruit of these ideas would be an injustice; the second, an error—and, we must confess it, *an error which has been too long maintained.*"

Whether this is prose or poetry, I leave to the judgment of others. It seems to me to be, at any rate, very important and seasonable truth. Whether it will be heeded in our day by the Observers, Recorders, Evangelists, &c., who have the ear of the class here of which *Le Semeur* is the oracle in France, I can not predict. You will find in it, doubtless, occasion for a fresh sneer at the " good time coming."

If I were to-day blessed with an opportunity of speaking intimately and fully to a chief of that different but powerful class with whom your paper is an oracle, because it flatters and justifies their over-mastering impulses—if I could sit down beside some man who is tottering down to the grave beneath the burden of fourscore years, yet eagerly adding hundreds of thousands per annum to a hoard of wealth already counted by millions, and hugging himself with the conceit of his own generosity, because he gives perhaps thousands each year to relieve distress, diffuse knowledge, or commend religion and morality, I would wish to plead with him after this fashion : " Brother of mine ! you are madly throwing away the most golden opportunities ! you are criminally disregarding the most solemn duties ! Talk not of your contributions to this or that charity, this or that missionary or philanthropic society : all that may be very well ; but it falls immensely short of your *whole* duty. You hold *all* your wealth as the steward of the Great Benefactor ; you are bound, by His commands, declared in Nature and in Revelation, to devote *all* your means, over an adequate support and provision for those specially dependent upon you, to the relief of misery, the diffusion of comfort, the increase of human happiness. But not your money nor your provisions only ; your best efforts, counsel, influence, deportment, familiar intercourse, are demanded by the law of Love to God and Man as free-will offerings to the cause of Human Well-being. Not merely to mitigate the woes of Want and Suffering by alms, but to dry up the fountains of human sorrow—to seek out and eradicate the *causes* of wide-spread degradation and misery—to replace the influences which produce or aggravate evil by such as shall tend steadily and strongly to create good—these are within the clear bounds of your duty. I ask you, therefore, to *unite in so recasting Society that it shall be thoroughly adapted to the performance of these duties*—so that it shall constitute a true mirror, in which the virtues we require of men shall be readily and truly reflected—or rather, a true element, in which they shall be readily and freely generated and developed." Let any man but sit down seriously and impartially to consider whether the Social Organization in which we live is such a one—whether it is calculated to develop the good and repress the evil in our nature—whether its natural influences are on the side of generosity, industry, frankness, or of selfishness, scheming, and duplicity, and he can come to but one conclusion.

I do maintain that, if the Law of Love given through Christ shall ever become in reality the guiding principle of mankind, or of any considerable section or community, a Social Reform will be the inevitable result. To call *that* a Christian State in which the few roll in wealth and luxury while the many are pinched by frost and hunger—where the few own all the Soil, and the many must hire it of them at exorbitant prices, or cultivate it for them for wages which will barely hold soul and body together—where those who can command work whenever they choose are under no obligation to do any, and where those who *must* work or starve are often unable for weeks to obtain a single day's employment—where the palace of the rich Christian overshadows a hundred hovels tenanted by ignorance, want, and wretchedness, their inmates forming a class as distinct from his in every Social usage and characteristic as the Pariahs from the Brahmins of Hindostan—is grossly to libel Christianity. I can not see how a man profoundly impressed with the truth and importance of Christ's teaching, as those of a divinely-sent messenger and guide, can fail to realize and aspire to a Social polity radically different from that which has hitherto prevailed. Unless we are to understand as mere rhetoric, of the most exaggerated kind, his " How hardly shall they that have riches enter into the Kingdom of God," (Mark x., 23), " Sell that thou hast and give to the poor, and thou shalt have treasure in Heaven," (Matt. xix., 21), &c., I do not see how it is possible for any one to suppose that He contemplated or could fail to condemn a perpetuation of the social distinctions of master and servant, rich and poor, landlord and landless, &c., to any thing like the extent, or in any thing like the spirit, which are now manifested all around us, and even in (alas, that it should be so !) the households of many among the most exalted and esteemed of the professed followers of Christ.

But I have not urged the justice and necessity of a Social Reform mainly from the Religious point of view, because I was aware of the proneness on your side to make this a question of creeds and catechisms—to make its decision hinge on dogmatic theology, instead of practical Christianity. I protest against the introduction of sectarian shibboleths whereby to try the merits of this controversy. "Our fathers worshiped in this mountain"—"We have Abraham to our father"—"Art thou greater than our father Jacob?" are not tests by which either party to this discussion is to be justified or found wanting. I do, indeed, believe that, if the Bible were the truly-heeded and fairly-construed arbiter, its decision would be emphatically in favor of that side which harmonizes best with the rigid Agrarianism of Moses (Levit. xxv., 23–28, etc ), the stern denunciations of the lust of wealth by the prophets (see Isa. v.8, etc.), the practical ultra-Socialism of the early Christians (Acts ii , 44–46). But I know how easy it is, how natural it is, for those who seek to be justified in the neglect of unwelcome duty and in their attempts to blend the service of God with that of Mammon, to court the raising of a cloud of theological smoke and dust calculated to obscure the whole field of Duty. Against all this I earnestly protest. I decline to be made a party to it in any way. Make out, if you will, as your argument assumes, that all Unitarians, Universalists, with others who do not deem Man essentially and totally depraved—all who are believers in Mesmerism or Phrenology, are Infidels, and still *my* positions are unaffected, my arguments unshaken. Prove, if you can, that Nature's laws are not of God but of the Devil—and what then? Are my positions weakened? Long before this controversy commenced, you know perfectly well that I advocated Association on my own grounds, and you distinctly assented that I *should* so advocate it in this discussion, and that you would meet me on the case as I should present it. Have you done so? Look back on your whole course through this controversy! Look, then, to this passage (already quoted) from Godwin, page 73, and to the whole page asserting, explaining, and enforcing it.

"*The School of Fourier* [that is of the Associationists, who are distinctively termed Fourierites] *profess but one thing :* THE ORGANIZATION OF LABOR IN THE TOWNSHIP. It has no other *object*, no other *faith*, as a School. Individuals are, of course, always at liberty to promulgate whatever opinions they may see fit."

When, therefore, you tell me that this or that Associationist makes Passional Attraction his starting-point, I answer, "What is that to me? He is welcome." When you state that I "profess to *disavow*" that law, you state what *I* have not warranted. Undoubtedly, I should dissent from any presentment of that law from *your* pen, still more from such deductions therefrom as you would consider fair and logical; but I do not feel called upon either to disavow or affirm that law. I do not deduce the necessity, feasibility, and beneficence of Association from any abstract speculation or theory respecting the essential nature of Man, but from what is known of his history and character Whatever the "intrinsic depravity" of his nature, no one disputes that he who has grown up from birth to maturity in Scotland, for instance, is *likely* to be a far superior being to his fellow educated on the Slave-Coast, and so of Connecticut and New Zealand, of Union Square and the Five Points, although the "intrinsic depravity" is necessarily the same in each case. But does any man seriously contend that Scotland, or Connecticut, or Union Square, affords the best possible conditions for the formation of an exalted Human Character? May we not rather fairly presume that what has been done is but a foretaste of what may be? If it be true—as who can doubt?—that a community even so imperfectly and partially supplied with the means of Education, Refinement, Moral and Religious Culture as ours, must naturally exhibit an immense and continual improvement on the Social aspects of Tartary or Abyssinia, why should not a Social Condition affording to *every member* advantages equal to those enjoyed by the most favored in our present society lead to corresponding results? In short, concede me only that all our Seminaries, Sermons, Sunday Schools, etc , are not empty and intolerable farces—that human beings as they exist throughout the world may rationally and advantageously be instructed, admonished, developed, and you can not bring Human Depravity to bear effectively against Association. If the Divine prayer, "lead me not into temptation," and the not dissimilar entreaty of "Agur the son of Jakeh"—"Give me neither poverty nor riches. * * * lest I be full and deny thee, and say, Who is the Lord? or lest I be poor and steal, and take the name of my God in vain," be not empty words—then it is desirable to call into existence a Social state and Social laws very different from those under which we have hitherto lived and are now living—a condition which shall bridge the gulf now yawning betwixt Wealth and Poverty, and immensely diminish the temptations of Want which Agur states so forcibly and clearly. That there will be Sin and Suffering under the very highest Social condition, speedily or even at all attainable by frail Mortality, does not at all disprove the feasibility or importance of the changes involved in the idea of Association.

What you say of Marriage and the kindred topics, in view of all that has already been urged in the course of this discussion, I cheerfully leave to the discernment of our readers. They know whether I have or not maintained that, whenever an individual impulse shall prompt to acts inconsistent with general good —Theft, Hatred, Adultery, and Murder—that impulse is to be obeyed or repressed. I do, indeed, believe that men are daily hurried to shameful graves by dissipation, by suicide, by the gallows, who are intrinsically no worse than those who live and die in odor of sanctity, and, with equal opportunities and facilities, would have been equally respected and honored to the last I may differ from you in disbelieving that Human Nature, truly instructed and developed, would ever tend to debauchery, theft, or murder, but we *do not* differ on the point that propensities to evil are to be sternly repressed, if they can not otherwise be overcome—repressed by force and penalty, if necessary. I submit to be taught by experience as to how far and under what conditions this necessity shall be found to exist. I know that it was once necessary, in view of the actual condition of mankind, to threaten and to inflict the most tremendous judgments against Idolatry, or the worship as Divine of man-made images and the most revolting creatures of diseased human fancies; I see that, among the very descendants of the nation thus sinning and thus punished there is now no shadow of necessity for even a condemnation of Idolatry, though theirs is the same Human Nature as of old. Is it preposterous to believe that, with a true and thorough development of their intellects and their affections, other vices and crimes now seductive may in like manner become abhorrent to mankind? Was not "the proclivity of Man's *nature* to act in violation of the rule of Right" the same with regard to Idolatry that it now is with regard to sins still popular among Jewish and Christian communities? And if yes, How does the fact of Man's depravity, such as it is, prove that he will always continue prone to Adultery, or Theft, any more than he now is to Idolatry?

Your assertion that "Mr. Godwin contends" that "the bonds of Marriage * * * ought to have no force beyond the consent of the parties whom they bind," is, in my confident belief, grossly untrue, but I shall not dwell upon that, however obvious and sinister its purpose; and, as to the prevalence of personal purity or constancy, I will very willingly compare the Associationists with their adversaries, the world over. That individuals among them have erred in this respect, as in others, is doubtless true; that some have perverted the doctrine of Passional Attraction to subserve illicit desires is possible, though I have not heard of such an instance. But where there has been one such case, there are thousands on record where the pages of the Bible have been pressed into similar service—where the scarcely rebuked Polygamy and Concubinage of the Old Testament have been cited as Divine authority for similar conduct in our day. How unjust and unauthorized this is, I need not stop here to exhibit.

Your pretence that "this discussion" has "*compelled* the Tribune to disavow and abandon some of the most vital and essential elements of the Association theory," will be read by thousands who will freshly remember the express and indispensable stipulation at first made by me, that the subject discussed should be "Association as I understand it"—the difficulty I had in bringing you to assent to this—the difficulty *you* had in justifying, even to yourself, your palpable determination from the first to violate your engagement—and the course you have pursued ever since. You knew well at the outset, that I intended to advocate Association from my own stand-point, and that this was somewhat different from that of Fourier or Brisbane—you knew that I had small regard for abstract metaphysical speculations in comparison with practical realities—you knew well that the American Associationists as a body had repeatedly and solemnly disclaimed the doctrines with regard to Marriage, &c., which had been deduced by their adversaries from the writings of Fourier—that they had declared generally that they did not adopt all of Fourier's speculations, but only such parts as they deemed well-grounded—you knew (for you had Mr Godwin's book before you), "*The Organization of Labor in the Township*" is the one Object, one Faith, of the Associative School; beyond which each member of it accepted or rejected, propounded or questioned, whatever commended itself to his individual reason and conscience. All this was perfectly familiar to your mind; and how can I resist the conviction that you deliberately intended to prejudice our readers against certain propositions for the practical melioration of the hard lot of the ignorant, the destitute, the depressed, by exciting a theological odium against a part of the *arguments* by which some of their advocates commended those Reforms? Let Justice decide between us.

You seek to parry the existing contrast between New Lebanon and Ireland, which I adduced as examples of the practical working of Associative and Competitive life respectively, by speaking of the Shakers as "directly under the despotic will of a single person," &c. I know no warrant for this charge—do you? As to Marriage, the Community at Zoar (Ohio), cherishes Marriage, yet its increase in wealth has been more rapid that that of the Shakers, and its present command of the means of living is as ample as theirs. Surely, all must see that a Social state in which a strong and omnipresent public sentiment demands that each able member shall be a producer, and not a mere consumer of wealth—which renders each the ally, none the antagonist of his brother toiler—which removes the temptation to lie in wait for the products of others' industry instead of producing more—*must* naturally tend to opposite results from those whereof unhappy Ireland is now the most conspicuous example. "Do men gather grapes of thorns, or figs of thistles?"

It is of course easy for you to assert that a denial of the right to monopolize the Soil in unlimited quantity is equivalent to a denial of any right to Property; and it would be just *as* easy to say that he who denies the right of one man to have a thousand wives, and to dispose of them as his interest or caprice should dictate, denies the right to have any wife at all. Such points are not settled by mere assertion. I do indeed hold, that a man has a natural right to produce and acquire property, and I therefore condemn the system of Land Monopoly, which robs the producer of one-half to seven-eighths of the fruits of his toil, and often dooms him to absolute starvation on the soil which he has faithfully and effectively cultivated. The right of owning property, or of owning land, is one thing; the right to own thousands, and even millions of acres of land, is another. The public is learning to distinguish the one from the other.

As to "working by music," &c., which you pronounce so "absurd," and that to "urge it as a means of making hard labor attractive, is nonsense," I will barely quote a passage from a not very obscure nor Agrarian authority. The historian Robertson, in his account of the Aborigines of Peru, who were among the most innocent, refined, and happy, of the nations whom (nominally) Christian avarice, lust, and butchery have exterminated or reduced to abject wretchedness, says that they held their lands as the common property of all, making frequent allotments and reallotments thereof, somewhat resembling the land-system of the Israelites under the Mosaic economy. He proceeds:

"All those lands were cultivated by the joint industry of the community. The people, summoned by a proper officer, repaired in a body to the fields, and performed their common task, while songs and musical instruments cheered them to their labor. By this singular distribution, as well as by the mode of cultivating it, the idea of a common interest and of mutual subserviency was continually inculcated. Each individual felt his connection with those around him, and knew that he depended on their friendly aid for what increase he was to reap. A state thus constituted, may be considered as one great family, in which the union of the members was so complete, and the exchange of good offices so perceptible, as to create stronger attachment, and to bind men in closer intercourse than subsisted under any form of society established in America."

Whether History (and I could quote columns like this) should presume to weigh against your dictum that all such notions are "nonsense," "too absurd for argument," our readers will determine.

—Midnight draws upon me, and the last words permitted me in this discussion are now to be penned. Let me barely restate, in order, the positions which I have endeavored to maintain during its progress, and I will calmly await the judgment to be pronounced upon the whole matter. I know well that nineteen-twentieths of those whose utterance create and mold Public Opinion had prejudged the case before reading a page with regard to it—that they had promptly decided that no Social Reconstruction is necessary or desirable, since they do not perceive that any is likely to promote the ends for which they live and strive. Of these, very few will have read our articles—they felt no need of your arguments, no appetite for mine. Yet there is a class, even in this modern Babel of selfishness and envious striving, still more in our broad land, who are earnestly seeking, inquiring for, the means whereby Error and Evil may be diminished, the realm of Justice and of Happiness extended. These will have generally followed us with more or less interest throughout; their collective judgment will award the palm of manly dealing and of beneficent endeavor to one or the other. For their consideration, I reiterate the positions I have endeavored to maintain in this discussion, and cheerfully abide their verdict that I have sustained, or you have overthrown, them. I have endeavored to show, then,

1. That Man has a natural, God-given Right to Labor for his own subsistence and the good of others, and to a needful portion of the Earth from which his physical sustenance is to be drawn. If this be a natural, essential Right, it can not be justly suspended, as to any, upon the interest or caprice of others; and that Society in which a part of mankind are permitted or forbidden to labor, according to the need felt or fancied by others for their labor, is unjustly constituted and ought to be reformed.

2. That, in a true Social state, the Right of every individual to such Labor as he is able to perform, and to the fair and equal Recompense of his Labor, will be guarantied and provided for; and the thorough Education of each child, Physical, Moral, and Intellectual, be regarded as the dictate of universal Interest and imperative Duty.

3. That such Education for All, such Opportunity to Labor, such security to each of a just and fair Recompense, are manifestly practicable only through the Association of some two or three hundred families on the basis of United Interests and Efforts (after the similitude of a Bank, Rail-road or Whale-ship, though with far more perfect arrangements for securing to each what is justly his; inhabiting a common Edifice, though with distinct and exclusive as well as common apartments, cultivating one common Domain, and pursuing thereon various branches of Mechanical and Manufacturing as well as Agricultural Industry, and uniting in the support of Education, in defraying the cost of Chemical and Philosophical Apparatus, of frequent Lectures, &c., &c.

4. That among the advantages of this Organization would be immense Economies in Land, Food, Cooking, Fuel, Buildings, Teams, Implements, Merchandise, Litigation, Account-Keeping, &c., &c.; while, on the other hand, a vastly increased Efficiency would be given to the Labor of each by concentration of effort and the devotion to Productive Industry of the great numbers now employed in unproductive avocations, or who are deemed too young, too unskilled, or too inefficient, to be set at work under our present Industrial mechanism.

5. That, thus associated and blended in interests, in daily intercourse, in early impressions, in cares, joys, and aspirations, the Rich and Poor would become the brethren and mutual helpers for which their Creator designed them—that Labor would be rendered Attractive by well-planned, lighted, warmed, and ventilated work-shops, by frequent alternations from the field to the shop as urgency, convenience, weariness, or weather should suggest; and that all being workers, all sharers in the same cares and recreations, none doomed to endure existence in a cellar or hovel, the antagonism and envious discontent now prevalent would be banished, and general Content, Good Will, and Happiness prevail, while Famine, Homelessness, unwilling Idleness, the horrors of Bankruptcy, &c., would be unknown.

—These hastily and imperfectly condensed, are my positions, my convictions. I believe that Christianity, Social Justice, Intellectual and Moral Progress, Universal Well-being, imperatively require the adoption of such a Reform as is here roughly sketched. I do not expect that it will be immediately effected, nor that the approaches to it will not be signalized by failures, mistakes, disappointments. But the PRINCIPLE of Association is one which has already done much for the improvement of the condition of our Race; we see it now actively making its way into general adoption, through Odd-Fellowship, Protective Unions, Mutual Fire, Marine, and Life Insurance, and other forms of Guaranteeism. Already commodious Edifices for the Poor of Cities are planned by Benevolence, unsuspicious of the end to which it points; already the removal of the Paupers from localities where they are a grievous burthen to those where they can substantially support themselves, is the theme of general discussion. In all these and many like them I see the pur-

tents of "a good time coming," not for the destitute and hopeless only, but for the great mass of our fellow-men. In this faith I labor and live: share it or scout it as you will.
Adieu! H. G.

---

From the Courier and Enquirer, May 20th, 1847.

## REPLY TO LETTER XII.

The Tribune closes its defense of Association by charging us with gross unfairness for the manner in which we have opposed it. We pass unnoticed the offensive terms in which this charge is made, and content ourselves with showing its entire injustice.

The Tribune first complains that we have not met the case which it has presented. We appeal to the whole course of the discussion, in refutation of this statement. We are not aware of a single position taken by the Tribune upon this subject, that we have left unnoticed. We have given to every argument it has urged in defense of the system, all the attention it seemed to merit. We began by discussing its fundamental theory of Natural Rights—its primary denial of the right of property in Land; and we have followed, throughout, the line of argument which it adopted. The Tribune ascribed all existing evil to the false arrangements of Society; we contended that even those false arrangements grow out of the selfishness of the human heart. The Tribune demanded a new Social form which should abolish the *cause* of existing evil; we insisted that, as evil did not spring from social forms, so no change of those forms could destroy it. The Tribune condemned the present system of isolated households and individual effort, and demanded the substitution for them of a Community of interests and of life; we sought to prove that such a Community would be impossible so long as human nature remains unchanged. The Tribune urged Association as the means of effecting that change in human character which alone would render Association possible; we proved that this confounded cause and effect, and that the personal reform of individual men must *precede* such a social reform as the Tribune seeks. The Tribune contended that in Association Labor would receive, as its reward, a fixed proportion of its product, and that this would be greater than under the present system; we proved that the reward of labor is regulated by certain principles of permanent force, which Association could not change, and that then, as now, when labor was abundant and laborers scarce, the wages of labor would be high; and that, when laborers increased more rapidly than the work to be done, their reward would diminish. And so we proceeded step by step, meeting every claim urged by the Tribune in defense of the system; refuting its pretensions to exclusive philanthropy; pointing out obstacles for which it made no adequate provision; and discussing fully and fairly the whole System, in all its details, as presented in its columns. We met the Tribune, throughout, upon its own ground; yet, in nearly every instance, our objections were denounced as "*cavils;*" our arguments remained untouched; and now, in its closing article, the Tribune repeats all its original positions, and charges us with having failed to meet them. We are quite content to submit this point to the judgment of our readers.

But the Tribune complains, further, that we have *gone beyond* its line of argument; that we have not occupied exclusively the "stand-point" from which it saw fit to view the system. We can perceive no justice in this claim. The Tribune is contending that the shield is made of silver; we assert that it is of brass. Is it not absurd to insist that we shall look at it only from the Tribune's point of view? We have examined it from that "stand-point," and now we claim the right to look upon the other side. We met the arguments which the Tribune urged, but we are not bound to stop with that. The Tribune's "stand-point" may be different from that of Fourier and Brisbane; it may look at the system from other ground than that they occupy; *but is not the* SYSTEM *which they advocate the* SAME? The Tribune may adopt it for one reason, and they for another; but this difference in no way touches the question—*What is its essential character?* This is the point to be determined; and we claim the right to examine its pretensions and principles, not simply with the Tribune's eye-glass, but with the best telescope we can command.

Besides, the Tribune should remember that it referred us to the writings of Fourier, and Brisbane, and Godwin, for definite information upon precisely those points, which, it *now* insists, we had no right to touch. We had made inquiry as to the provisions of Association for the education of children; for religious worship; for the regulation of domestic and social intercourse, the relations of the sexes, &c., &c. We sought some definite and explicit statement of the modes of life in this new social order, as essential to its full and fair discussion; and we stated a great variety of obstacles which seemed to us to lie in the way of its success. The Tribune replied (Dec. 28th) in these terms:

"With regard to Labor, to *Education*, to *Religion*, &c., had you read attentively any of *the writings of the Associationists, you would have seen how your obstacles are surmounted.*"

And subsequently (Jan. 13th) it said:

"I give you the full benefit of your citations from Mr. Brisbane's book, and of your excuse for them."

Here is no intimation that our inquiries were irrelevant. Nothing was said *then* of our having violated an "express engagement" by making them. But when the Tribune saw the answers which its own references had given to our inquiries, it suddenly discovered gross "unfairness" in the course we had adopted. Our readers will have no difficulty in discerning the real cause of the Tribune's dissatisfaction.

We have proved in preceding articles of this discussion, that the whole SYSTEM OF ASSOCIATION is founded upon, and grows out of, the fundamental principle, known as the 'law of PASSIONAL ATTRACTION. The argument by which this position is established remains untouched: and we shall not therefore repeat it. In our last article we proved that, in this system, the *Law of Man's Nature* is made the supreme rule of his conduct and character;—that it recognizes no higher law than that of inclination, no authority above that of passion, and of course ne essential distinction between right and wrong,—no standard of duty except that of impulse. Of course the idea of human responsibility is utterly destroyed; and all the sanctions of moral and religious truth, as derived from the Word of God, are abrogated and cast aside. These deductions flow inevitably from the law of Passional Attraction; and that law we have proved to be fundamental in Association. We have not made this, as the Tribune assumes, a matter of "assertion," but of proof: and we are entitled to demand that the Tribune shall either acknowledge its conclusiveness or demonstrate its fallacy.

But the Tribune will do neither. It will "neither *affirm* nor *disavow* that law," though it "would undoubtedly dissent from any presentment of it" from our pen, and "still more from such deductions therefrom" as we should think "fair and logical." Why does not the Tribune state its reasons for such dissent? Have we presented that law untruly, or made unfair and illogical deductions from it? If so, the fact can easily be shown. If not, the fact of the Tribune's "dissent" is of but little consequence. But the Tribune adds :—

"Make out if you will that all who do not deem man essentially and totally depraved, are *infidels*, and still *my* positions are unaffected, my arguments unshaken. Prove, if you can, that Nature's laws are not of God, but of the Devil—and *what then?* Are my positions weakened?"

The Tribune's positions may not be weakened by that fact;—but *after* its arguments have been refuted, and its positions demolished, by other considerations, this point, it seems to us, becomes pertinent and important. We have met all the arguments which the Tribune has advanced, and proved that *they* are not sufficient to vindicate the System: and now, *after that has been done*, if the System can be shown to rest upon principles which are "*of the Devil*,"—if its vital and essential elements can be proved to be those of infidelity, its claims upon the favor of religious people at all events must, in our judgment, be somewhat "weakened." The Tribune can not escape the responsibility of the System it advocates, by so shallow an evasion as this. The fact that it chooses to shut its eyes to the *religious* bearings of the subject,—that it prefers not to urge Association "from the religious point of view," will not prevent others, who deem its moral and religious bearings of paramount importance, from examining its principles and pretensions from that fixed and abiding platform. Nor will its protest against testing the merits of Association by "sectarian shibboleths," by "creeds and catechisms," by "dogmas of theology," be of more avail. In spite of the contempt thus expressed by the Tribune, for matters of *belief*, and in spite of the "slight regard" it professes for "abstract speculation or theory" upon any point of moral and religious duty, it will still be held responsible, by all considerate minds, for the infidelity of faith as well as the licentiousness of life, involved in the system which it so earnestly advocates. Belief, abstract theory, must always go before practical conduct. A man may indeed live a correct life and yet entertain a very erroneous faith;—but generally his belief will shape his conduct. A System, moreover, can never be better than the principles on which it rests. Its practical operation never can be good, when its predominant, ruling principles are false and pernicious. There is, therefore, no more proper or decisive mode of determining the character of any System, than by bringing to the test of established truth the fundamental principles out of which it grows. This is the test,—the *experimentum crucis*,—by which we would try the character of the SOCIALISM which the Tribune advocates: and it is precisely the test from which the Tribune shrinks. It protests against having any thing to do with "creeds" and "catechisms" and the "dogmas of theology"—meaning by these expressions, the doctrines and principles of the Christian faith.

Now there are certain fundamental truths, so distinctly set forth in the revealed Word of God, and so clearly recognized as true by the moral reason of every man, that they are received as fixed and forever established, by the great mass of the Christian world. These principles may therefore be most justly used as absolute tests, in the examination of any System which has any relation to the moral and spiritual interests of mankind. The principles of the System of Association are in the most direct and irreconcilable hostility to these principles of Christianity. They involve, as we have already shown, a denial of the existence of Sin, as an active power, in the human heart. They teach that the law of Man's *Nature* is the highest rule of his conduct. They recognize no law of duty superior to the law of passion and inclination. They subject all truth and all obligation to the dominion of individual impulses, and thus destroy the essential distinction between right and wrong. They teach that evil is simply the consequence of attempting to repress human passion,—that it is chargeable upon those Social forms which seek that repression; and they thus deny the responsibility of individuals for their conduct and character. They teach that the great aim of man and of society should be to develop and gratify the radical passions of the human heart; and they thus contradict directly the Christian injunction of *self-denial*. The SYSTEM claims to be adapted to all the wants of humanity: —claims to be divine in its origin,—based upon fixed and eternal principles, and perfect in its provisions for the well-being of man It claims to have made provision for all the interests of all the members of Society: and yet it makes no provision for religious teaching, discards all reference to higher than human sanctions, and assents to the teachings of Christ and his apostles, only after it has *forced* them to echo its own principles and reflect its image. Such a SYSTEM we have no hesitation in characterizing as *infidel* in its principles, and therefore dangerous to all the best interests of Society and of man, in its operation and effect. The Tribune may think this no valid objection to it,—but others will not so regard it. The Tribune may refuse to look at it from this point of view,—may shut its eyes to the aspect of the scheme when seen from this stand-point, and may assert that all this has nothing to do with its "immense economies," its "spacious edifices," its gardens, orchards, attractive industry, and miscellaneous but fantastic magnificence; but it can not convince reflecting men that it is either unimportant or irrelevant.

But the Tribune again quotes Mr. Godwin's statement, that

"The school of Fourier propose but one thing, *the Organization of Labor in the Township :*"

while it suppresses entirely his additional declaration, to which, more than once, we have called its notice, that,

"Let a *Township* be once organized according to our principles, and the reform will soon *spread over the entire nation :*" and that "Law, Government, and *Religion*, will *all* be more or less affected by a unitary regime of industry."

Thus, the very author cited by the Tribune, disproves the position which it seeks to establish, and confirms our statement, that "the Organization of Labor in the Township" is sought simply as the stepping-stone to the entire reorganization of Society. And equally explicit upon the same point is Mr. Brisbane's declaration:

"It is evident that the whole question of a *universal social* reform, resolves itself into the *right organization of one single township.*"

To say that each member may accept or reject whatever he pleases of the principles of the System, is simply to say that each member may abandon the System whenever he pleases. There is nothing in the mere principle of combined exertion, of united effort, for the attainment of a common object, which can distinguish Association from hundreds of institutions already in existence. It is not this which marks it as a new scheme for the entire reorganization of Society.

But all these points have already been fully met, in the preceding articles of this discussion; and we refer to them now, only because the Tribune reiterates its positions, without the least reference to the arguments we have urged against them.

We have still to advert to one point of great practical importance, which has hitherto been but slightly touched: we mean THE INFLUENCE UPON SOCIETY OF THE PRINCIPLES OF ASSOCIATION, as they are presented and urged in the columns of the Tribune. Its advocacy of this Social System is regarded by many as wholly unaccountable—as the result of some strange whim, for which no reason can be found in its general tone and teaching. This, in our judgment, is a mistaken notion. The fundamental principles of Association,—its essential doctrines, as we have set them forth in this discussion,—are far more earnestly cherished by the Editor of that paper, than any of the party measures, or temporary expedients, which he advocates. The principles which lie at the bottom of this new Social System, in our view, shape the entire policy of the Tribune. They dictate all its sentiments; prompt all its comments upon men and measures; pervade its most trifling notices of the most common events; govern its estimate of all schemes of public concern; and create the very atmosphere in which it has its being.

Take, for example, the principle, as laid down by the Tribune at the outset of this discussion,— that *every man born within the limits of New-York has, by a law of nature, a perfect right to his equal share of its soil*. This position, as we have proved conclusively, denies the right of owning Land, and includes a denial of the right to own any thing. It strikes at the root of the right of property. Now, with the Tribune, this principle is not a mere abstraction, an opinion entertained, but not acted upon. That paper *takes it for granted*, in all its discussions. It assumes the principle, and shapes its practical teachings in accordance with it. Its columns teem with denunciations of "Land monopoly." It brands the right of property in Land as the "monster evil" of society. It calls upon the Legislature to fix a *limit* to the right of owning the soil, and demands of Congress, in complete abandonment of a principle it once cherished, that the Public Lands shall be given away to any who may settle upon them. And still more apparent is the effect of its advocacy of this principle upon the political and social aspect of this State. Great numbers of our people live upon farms which are owned by others. They have been taught by the Tribune, that Land is a "God-created element," which should not be monopolized; that the right to live is paramount to the right of owning land; and that they who labor upon the soil, and redeem it from its primeval rudeness, are its rightful owners. The conclusion from all this is inevitable; they, upon this principle, have a perfect right to the farms they hold. And throughout a very large district in this State, the inhabitants have determined to *enforce* that right—to claim and retain the ownership of these farms, in the face of all Law, and in spite of those upon whom has been devolved its execution. And in the prosecution of this purpose, sheriffs have been shot; the owners of the farms have been beaten; their agents have been maltreated; armed bands have been organized to seize upon the landed estates of others; and the whole civil and social fabric has been threatened with entire destruction.* These are the legitimate fruits of the doctrines proclaimed by the Tribune. They may have been acted upon before the Tribune became their advocate; but they are nevertheless *its* principles, and it is exerting all its power to give them still wider influence and more undoubted sway.

Then again, under the influence of this principle, and under the immediate supervision of the Tribune, a political party has sprung into existence calling itself the party of "National Reform," and exhorting its members to "*vote themselves a farm.*" Hostility to what the Tribune styles the "Land monopoly," is the fundamental element of their creed: and already is the Tribune boasting of the political strength they have acquired, and looking forward to the day when their demands shall be carried into full effect. The practical results of the Tribune's theories may be seen in these organized movements of the day, and still more clearly in the spirit of radical, bitter *hostility* between the Rich and the Poor, which has rapidly acquired strength and vigor, under their constant and

---

* The history of the *Anti Rent* Rebellion in the State of New York is so well known, in all its details, to the public, that no more special reference to its particular incidents, is here deemed necessary.

skilful promulgation. These are the direct fruits of this principle of "Association as the Tribune understands it." That paper, indeed, disavows any denial of the right of property: but we have proved that this denial is involved in its fundamental position, and our argument is yet unanswered. The Tribune, moreover, forgets its declaration of a few months since, that

"Mine and Thine are distinctions which inhere *in our present* relations, feelings, social necessities: *yet they are beginning to be felt as a* YOKE AND A BURDEN."

This, certainly, is a distinct avowal of the hardship and injustice of a system of property, and alludes clearly enough to the "good time coming" when all distinctions of *meum* and *tuum* shall be abolished.

In the same way, and to a still greater extent, may be traced the influence upon the Tribune, and through its columns upon Society, *of that very* LAW OF PASSIONAL ATTRACTION, which, when stated in a definite form, the Tribune will "neither affirm nor disavow." We have hitherto so fully and so clearly proved that this Law lies at the very basis of Association, and that, if it be rejected, the entire system must be abandoned, that nothing more need be said upon that point. This law affirms that "the *attractions and repulsions* of every being in the creation are exactly in proportion to their respective *functions* and *real destinies* in the universe:" or, in other words, that the impulses and desires of every man indicate precisely the position he should fill, the actions he should perform, the character he should maintain in society. And it is made the great end of Social Reform to introduce such a form of society as should permit, without disturbance or injury, this full and free development of the passions and impulses of man. In our last article we showed, with sufficient clearness, that this principle recognizes every act as *right* which is in accordance with the nature of man; and that those things only are held to be *wrong* which are not in accordance with his nature, and that they are wrong *so far* only as they produce evil consequences. *The idea of* MORAL GUILT—of any distinction between right and wrong aside from their consequences—is entirely rejected. No absolute, fixed standard of moral character is recognized in this system. The Tribune, indeed, professes to be "in favor of repressing an individual impulse whenever it shall prompt to acts *inconsistent with the general good:*"—but even this position tacitly repudiates the idea of any inherent distinction between *right* and *wrong*, in human conduct, aside from the results they may produce.

The Tribune's whole theory of CRIME and of PUNISHMENT springs directly from this principle. It regards crime as simply the result of a *diseased* nature: it treats it as involving misfortune, but not as implying guilt. Thus it is only a few days since (May 5th), that the Tribune spoke of *thieves* as men "guilty of *diseased appetites and perverted faculties:*" and it constantly assumes, even when it does not directly assert, that crime is produced by circumstances, and that Society, instead of the individual, is responsible for it. In its last article it seeks to defend this position, and to show that a change in condition will destroy the cause of evil, by citing the fact that the Jews were once guilty of worshiping idols; and that, as changed circumstances have banished this sin, so a changed condition may uproot any evil tendency in the human heart. But here is a sophism, founded upon a confusion of terms. The adoration of images was simply the *form* which an idolizing spirit among the Jews assumed, in its outward manifestation. A change of circumstances may have changed the form, but is the Tribune sure it has destroyed the *spirit* of idolatry? Or may not that spirit still make itself apparent in an inordinate love of money, or in some other form? Now in Association, adultery, theft, &c., may not be deemed the crimes they are now considered: but will the lust, the covetousness, the self-seeking out of which they grow, be banished from the human heart? If not, no reformation of the character will have been effected:—the developments of passion may be modified or changed; but its inherent character remains the same. Crime is not, as the Law of Passional Attraction would teach, the result of circumstances. It can not be charged upon Society. It springs from the heart of man, and each man is individually responsible for it as it exists within him.

But the influence of this fundamental principle of PASSIONAL ATTRACTION is also manifest in all the Tribune's teachings concerning the CONJUGAL and the FAMILY RELATIONS. We have already proved, by a close and logical deduction, that this Law, when carried into this department of social life, utterly abolishes Marriage as an institution of fixed force and abiding sanctions, and substitutes for it the arrangement of *groups* and *series*, as being better adapted to the wants and requirements of human nature. We proved also that Fourier himself recognized this necessity, and, in his social system, made provision for the full indulgence of inconstant passion. Those in Association who should choose to remain constant could do so; while those whose impulses should prompt to change, would also have abundant opportunity to gratify their inclinations. This state of things is defended on the ground that the relations between the sexes are entirely conventional—the creatures of society; that inconstancy, being an impulse of nature, is wrong only because society so considers it, and because, under existing arrangements, it leads to confusion and disturbance; and that in a social form adapted to it, and in an atmosphere of opinion which would permit it, it would cease to be *hurtful*, and therefore cease to be *wrong*. The Tribune, as already quoted, assents to this position, intimating only its belief that inconstancy, in a true society, would not be desired, but conceding virtually that *if* desired in such a state, it should be allowed.

This is a point, we are aware, on which the Tribune is never explicit; and we shall dwell upon it, therefore, a little longer. Under the present system, as the Associationists urge, parties are often brought into conjugal union who have for each other no true affection; and, in many cases, the passion which prompted the union dies or changes to some other object. Society now requires the marriage relation, nevertheless, to be maintained, and thus compels parties to live together after all mutual regard has disappeared. This compulsion, they alledge, is at war with nature—in violation of the principle of passional attraction; and, in a true society, it must, therefore, be done away. Marriage, as a fixed and abiding institution, is thus abolished, and it only remains to provide a substitute. *This substitute, as we have already shown, flows naturally from the Law of Passional Attraction.* Let those persons, and those only, be united who are impelled to that union by the impulses of their nature; let them remain united only while those impulses prompt them to do so; and let them be released, and allowed to form new connections, in free obedience to the same promptings of their nature. Of course such an arrangement could be carried out only in a social form adapted to it. Certain conditions are indispensable to its introduction. Thus, for example, public sentiment would reprobate such conduct now; a wife, being dependent upon her husband for support, would, if he should leave her, be left destitute; their children, under the same circumstances, would be unprotected; and other obstacles exist, under the present social system, which would render impossible such a scheme as is here proposed. Therefore, say the Associationists, we do not seek any such object *now*: we do not propose to interfere at all with marriage *now*: we leave that whole subject *for the present* untouched. This is the Tribune's position. That paper, conceding that these are Fourier's views, asserts that they have been expressly disavowed by the American Associationists, "as a body." We have never met such a disavowal, nor do we believe it has ever been made. The Associationists have, indeed, declared that *some* of Fourier's speculations *individuals* among them do reject; but what these are they do not say, nor, *as a body*, do they disclaim any part of the system, or any of the principles on which it is based. Besides, the "SYLVANIA ASSOCIATION," with which the Editor of the Tribune was officially connected, in a programme of their faith and proposed practice, declared explicitly that

"*The Sylvanians reject* NOTHING *of Fourier's teachings*;" but that, after organizing labor, and carrying into effect other preliminary reforms, they intend to "*proceed to the study of the more metaphysical and speculative parts of Fourier's doctrine, and to the application of these to their own upbuilding in the ways of Truth, Wisdom, and Love.*"

We find here no *rejection* of any part of Fourier's doctrines, but a distinctive statement that, at the proper time, they would be applied to daily life; and this prospectus bears the name of H. Greeley, as the Treasurer of the Association. The views and purposes of the "American Associationists," in regard to this matter, are set forth, in an article written by Mr. Brisbane for the *Democratic Review* (Feb., 1846), expressly to correct alledged misapprehensions upon the subject, and from which we make the following extract:—

"Let me explain briefly the views which the Associationists hold on the subject of *Marriage*, and a few other leading points.

"As regards Marriage the Associationists have not treated it, scarcely even adverted to it. They leave marriage as it is, and maintain it in its present condition, for they are fully convinced that it is *not a question for the present age.* \* \* \* We do not wish to change or abolish marriage to correct the abuses which we see at present connected or interwoven with it. We wish, *first*, to change all the social, political, and household evils that surround it; and *when this is accomplished*, we shall then be in a position to form a clear and correct opinion *as to what is to be done next*, if other evils still remain.

"We believe that it is for the women of a future generation—*when all the preliminary reforms of which we spoke are carried out*—when woman possesses her pecuniary independence—when she enjoys all her rights, and gains her own livelihood by her own efforts, in a system of dignified and attractive industry—when she is fully and integrally developed, morally and intellectually, and when *the paternal protection of society*, or a social providence, is *extended to all children*; it is, we believe, for the noble women of the future, of a regenerated race, to decide upon this most delicate and intricate question.

"In short, we leave this whole question to the soul of fully-developed, fully-educated, and fully-independent woman, in a true social order; we are convinced that that soul will then be noble, pure, and elevated, and that *the decrees which go forth from the heart will be the voice of God, speaking through the divine affections which He has implanted in humanity, will be a true guide and a true revelation upon this great subject.* These are our intimate convictions; this is the ground which we take."

Now it is clear from this formal statement,

1. That the Associationists contemplate some future change of the Marriage relation, although *for the present* they leave it untouched; and that they do not, therefore, consider it as a permanent institution, divine in its sanctions, and of abiding obligation.

2. That the character of this future change of the Marriage relation is to be determined by *the " decrees of the heart" of woman*, in a true social state—that is, in one adapted to the development and dominion of these decrees; in other words, that it is to be shaped and governed by the *Law* of PASSIONAL ATTRACTION.

3. That certain reforms are needed as *preliminary* to this change; that Labor must be organized; that woman must enjoy her perfect right of property, and thus become independent of man; that society must make provision for all children; and that woman must be in a condition of *perfect independence* in regard to property, person, and affection.

4. When these "preliminary reforms" shall have been effected, then the Marriage relation will be brought into perfect accordance with the " decrees of the heart."

Now it should be noted that the Tribune, although it disavows the intention of such a change, *zealously advocates the reforms here set forth as* PRELIMINARY *to the subversion of the Marriage relation, and the substitution for it of the groups and series dictated by the Law of Passional Attraction.* It constantly urges upon the public, and upon the legislature, the enactment of laws giving to woman the entire control of her property, and making her, in all that relates to her support, perfectly independent of her husband. It boasts of the progress its sentiments, on this subject, have already made upon the public mind, and of the steps already taken to give them legal and permanent force. It is thus zealously striving to bring about precisely that state of things which is *preliminary* to a reform of the Marriage relation, in which the impulses of woman, freed from all dependence, and from all anxiety, released from all constraint, with all her passions fully and "integrally" developed, acting solely from the promptings of her nature, shall control the relations between the sexes; and in which nothing—no influence of any kind or from any quarter, no dread of public censure, no regard for divine sanctions, no fear of evil results, nothing that now operates as a constraint and check upon unbridled impulse—will prevent the intercourse of the sexes from being just as free as the women of an Association, thus educated, and thus surrounded, can be induced to permit! The Tribune may not consciously aim at this result, but it is *paving the way* for those who *are* aiming at it; it is clearing the path for its attainment; it is urging the precise steps preliminary to this result; it is gradually and adroitly preparing the public mind for this consummation. It is silently destroying the conviction, at the heart of society, that MARRIAGE is a sacred institution, ordained by God, and intended to be fixed and permanent. It is creating the sentiment that the institution of Marriage imposes unjust restraints on human nature, and that it must, therefore, be modified. It is thus doing the work, and advancing the dominion, of that Law of PASSIONAL ATTRACTION which lies at the basis of the entire system of Association. It may disclaim this law in terms; it may even be unconscious of its influence; but in all its teachings, in politics, and in morals, it manifests its spirit and assumes its truth.

Here we close the discussion of Association, to which we were challenged by the Tribune. We have not given the system that methodical and complete examination which can alone do justice to its principles and pretensions. Our remarks have been desultory and discursive, because the form of controversy compelled us to follow in the path which our opponent chose to take. Very many points of more or less interest, we are thus enforced to leave untouched. The provisions of the system for civil government; its "sacred legion" for the performance of the "filthy functions" of society; its asserted power to reclaim deserts, to redeem alike the torrid and the frigid zones from their excessive heat and cold; these claims, like many others which the system presents, must remain unnoticed. Its practical aspects and essential principles have formed the only topic of this discussion; and with regard to them, we think the following leading positions have been established by evidence and argument which the Tribune has failed to shake :—

I. Association ascribes all existing evil to what it terms the "FALSE ORGANIZATION *of society*," and it seeks to cure it, therefore, by giving to society a *new* and widely different organization from that which now prevails.

II. This reorganization of society is to be universal, and embrace all departments of social life. All social forms and institutions, it is alledged, are radically wrong; all, therefore, must be radically and completely changed.

III. LABOR is the first thing to be reformed. Existing society authorizes the "monopoly of land," and thus excludes a part of its members from sharing this God-given element, and from working upon it, and enjoying the fruits of their labor. Association proposes, therefore, to *abolish* private property in land; to make the soil the *joint* property of masses of men, all of whom can work upon it and share its fruits, but none of whom can have in it any private and exclusive ownership; and by this means to *increase* and render *fixed* the reward of mere labor, without making it, in any degree, dependent upon capital.—We have proved (1.) that Capitalists never can be induced to enter into this arrangement : (2.) that the denial of the right of private property *in land* involves the denial of the right to own any thing : (3.) that the very root and foundation of all civilization and progress are thus destroyed : (4.) that such a community of property and labor, if it were feasible, would beget discontent and strife, and so involve the elements of its own destruction : (5.) that the reward of labor can not be made *fixed*, because it must always, *ex necessitate rei*, depend upon the fluctuating ratio of the supply to the demand; and (6.) that the effect of this system of owning the soil, if carried out, would render *Capitalists* the sole owners of all the land, and laborers everywhere their tenants and serfs. Its only effect would be, therefore, vastly to *increase* the evils which it seeks to remedy.

IV. The ISOLATED HOUSEHOLD is the next false institution of the present Society, to be reformed. As a general thing, each family now inhabits a separate house. Association proposes that this shall be abandoned, as expensive, selfish, and inconvenient; and that all shall live in one *common house*, having their cooking, washing, and all other domestic service performed in common; eating, as a general rule, at a common table, and leading in all essential respects a common life. Such an arrangement, we have contended—(1) Would destroy that most potent spur to human effort, the desire of creating and enjoying an independent and separate *home*; (2) That it would bring together persons of habits, tastes, convictions, prejudices, motives, and general characters utterly incompatible with each other; (3.) That it would fail to bring such discordant materials into the harmony of feeling, faith, and conduct essential to success : and (4.) that it would, so far as it should prove successful, destroy all individuality of character, and bring all men to a dead level of uniformity. It would be, therefore, in the first place, *impossible*; and, if not so, injurious to the best interests of all concerned.

V. The EDUCATION OF CHILDREN is the next thing to be reformed. Now, infants are taken care of by their parents, or by hired nurses :—they are subjected to their absolute control; they inherit their tastes and dispositions; there is no uniformity in their Education, and therefore none in their belief or characters—and thus are perpetuated, from one generation to another, all the evils of the existing social state. Association proposes to commit all the infants to common nurses; to educate young children upon a common plan, and under the direction of an Elective Council; to release them from all constraint, leaving them to obey *none* but " superiors of their *own choice*;" relieving the parents from all care of them, and the children from all obligation to obey their parents; and so forming their characters, and guiding their conduct in a way precisely opposite to that which now prevails. This System, we have shown—(1,) neglects entirely to take into account the strong instincts of parental and filial affection; (2,) that it, therefore, would prove impracticable; (3,) that it aims, avowedly, to *annul the* DUTY *of* Filial Obedience; (4,) that it *denies* explicitly the RIGHT of Parental Authority; and (5,) that it thus strikes a deadly blow at the very heart of the PARENTAL RELATION, as its nature is set forth and its duties defined in the Word of God.

VI. The Relation of HUSBAND and WIFE is now a fixed and permanent one:—yet it often unites parties who have for each other no mutual love, and keeps asunder those whom mutual passion impels to union. Public sentiment, legal enactments, the pecuniary dependence of woman, the embarrassing care of children, and all existing social usages combine to perpetuate and enforce this unnatural and unjust constraint. Association proposes to reorganize the Marriage relation; to remove all the obstacles to the free sway of natural impulse; and to commit the intercourse of the sexes to the laws of human nature and individual passion, freed from all the restraints and checks they now encounter. In order to effect this, it imposes on Society the care of the children; repeals all legal disabilities; confers upon women perfect liberty in person, property, and affection; enlightens public sentiment; and so renders easy and unobstructed the full and free gratification of inconstant, as well as of constant, passions. We have demonstrated—(1,) that this is the aim and final purpose of this system of Social Reform; (2,) that, in not regarding Marriage as a permanent institution of divine origin and sanctions, it rejects the teachings of Christ; and (3,) that its result would be the complete destruction of the MARRIAGE RELATION, and the substitution for it of a systematized Polygamy, less regulated, less restrained, and therefore far *worse* than has ever been witnessed in any nation or in any age of the world.

VII. The FAMILY, under the present Social system, is an institution narrow in its scope, selfish in its spirit, and injurious to social and human progress. It rests upon, and is sustained by, the Isolated Household, the Parental Relation, and the Relation of Husband and Wife. So long as these exist, it will exist also. But Association proposes, as we have already seen, to *reorganize*, and in effect, *destroy* all these relations. When that has been accomplished the FAMILY RELATION must, of course, fall to the ground, and the Family *spirit* will be *absorbed* by the spirit of the Association. In all this we have insisted—(1,) that the System seeks the destruction of an institution of divine origin—one that lies at the basis of all human improvement, that nourishes and develops all the best affections and sympathies of the human heart, and that does more for the preservation of order, of purity, and of civilization than all human institutions put together; (2,) that its purposes are therefore hostile to the well-being of society; and (3,) that, if carried out, they would sweep away the best and surest safe- of the public good, and break down one

of the strongest barriers ever erected against the destructive torrent of vice and misery.

VIII. Under the existing System, the RESTRAINT OF HUMAN PASSIONS is made the great end of all Social Institutions. Education, Law, the Church, the Family, all formal provisions for the public good, enforce the duty and necessity of *repressing* the passions and impulses of human nature. Association denounces this as a false and fruitless method. The natural impulses of man, it asserts, are *good:* evil results only from their repression. A true Society, therefore, should provide for their perfect and complete development. This is accordingly proposed as the great and controlling object of the new Society which the System seeks to introduce. *The impulses of every human being, in the language of Association, point out exactly his real functions and his true position in Society.* This law, therefore, is *to* CONTROL, in every respect, *the proposed reorganization of all Social Forms.* Labor, Education, the Family, all modes of Life and of Work, are to be brought under its complete command. (1.) In Labor, men are to work, not under the guidance of necessity, but according to their likings;—not separately, as their personal interests may dictate, but in *groups* and *series*, according to the Law of Passional Attraction. (2.) In Education, children are to learn, not what they are directed, but what they like;—they are to obey, not their parents, but only "superiors of their own choice;" and in all things, their path is to be indicated, not by the judgment of older and wiser persons, but by their own "passional attractions." (3.) In the Conjugal Relation, according to this fundamental law, those persons are to be united whose impulses prompt a union;—if those impulses are constant, the union may be constant also;—if they die, the union may be dissolved;—if they change to other objects, they may still be gratified;—and all the obstacles which public sentiment, the care of children, and the fear of consequences now oppose to such an arrangement will be removed; and, in the language of Fourier himself, the author of the System,—

"A wife may have *at the same time* a *husband* of whom she may have two children:—2. A *genitor* of whom she has but one child: 3. A *favorite*, who has lived with her and preserved the title; and further, simple *possessors* who are nothing before the law. This gradation of the title, establishes a great courteousness and great fidelity to the engagement. *Men do the same to their divers wives.* This method prevents completely the hypocrisy of which marriage is the source. Misses would by no means be degraded for having had "gallants," because they had waited before they took them to the age of eighteen. They would be married without scruple. * * *Our ideas of the honor and virtue of women are but prejudices which vary with our legislation.*" *

---

* It has been repeatedly asserted by some of the advocates of Association, that in after life FOURIER *changed* his views upon this subject, and *disclaimed* the opinions set forth in this extract, the authenticity of which is conceded. They were challenged to produce any evidence of this assertion. The only paragraph which has ever been cited in its support, is the following—which we give at length, in order to preclude any charge of partial or unfair dealing:—

"In 1807, my progress in the theory of Harmony, extended only to the relations of material love, which being the *easiest to calculate*, became naturally the object of the first studies.

(4) All the forms, and all the relations of Society, are to be adapted to the wants of human nature;—to be shaped in exact accordance with the requirements of the law of Passional Attraction; so that, instead of RESTRAINT, the complete SATISFACTION of all the passions, shall be the controlling object of all Social forms.—It has been our aim, in this discussion, to prove that these *results* are actually involved in the principles, and contemplated in the practice of the SYSTEM. It has not been necessary to do more than this; as the Tribune has not seen fit to follow the inquiry into this branch of the subject.

IX. In all its principles and all its arrangements, the SYSTEM of Association recognizes no higher rule of human conduct, no other standard of right and wrong, than that of the LAWS OF HUMAN NATURE. These laws, in its whole reorganization of Society, are final and imperative. In this respect, we contend, it is essentially and at bottom, a system of INFIDELITY, inasmuch as it discards the vital and absolute distinction between Right and Wrong;—recognizes no such thing as Conscience;—involves a denial of God as a moral being—the governor of the universe;—and is directly hostile, in its essence, to the most vital doctrines of the Christian Faith.

That this is the true outline and character of the SYSTEM OF ASSOCIATION, first promulgated by Fourier, and now urged upon the adoption of the American people by the Tribune, we claim to have proved in the foregoing articles of this discussion. We do not assert, nor do we believe, that the editor of the Tribune aims at these results. On the contrary, if he believed that they were involved in the System, we have no doubt he would promptly discard it. But in our judgment, *they flow necessarily from the fundamental principle of the System*; and every step taken toward *its* supremacy, is a step toward *their* establishment. The Tribune, whether consciously or not, advocates THE SYSTEM in which they are involved; and it is justly, therefore, held responsible for its principles and their inevitable results. The System of Association, if fully carried out, would effect the most complete *overthrow* of existing institutions the world has ever seen. A universal Deluge would not more thoroughly change the face of the Earth, than would this Social revolution change the face of Human Society. Law, Labor, Education, Social forms, Religion, Domestic life, *every thing* in the world as it now exists, the best institutions as well as the worst, would be swept into a common vortex, and all Society would be thrown back into a worse than primeval chaos. Churches, Courts of Law, Halls of Legislation, the Homes of Men, all private rights, and all the forms of Social life, would be banished from the Earth, and the whole work of Social Creation must be performed anew. So momentous a change as this the world has never seen,—one so radical, so sweeping in its nature, so overwhelming in its results. And the principles which, if *fully* carried out, would involve these tremendous consequences, when *partially* carried out, produce, of course, corresponding injury. They are subtle, plausible, and to many minds attractive; and, in our judgment, by adroitly and zealously pressing them upon public favor, the Tribune is weakening the foundations and pillars of the Social fabric; is silently poisoning the public mind with false notions of natural rights and of personal obligation; and is sowing broadcast the seeds of discontent and hate, of which future generations will reap the fruits, if not in the bloody field of carnage and terror, in the anarchy and social disorder which are equally fatal to all human advancement and all Social good.

Throughout this discussion the Tribune has charged us with being hostile to all Reform, and especially to every attempt to meliorate the hard lot of the degraded poor. The charge is as unfounded as it is ungenerous. We labor willingly and zealously, as our columns will testify, within our sphere, in aid of every thing which seems to us TRUE REFORM,—founded upon just principles, seeking worthy ends by worthy means, and promising actual and good results. We regard it as our duty to do all in our power to benefit our fellow-men:—but we are not of those who "feel personally responsible for the turning of the Earth upon its axis," nor do we deem it our special "mission" to reorganize Society. We believe much good may be done by improving the circumstances which surround the vicious and the wretched:—but the essential evil lies behind that, and must be reached by other means. We should not differ from the Tribune as to the Christian duty of the rich toward the poor:—but we can not denounce them as the tyrants and robbers of those who have been less industrious and less fortunate. We would gladly see Society free from suffering, and all its members virtuous and happy:—but we believe Social Equality to be as undesirable, as it is impossible,—holding, rather, with Plato and Aristotle, that a true Society requires a *union* of unequal interests, mutually sustaining and aiding each other, and not an aggregation of identical elements, which could give nothing like coherence or strength to the fabric. We believe in human improvement, but not in a Progress which will have nothing *fixed*, which consists in leaving behind it every thing like established principles, and which measures its rate, by the extent of its departure from all."

---

"It was only in 1817 that I discovered the theory of Spiritual Love, in its simpler and higher degrees.

"No one ought to be astonished, if in a statement written only eight years after the first discovery, I considered Love only in its material relations, the theory of which was still exceedingly *incomplete*.

"A new Science can attain its free development only by degrees, and for a long time is subjected to the influence of the tendencies prevailing around it. Situated as I was in the midst of civilizers, who are all sensualists, or nearly so, it was almost inevitable that in my first studies of Love, as it will exist in the combined order, I should stop at the material part of the subject which alone opens a vast field for scientific calculations. Afterwards, I came to the spiritual part of the theory, which is much more difficult to unfold, I could not carry on both these branches together, and was obliged in 1807 to treat the relations of Material Love *into the system of which I had at that time an insight.*"

It will be seen here, that FOURIER instead of *disclaiming* his former views and asserting that he *had changed* them, simply remarks that his scheme was then "*incomplete*," and explicitly declares that in 1807 he had "an insight" into the scientific principles of the "System of Material Love." Nor have the American Associations ever repudiated, so far as we are aware, or disavowed these opinions. So far as they go, they are held to be just: the only complaint is that of FOURIER, that the system is incomplete."

pillars which wisdom and experience have erected. We can not regard with favor any principle or any scheme, no matter how plausible its pretensions, which involves the destruction of the FAMILY RELATION, or subjects the MARRIAGE union to the caprice of individual passion:—for not only the dictates of wisdom and experience, but the explicit injunctions of God himself, are thus rejected and disavowed. We would not venture upon the tremendous experiment of taking off from human passions all the restraints which Society, Law, and Religion have hitherto imposed, however plausible the plea that the Law of Passional Attraction will again bring them into more complete harmony, and with "pacific and constructive" power, build up, as by enchantment, a new and more perfect Social form. As soon would we unchain and turn loose upon unprotected women and children a thousand untamed tigers, or lead mankind, in search of its lost paradise, into the very heart of hell,—in the hope that some Orphean lute might charm wild beasts from their nature, and convert even the furies of the infernal world into angels and ministers of grace. The walls of Thebes may have risen to the sound of Amphion's harp; but he himself was a son of the Highest, and received his lyre and acquired his skill in such creative melody, from the direct teachings of its Sovereign God. So, in these latter days, must the principles of all true REFORM come down from Heaven. We have no faith in any System that does not aim at the extirpation of MORAL EVIL from the heart of Man: or that sets aside, in this endeavor, the teachings of Revelation; the Eternal principles of spiritual truth therein proclaimed; and the method of redemption therein set forth. The CHRISTIAN RELIGION, in its spiritual, life-giving, heart-redeeming principles is the only power that can reform Society: and it can accomplish this work only by first reforming the individuals of whom Society is composed. Without God, and the plan of redemption which he has revealed, the World is also without HOPE.

THE END.

This book is a preservation facsimile.
It is made in compliance with copyright law
and produced on acid-free archival
60# book weight paper
which meets the requirements of
ANSI/NISO Z39.48-1992 (permanence of paper)


Preservation facsimile printing and binding
by
Acme Bookbinding
Charlestown, Massachusetts

2005

CPSIA information can be obtained at www.ICGtesting.com
Printed in the USA
LVOW03s0420160915

454271LV00017B/539/P

9 781173 819088